# Creating Worldviews

# Creating Worldviews

## Metaphor, Ideology and Language

James W. Underhill

Edinburgh University Press

© James W. Underhill, 2011, 2013

Edinburgh University Press Ltd
22 George Square, Edinburgh EH8 9LF

First published in hardback by Edinburgh University Press 2011

www.euppublishing.com

Typeset in 11.5/13 Monotype Ehrhardt
by Servis Filmsetting Ltd, Stockport, Cheshire,
and printed and bound in Great Britain by
CPI Antony Rowe, Chippenham and Eastbourne

A CIP record for this book is available from the British Library

ISBN 978 0 7486 4315 8 (hardback)
ISBN 978 0 7486 7909 6 (paperback)

The right of James W. Underhill
to be identified as author of this work
has been asserted in accordance with
the Copyright, Designs and Patents Act 1988.

# Contents

# Acknowledgements

I wish to thank Triada Publishing House for allowing me to publish extracts from Petr Fidelius's Czech book on communist rhetoric, *Řeč komunistické* (1998); Walter de Gruyter editions, for allowing me to publish extracts from Joseph Goebbels's diaries (volume 1, part one, published by K. G. Saur in 1987); and Cambridge University Press, for allowing me to publish extracts from David Crystal's *Language Death* (2000). I would also like to thank the Reklam publishers for allowing me to publish extracts from the German original of Victor Klemperer's *LTI* (1975), a study of Nazi rhetoric and discourse, as well as the English publisher, Continuum, who have kindly allowed me both to reproduce extracts from Martin Brady's English translation of this extremely arduous work (2006), and to provide my own translations where the German makes a 'natural-sounding' translation of Nazi-speech almost impossible.

For stylistic help with the English text, I would like to express my warmest thanks to Shaeda Isani, Dawn Rivière and John Reid. The presentation of the Czech language was greatly improved by Tamara Ibehová, and the German would not have escaped slips and errors without the invaluable help of Steffi Arzt, Marko Pajević and Cornelia Chladek. I should, however, be held responsible for any errors in analysis or translation. My debt to the late Henri Meschonnic, who guided my research on language, translation and poetics for six years in the 1990s will be perfectly obvious in the following pages, and therefore makes thanks here superfluous. Thanks also to the editorial staff of Edinburgh University Press for their help, support and astute insights.

For my Dad

# Part I  Metaphor

# CHAPTER I

# Metaphor and World-Conceiving

## WORLDVIEWS

F ew scholars would argue with the idea that words and world-views are intertwined and that language and thought are related. But when we speak of language, what do we mean? Are we thinking of the language system, or the particular style or type of language used? Most sociologists, political analysts and philosophers are concerned with the ideological content of concepts. Theodor Adorno (1991a, 1991b, 1989), Raymond Williams (1983), Michel Foucault (2004), George Lakoff (1996) and Andrew Goatly (2007) are but a few of those who remind us that words are not innocent and that political systems, reigning ideologies and competing world-conceptions seek to shape and delimit the content we attribute to words like 'citizen', 'individual', 'state' and 'nation'. Even those concepts we cannot help feeling belong to the personal world, the private world of intimacy, which should (so we would like to believe) remain untouched and aloof from the political sphere – concepts like 'love', 'the family', 'the body' and 'purity' – are taken over and integrated into the worldview of a dominant conceptual paradigm.

Writers such as Adorno, Williams and Foucault are working within the framework of the social sciences, and therefore tend to consider the individual as the 'product' of social systems. Language, or what such writers often call 'discourse', is considered as a means of social pressure: depending upon the level of coercion, such writers will speak of socialisation, indoctrination, propaganda and manipulation.

Literary scholars, in contrast, refuse such a bleak and deterministic view of language and the individual's place within the tradition. Shakespeare, Goethe and Molière helped to shape their languages, giving the members of their own linguistic communities new vibrant visions of the world; and if writers' words and turns of phrases, rhythms, rhymes and metaphors continue to stimulate the way we express ourselves in everyday speech today, it is because the vitality of those authors' worldviews has not died within our language. To a greater or lesser extent, their ways of viewing the world continue to contribute to the ways we view the world. As the great German linguist Wilhelm von Humboldt (1767–1835) put it, poets and philosophers strike their roots into reality, and in doing so, they cultivate and shape our vision of the world. Poets have the capacity to shape our interior world, the intimate space within us, just as much as ideologies structure the frameworks within which we live and work.

It would, however, be a mistake to consider that literature can be exiled to the private sphere. As readers and literary critics often affirm, writers transform our conception of the public sphere. Writers, whether 'engaged' or not, contribute to our conception of politics. For this reason it is argued that Orwell or Kundera have their own worldviews. Indeed, it would seem clear that 'the Orwellian worldview' and the 'Big Brother' State are ideas which have taken root in reality, that is, in the sphere of political debate. Any Internet search engine will provide ample proof of this fact, and it is noteworthy that most Internet references to Orwell (in English, French, German and Czech) concern politics, and not the author himself. Orwell's concepts have, as it were, taken flight from literary circles; they have set up nest in the public sphere and become fixed points of reference.

At first glance, it would seem fair to set at opposite extremes this literary conception of worldview and the conception held to be a truism by many linguists, that is to say, that each language system is in itself a conceptual 'world'. Though generative linguists, and, in recent years, the second generation of cognitive linguistics, have tended to downplay linguistic diversity, many linguists believe that each language system opens up for us 'a whole new world', a world in which the 'objects of understanding', the concepts with which we speak and think, are shaped differently.

This belief in 'linguistic relativism' must be distinguished from philosophical relativism. And linguistic relativism has nothing whatsoever to do with the intellectual nihilism which became fashionable on American and British campuses in the 1970s and 1980s: that mode of reflection was inspired by a scant reading and febrile understanding of thinkers such as Derrida. The cultural relativism which rejects truth, questions the nature of meaning itself, and which engenders a deep and stubborn cynicism concerning the capacity of language to act as a means of making sense of the world bears nothing in common with the affirmations of the great American linguists Sapir and Whorf (or their contemporary counterparts Trabant and Wierzbicka). Sapir and Whorf were not concerned with challenging the capacity of English-speakers to make sense of the world: they simply pointed out that other language systems followed different paths in describing reality. Other languages 'make sense' using different means. Sapir and Whorf believed that language allows us to assimilate the world into consciousness, but our 'world' will always be 'given' to us in the form of a representation, a model rather than a graspable reality which can be mastered.

Reality, the objective world which science legitimately seeks to define and explain, is not in question. Sapir and Whorf simply contended that we use different means to grasp reality when we conceptualise the world and try to make sense of it for ourselves, and when we speak about it in our meaningful exchanges with others. While political analysts, such as Williams, consider the origins of nouns such as 'citizen' or 'individual' and adjectives such as 'private', linguists and philologists such as Humboldt (1999), Sapir (1949, 1985), Whorf (1984) and Trabant (2003, 2008) are concerned with the varying ways in which concepts evolve in different languages.

For all these thinkers, worldview and language prove to be central concepts. But this forces us to face up to the fact that there are at least three dimensions of worldview in play here:

1. The worldview of the language system, that mode of understanding which provides us with concepts and which organises
   the relationships between those concepts.
2. The worldview of each cultural mindset, a worldview which
   paradoxically must take root within a given linguistic worldview
   but which can migrate between language systems (as the spread
   of Catholicism, Protestantism, Buddhism and communism
   clearly demonstrates).
3. The worldview of the individual which finds its highest expression in the works of great writers who cultivate their language as
   Tolstoy, Dostoyevsky, Goethe, Shakespeare or Orwell have done.

It would be a mistake to take distinctions for classifications, separate categories. This subdivision will only serve if it is understood
as a means of discerning different conceptions of the relationship
between language and thought, between words and worldviews.
The sociologist reminds us that nobody can escape their culture,
and from this angle, it becomes plausible to consider men and
women as the 'products' of a given social system. Conversely,
however, the writer and the literary scholar remind us that all
fiercely free-thinking individuals are capable of expanding the
sphere of their own intellectual freedom by pushing back the limits
of their own language system at any given moment in history.

Ultimately, it makes little sense to consider the individual as
the passive object or 'victim' of ideology (as the causal logic of
the social sciences often invites us to do). All citizens are actors,
whether they play passive or active roles in adopting, imposing or
resisting dominant political discourse. In the same respect, though
each language opens up to us a 'world', and though we do, in a
certain sense, 'make our homes in the world' when we speak our
language with others, each language system opens up a sphere for
creative conceptual thought. Freedom and expression are inextricable. Individuals choose either to accept or to resist and to modify
the concepts that their mother tongue and cultural mindset provide
them with. And a third alternative remains open to the individual:
creative thinking, what Humboldt called the 'work of the spirit'
(*Arbeit des Geistes*). The individual can strike out on new paths to
invent radically new frameworks of understanding.

I have subdivided the concept of 'worldview' elsewhere (Underhill 2009b), because it became obvious to me that distinctions would be crucial, if thinkers of various academic disciplines were ever to come to any degree of understanding as to what was meant by the relationship between 'language' and 'worldview'. For this reason I suggested that it was necessary to distinguish between five subcategories for the term. While the concept of an ideological worldview can be encapsulated in one single term, 'conceptual mindset', the worldview of the language system and the worldview attributed to writers and individual speakers both required a further subdivision into two distinctions. This provides us with the following taxonomy:

1. **World-perceiving**, designating the frameworks of understanding which direct and shade our perception of the world.
2. **World-conceiving**, designating, the conceptual frameworks which enable us to communicate with others and engage in the discussion of ideas, impressions and feelings.
3. **Cultural mindset**, designating the worldview specific to a political regime or religion (and the concepts of 'man', 'woman', 'family', 'organisation', 'social stratification', 'social objectives', 'history', 'destiny', and so on, which take their place within the 'logic' of that mindset).
4. **Personal world**, designating the fairly stable system of concepts which organise and structure the worldview we can attribute to individuals and writers (for example, that worldview we attribute to Thomas Hardy, F. Scott Fitzgerald, Virginia Woolf or Jean-Paul Sartre).
5. **Perspective**, designating that fluctuating conceptual and emotional response we have in interacting with the world, whose shape is constantly being reaffirmed and reinvented by each one of us as we ourselves change and develop.

## PATTERNING

In one sense, worldviews can never be pinned down. In this respect they resemble Heraclitus's river, in which we can never bathe twice. Just as the river changes, flowing downstream, so we ourselves age and change. In the same way, however pervasive, however over-arching worldviews may be, it would be a mistake to believe that they can exist outside of the fluctuating minds of men and women. Languages (English, French, German, Czech or any other) do exist, certainly, but they have no real existence outside of the minds of those who speak them. Of course, texts do exist. These very paragraphs prove this. But only the mind can reorganise the text into a meaningful discourse. This present text only 'exists' because English resonates within my mind as a vibrant living language and because it resonates in a largely similar way within your own personal version of English, within your idiolect. It is our dynamic understanding of the relations between concepts that makes it possible for us to recognise the words of the text and to link them together to form a coherent, meaningful whole. Living languages live on in us. The meaning of words appears both fragile and intangible as soon as they are lifted out of context. Words are not the bricks in a construction which can be assigned definitive meanings outside of speech. If they were, polysemy and homonyms would be unthinkable. Words take on meaning in context by virtue of complex and subtle links and paths which are activated within the mind. Concepts can of course, be lifted out of language and discussed, but in separating them from their linguistic, their historical and their cultural context, we deprive them of much of the meaning which resonates within them when we observe them functioning within the language system, within discourse.

For this reason, Humboldt insisted that in order to understand the worldview of a foreign language the linguist must not only amass words, grammatical rules, morphological tendencies and concepts. This accumulation of isolated data was indeed important for Humboldt, but more important than this was the act of entering into the understanding of the way a language harnesses and organises concepts. How, for example, is the concept of space used to construct time in different languages? Is it possible to compare the construction of *Vorgestern* in German (literally 'before yesterday') with *avant-hier* in French? Can we find the same linear concept of time and of history in Czech and German? Do people in those languages speak of the 'march of history' and of conflicts between 'reactionaries' and 'forward-thinking' individuals? How does space shape our ideas on religion? Are the complex conceptual extensions of the 'moral path' which are found in the Bible translated in the same way into German and French as they are in English? Do other languages provide translatable concepts for 'wayward behaviour', 'lost persons', and people who 'turn their backs on truth' and 'fly from the face of God'? Does the Arabic of the Koran offer similar or alternative metaphoric mappings? Such questions force us to question our own worldview and the way it is linguistically constructed.

The linguistic project over the last two centuries has made so much progress in categorising individual elements of language (morphemes, phonemes, etc.), that we have tended to ignore Humboldt's imperative to investigate the interaction of elements within the language system as a whole. Humboldt used the term *Wechselwirkung* to designate this interaction of linguistic elements. This concept has been best defended in French by the contemporary thinker-translator-poet, Henri Meschonnic (1932–2009), who speaks of *le continu du langage*. In English-speaking countries, the best (but inevitably insufficient) concept which might be used to designate this living interaction of concepts is the term 'patterning', introduced by Sapir and developed in the unpublished works of Whorf (see Lee 1996).

Patterning must be understood as the links which bind concepts together. In Czech, for example, the terms for rights (*práva*) and for truth (*pravda*) are linked etymologically. In French a clear link is made between 'reality' and 'truth' when we speak of something as being *vrai* or when we insist on something being 'really so' (*vraiment*). Patterning refers to the unconscious association of words. In everyday speech, for example, we link adjectives to nouns in predictable collocations when we speak of 'abnormal behaviour', 'dysfunctional families', 'upper' and 'lower classes' or 'political corruption'. Such phrases present themselves to the mind almost as reflexes. Indeed, learning a language would be a much simpler business if it were only a question of learning words. If this were possible, word for word translation would cause no problem. What takes so much effort and sensitivity in language-learning, is discerning and mastering the relations between words, the bonds between concepts. And since people are constantly playing with language, this involves tracing the way individuals explore new paths in describing the world, and in speaking about the way it functions and about their own place in that world.

Not only the concepts themselves but the links between those concepts often turn out to be highly political. 'Upper classes' and 'lower classes' may seem innocent enough to certain English-speakers, but communists clearly discerned in these terms a hangover from the aristocratic age which imposed hierarchical value judgements upon the class system. For this reason, Czech communists, for example, rejected the equivalent terms in their own language.

In the same way, fundamental 'universal' concepts will take on different meanings in different languages. 'Freedom' will mean one thing in relation to the Czechoslovak communist State and something entirely different in the framework of the Bush or the Obama administrations. For the American, freedom evokes the individual's place within the market and his or her right to free expression within the sphere of public debate. For the Czechosolvak communist of the 1960s and 1970s, freedom might evoke freedom from poverty, freedom from homelessness, and equal rights to education and job opportunities.

For the French of the nineteenth century, the concepts of 'the people' (*le peuple*) and 'the State' (*l'État*) were irrevocably bound up together; their destinies were believed to be inextricable. A parallel link can be found in Czechoslovak communism of the post-war decades. In contrast, Americans and British citizens have in general tended to privilege the individual over the people, and 'the people' has (rightly) been perceived as a politically charged term and (wrongly) been disparaged as such. 'The people', as a concept or ideal, has never attained the same status as a cardinal concept in English-speaking countries. There is no English historian who has both unearthed the roots and celebrated the destiny of the 'English people' as the great French nineteenth-century historian, Jules Michelet, did when he wrote his erudite and inspired *Le Peuple* (1846). And the discourse of the European Union (which was long the bastion of French bureaucracy) has, in recent years, followed the Anglo-American, Thatcher–Reagan neo-liberal rhetoric which, in celebrating individual achievement and enterprise, leaves little space for 'the people'. Consequently, the European peoples are increasingly being asked to identify with transcultural concepts of 'the individual', 'the citizen' and 'the consumer', the conceptual pillars of a neo-liberal globalisation celebrated within the English-speaking world.

Understanding worldviews involves entering into the patterning of a language, the conceptual frameworks and the paths offered up by the language system to its linguistic community. Ultimately, only that linguistic community can keep a worldview alive or transform it. Sadly, however, despite a wealth of critical theory, critical discourse analysis, sociology and political theory, little scholarship has taken up Humboldt's challenge to investigate the paths opened up to humanity by other languages.

Humboldt believed that each language explores reality in a manner which is essentially specific to it. But while he envisaged a linguistics that would take on board the investigation into the way we carve our understanding of the world using words, nineteenth-century linguistics became, under the influence of the Indo-European project, increasingly formalistic. Texts and discourse were often considered to be secondary. And the 'scientific' aspirations of twentieth-century linguistics have tended to marginalise political and personal aspects of language by encouraging linguists to strive for 'objectivity'.

In recent years, Anna Wierzbicka (2004, 1997, 1999, 2010) has been one of the rare exceptions among those who have maintained a parallel study of the way language shapes thought and the way thought shapes language. She is one of the few scholars writing in English to have explored what the Polish Lublin School has termed *Etnolingwistyka* (ethnolinguistics) and which the Frenchman, Henri Meschonnic, has termed *anthropologie liguistique*. Both Wierzbicka and Meschonnic are concerned by the way in which the language system and reigning ideologies and cultural mindsets affect thinking and expression, and the way in which individuals express their resistance to dominant discourse and develop alternative modes of thought. As a translator, Meschonnic believes that the individual writer of one language can transform the language system of another by importing a foreign mode of consciousness. He believes a text can transform the tradition, and that a discourse can transform the language system. Ultimately, Meschonnic believes that our language system has no real concrete existence outside the confines of individual discourses. Consequently, the primacy of the speaking subject over the abstract concept we form of a language and its (ever-changing) rules, appears to Meschonnic, a logical consequence. In the same spirit as Meschonnic and Wierzbicka, I hope this book will make a useful and thought-provoking contribution by helping us to reconsider the way language shapes us and the way we shape language.

## THIS BOOK

This book is concerned with the creation of worldviews: that is, with the way *we* create them, the way *we* introduce them, maintain them and transform them. My intention, in writing this book, is to invite readers into the kind of intellectual adventure that translators set off upon when they enter into foreign worldviews; because translators must inhabit more than one 'world', if they are to be able to build bridges between worlds with their translations. The difficulty of the task must not be underestimated. Humboldt believed it was never possible for us to fully enter into a foreign worldview, because we inevitably try to translate foreign concepts into our own. We attempt to assimilate foreignness into our own familiar frameworks of understanding. The temptation to believe that *parole* in French means 'speech' in English, that *langage* means 'language', that *Liebe* in German dovetails perfectly with 'love' in English, and that *citoyen* evokes the same connotations for French-speakers as 'citizen' for Americans, ultimately proves too great for us. And it is only when we find ourselves unable to convey our thoughts fully in a foreign tongue, that we realise that we are linking concepts and words in ways which appear curious, if not absurd, to the people we are speaking to.

Humboldt believed that understanding worldviews was a painstaking quest which required the exhaustive accumulation of empirical linguistic data. This process will inevitably exhaust the patience of certain readers. It is also understandable that some readers will be hoping that radically different, exotic worlds will be opened up for them. Whorf's own claims about the Hopi conception of time do indeed reinforce such hopes; but his theories were sadly based upon rather scant and inconclusive evidence, and no attempt at discourse analysis was made by Whorf (no doubt due to his insufficient knowledge of the Hopi language). The present work is written in an entirely different spirit. I will not strive to stress the exotic by downplaying similarities to be found in different languages. Indeed, studies of freedom in Polish and English (Wierzbicka 1997) or anger in those same two languages (Mikołajczuk 1998, 2004) uncover a significant degree of coincidence. Other comparative studies confirm the existence of a surprising degree of similarity to be found among languages. Despite startling differences, and creative innovations in the construction of the concept of the 'sexual act' in English, French and Czech, the metaphors used to construct the concept in each of the three languages often coincides. All three languages frequently conceive of love and the act of making love in terms of 'madness', or in terms of a 'game', for example (see Underhill 2007). Such similarities deserve to be studied in detail rather than being ignored as the startlingly bizarre and exotic differences between languages are highlighted and paraded in order to pander to the reader's taste for novelty. This book aims therefore to be modest in its claims, but rigorous in its empirical analysis of concepts.

How are we to enter into worldviews, then? What doorway or window shall we choose to seek entry? Since the 1980s, cognitive scholars have focused upon metaphor as one of the primary modes of conceptual organisation in language. In the present work, I have, therefore, selected metaphor as one of the possible entries into worldviews. No doubt other doorways exist. But cognitive scholars have rightly held up metaphor as one fundamental element of language, and it is because I consider metaphor to be crucial for the construction of worldviews, that the first part of the book will be devoted to appraising the contribution of cognitive scholars. In highlighting that contribution, I will juxtapose the aims, methodologies and concepts of other disciplines and evaluate their contribution to thought on the nature and the functioning of metaphor in language and understanding. The final chapters of Part I will be devoted to the research of schools (often in non-English-speaking countries) on the periphery of the cognitive project.

Such research is unlikely to be integrated into the cognitive project in the coming years, however, because an Anglo-centric trend has tended to emerge among the publications of the second generation of cognitive scholars. There has been a return to the almost religious quest for universals which, as Stephen Levinson points, out craves for sweeping conclusions but is often based upon a pitiful lack of empirical evidence (Levinson 2003: 63). The tendency to speak of 'language' without considering languages in recent years has led to what I have termed a 'languageless linguistics' in translating Jürgen Trabant's term *une linguistique sans langue* (Trabant 2007). Nevertheless, I believe that by demonstrating the originality of foreign work which either has been inspired by the cognitive approach to metaphor, or which approaches some of the fundamental questions related to metaphor from new angles, a debate on the nature of worldviews can be opened.

Part II of the book attempts to ground metaphor study in discourse analysis. In this attempt, the book does not stand alone. In recent years various scholars (Eubanks 2000; Goatly 2007) have employed metaphor analysis, by applying conceptual tools introduced by Lakoff and Johnson to the fields of discourse analysis and rhetoric. Their conclusions have proven fruitful and insightful. The three case studies in this book should also demonstrate the importance of discourse analysis for metaphor study. By framing the debate in terms of worldview, these studies should serve to show that metaphors are fundamental for all discourse and for the construction of our concepts. But at the same time they should explicate the ways in which individuals handle metaphor in their struggle to express their ideas and assert their arguments.

The first case study investigates the way in which metaphor proves fundamental in the construction of Czechoslovak communist rhetoric. It aims to unveil the conceptual clusters which allow the communist worldview to hold together and gain a degree of coherence and logic. By studying passages taken from Petr Fidelius's account of the State newspaper, *Rudé Právo*, the ways in which individuals contributed to the consolidation and the elaboration of party doctrine and socialist objectives will be analysed.

In the second case study, Victor Klemperer's critique of Nazi rhetoric will be reframed in terms of metaphor theory. By analysing the conceptual clusters and the conceptual paths travelled by the Nazi vision of the world, I will attempt to demonstrate that (in contrast to Fidelius's communist worldview), the Nazi worldview is inherently illogical and anti-rational. Seven 'perversions' will be discussed in this contribution to a critique of propaganda.

The third and final case study will attack linguistics with the tools provided by discourse analysis and metaphor theory. The aim of this study is both fundamental and ambitious. The objective is to demonstrate that all of our concepts of language are in fact metaphorically constructed. In other words, just as we can search for metaphors 'in' language, if we wish to pin down what we mean by language we must search for it 'in' metaphors. Moreover, the study of the construction of French as a concept should help us to understand that each language is constructed differently. The metaphoric construction of French, and most of all the florid lyricism used to celebrate that language, and the claims about the 'clarity' and 'purity' of French syntax and grammar, will seem outlandish to the English-speaker's imagination. Nevertheless, English-speakers, in contemplating their own idea of their mother tongue, cannot escape metaphors. The comparative study of ecolinguistics in French and English should serve to prove that it is the underlying logic of metaphoric constructions which leads people to make claims in both languages that we must act urgently 'to save' 'dying' languages. 'Living languages', 'dying languages': what are these but organic metaphors?

Discourse analysis and metaphor theory therefore challenge the conception of language used in linguistics. Linguists often wish to compare languages they do not speak. This involves superficial and sweeping generalisations of 'fundamental' or 'structural' levels of language. But what is represented as the 'deeper' levels of language often translates into rather superficial investigation. Metaphor takes us into discourse, and this study of the metaphors of language should serve to underline that if we wish to enter into visions of the world and into conceptions of language, then we must enter deeply into the patterning of concepts. We must trace the way they are harnessed, understood and expressed by living, speaking individuals. From this perspective, this study of language should highlight that the concepts of 'language' we construct are often far removed from the reality of speakers and writers.

Humboldt is often forgotten and often pushed to one side. This reflex is recurrent throughout history, but it is not so difficult to explain. Humboldt is the guilty conscience of modern linguistics. He is there to remind us that language is not simply about parts of speech, grammar, structure, rules and norms; language is about us. Speaking involves speakers. If metaphor serves to put us back on course, and leads us back into reflecting upon what language is and what we do with it, if it leads us to understand that without language, culture and history and common human endeavours are inconceivable, it will have done linguistics a great service. And it will attract a wide range of students and thinkers, who will see in linguistics not the dry analysis of objective laws and structural constraints, but the locus of becoming, the ongoing birth of worlds, worlds in which to live, worlds to create and to transform, together in speech.

# CHAPTER 2

# A Concern for Metaphor

One rich and wide-reaching element in language has become the focal point of much study in the past three decades: metaphor. If this element of language has aroused such interest, it is because there has been increasing recognition that all of our concepts are framed within metaphorical terms. Rather than a model of language based upon the linguistic sign (a model which implies that words designate things in the world outside of language), linguists today are more inclined to accept that there exists a figurative substructure to concepts. This in turn helps us to understand that concepts are not extra-lingual entities existing in the world and awaiting discovery by the mind and awaiting definition by philosophers. Thanks to progress in metaphor theory, it has become clear that concepts are the inventions of the mind as it works with and within language to construct meaningful configurations of thought.

Our model for the very concept of thought in English can serve as an example to demonstrate the figurative basis of abstract concepts. Sweetser (1990) investigated and catalogued an extensive subsystem of metaphors which enable us to define our concept of the human mind in terms of a *body system*. This model allows us to understand such expressions as 'His mind is going' and 'That's a weight off my mind'. Our concept for 'mind' may present some difficulties for translation. However, the fact that we can find such phrases as the French one, *avoir l'esprit vif* ('to have a sharp mind, a lively imagination'), bears witness to the fact that other languages also understand the mind in terms of a metaphorical 'body'.

Lakoff and Johnson (1999: 236–66) went on to explore the ramifications of this bodily concept of the mind for our concept of thought, concluding that expressions such as 'My mind was **racing**' and 'Harry kept going off on **flights of fancy**' show that we frame thinking in terms of moving. Ideas become locations, as in the expression 'We have **arrived at the crucial point** in the argument'. Understanding comes to mean 'following', as in the expression 'I'm stuck! I can't go any **farther along this line** of reasoning' (236). Curiously, this model of thought can lead us to disengage the thinking person from any responsibility for the direction of his or her thoughts. Reasoning becomes a force which imposes upon us 'a step-by-step journey' leading us towards a conclusion. It becomes a journey in which steps cannot be skipped, and along which any digression will be condemned as 'wandering away from the point' or 'going off at a tangent' (237).

One point of entry into the question of worldviews would be to compare the degree to which our concepts (and the metaphorical frameworks which engender them) coincide in different languages. If the world we perceive, think of and act within, is opened up to us by language, then the concepts which make up our language should be compared and contrasted with the conceptions of the world which emerge in different languages. This should allow us to ascertain the way each one 'channels' the direction of thoughts and even 'frames' the emerging configurations of thinking. Concepts and categories, Lakoff argued (1987), reveal something about the mind. Exploring the framing and organisation of our concepts amounts, therefore, to investigating the way the mind works.

Language should not, however, be conceived of as a 'doorway' into the mind. Such a metaphor would mislead us into supposing that language and thought are separate rooms, and that we pass through the former to reach the latter. Neither should it be supposed that we translate from thought into language, as the expression, 'putting your thoughts into words' leads us to suppose. Speaking and thinking form the two inextricable partners of a shared ongoing adventure. Categories reveal what Humboldt would have called 'the work of the mind' in language. Concepts are the layers of elaborated thought that are handed down for us to build upon as we learn to understand and to improvise with our mother tongue. If we adopt Lakoff and Johnson's hypothesis that language can 'reveal' something about the mind, then 'reveal' should not be taken to mean that language either 'reflects' something pre-existent or 'covers' something hidden. Both interpretations mean falling back into a misleading dualistic paradigm in which language is represented as the insufficient and inferior reflection of a purer, more objective conceptual world. At best, such a paradigm distorts our vision of thought; at worst, it perverts and hinders it.

The contribution made by Lakoff and Johnson to the discussion of the relationship between thought and language was to identify the weakness of the 'objectivist account of cognition', in which:

> Thought is characterized as symbol-manipulation. Concepts [they argued] are characterized as symbols in a system of fixed correspondence to things and categories in the world. Those symbols are made meaningful *only* via symbol-to-word correspondences. Correct reason is viewed as symbol-manipulation that accurately mirrors the rational structure of the world. (Lakoff 1987: 173)

In contrast to this approach, Lakoff argued that thought is *embodied*:

> The structures used to put together our conceptual systems grow out of bodily experience and make sense in terms of it; moreover, the core of our conceptual systems is directly grounded in perception, body movement and experience of a physical and social character. (Lakoff 1987: xiv)

Back in 1923, the German neo-Kantian thinker, Ernst Cassirer, who relied heavily upon Humboldt's conception of language, had expressed himself in very similar terms, arguing that the concept of the body and the frameworks related to its activity in the world were constantly at work in allowing us to invent conceptual frameworks for abstractions and the relationships we posit between those abstractions:

If we attempt to follow still farther the ways by which language progresses from its first sharply defined local distinctions to general spatial specifications and terms, we seem
to find here again that the direction of this development is
outward from the centre. The 'differentiation of locations
in space' starts from the situation of the speaker and spreads
in concentric circles until the objective whole, the sum and
system of local specifications has been articulated. At first
local distinctions are closely linked with specific material distinctions – and it is eminently the differentiation of the parts
of his own body that serves man as a basis for all other spatial
specifications. Once he has formed a distinct representation
of his own body, once he has apprehended it as a self-enclosed
and intrinsically articulated organism, it becomes as it were, a
model according to which he constructs the world as a whole.
In this perception of his body, he possesses an original set of
coordinates, to which in the course of development he con-
tinually returns and refers – and from which accordingly he
draws the terms which serve to designate this development.
(Cassirer 1968: 206–9)

Cassirer was well versed in the German linguistic tradition of
his time. But that tradition had largely forgotten Humboldt's
speculative linguistic philosophy which placed man at the centre
of language. Consequently, Cassirer's influence was limited. His
impact on language study was no doubt also hindered by the rise of
fascism, which finally forced him to flee his homeland in order to
take refuge in the United States.

In France, the conceptual foundations of thought were explored
and catalogued by Georges Matoré in his L'espace Humain (1962),
an impressive study which rigorously analysed the rhetoric and
reasoning of philosophers, literary writers and journalists, in
order to make a rich synthesis of what Matoré called the 'mental
geometry' of thought, the 'mental space' of language. By analysing the way French people use such primary forms as coordinates,
line, surface and volume to define their ideas, Matoré showed the
dynamic forces at work constructing the dimensions of the space
French people invent for themselves in the world around them.

Matoré asserted that space is 'constructed'. Space is not a physical material given: space is conceptualised. Furthermore, Matoré demonstrated our conception of space varies from period to period. In his own period, for example, Matoré traced the crisis of the continuous vision of experience and events, in which discontinuous modes of representation were brought to bear in order to force us to question the nature of order and organisation. This alternative mode of conception of space introduced a dynamics which undermined the representation of cause and effect, rejected the representation of events in sequences, and which highlighted shocks, tensions and fragmentation. Such a 'mental geometry' was doubly disconcerting. Not only were traditional processes for structuring events renounced, the observer of those events was cut loose from his or her anchorage in space and time. The events which we experience can no longer be conceived of in terms of objects moving through space, because such a conception rests upon the observation of experience from a detached stationary position. If we accept the modern view which posits a situated subject and a fluid perception of experience, the objective understanding of passing events becomes untenable. The 'individual' and the 'space' in which he lived were, Matoré argued, concepts which had come under attack. Unfortunately, Matoré, unlike Cassirer, was never translated into English, and his work, like so many other perplexingly original works, did not find its place within mainstream French thought in the 1960s and 1970s. Today, Matoré is virtually forgotten in France.

The work of Cassirer and Matoré can be considered precedents to the ideas advanced by Lakoff and Johnson and in some respects their conclusions take us beyond questions currently being raised in cognitive research. Nonetheless, Matoré has made no impact on the ideas of English-speaking countries and the influence of Cassirer was felt more in philosophy and in the social sciences, rather than in linguistics. We would not, therefore, be justified in assuming them to be precursors to Lakoff and Johnson in a linear conception of the history of ideas. The originality of Lakoff and Johnson and the far-reaching influence of their work cannot be questioned. These two researchers refocused discussion of language on the body, bodily metaphors and conceptual extensions which are body-bound. This direction in their thought upsets formal linguistics and objectivist views of reality which persist in representing language as a complex series of signs denoting existing objects to which all words are supposed to refer. Concepts like 'time', 'anger' and 'desire' do correspond to something we experience concretely or physically, but our perception of 'time', 'anger' and 'desire' is always constructed, organised by language. 'Anger' and 'desire' are not objects in the world awaiting designation: they are complex constructs which are defined and organised by the mind using the physical experience we have of the world as a basis for constructing metaphors. In this respect Lakoff and Johnson are siding with Sapir, who expresses the idea that the world is not a pile of assembled objects to which language must attach labels. Sapir argued that different languages were not, as is sometimes supposed, different sets of labels for the same things. Though the work of Lakoff and Johnson limits itself to English on the whole, their study of categorisation is implicitly relativistic in that it reveals that languages do not simply bear witness to an organised reality: language organises and structures our perception and conception of reality and experience.

Their approach also has the virtue of forcing us to question deterministic accounts which represent it as a system within which man is 'trapped'. This is a particularly dogmatic interpretation of the Sapir–Whorf hypothesis, however. It deforms the thought of both linguists to a large extent, despite having gained wide currency in many academic circles. In contrast to this pessimistic and dogmatic account of worldview, Lakoff, like Humboldt, affirms that language and thought are both essentially 'imaginative'. By this, Lakoff means that in both individual speech and language as a whole, those concepts which are not directly grounded in experience employ metaphor, metonymy and mental imagery. Our imagination takes us beyond the literal mirroring, or representation, of external reality. The rigorous analysis of metaphor offered by Lakoff and Johnson allows us to win back a concept that is often assigned a precarious place in modern thought: imagination is no longer a flight of fancy, it is a fundamental process of the organising mind. Metaphor, one of the fundamental modes of the imagination, cannot therefore be excluded from the analysis of experience, nor should it be regarded as a literary process of meaning transfer, a poetic but essentially 'disruptive' semantic process. Lakoff and Johnson (and the cognitive linguists who followed in their footsteps) refused the division of language into literal and figurative forms which tended to make metaphor the prerogative of the poets rather than the concern of linguists and thinkers in general.

The position Lakoff and Johnson adopt, does, it must be admitted, entail a certain confusion of traditional rhetorical categories. For example, Lakoff and Johnson would class 'personification' as a form of 'metaphor'. Likewise, though they distinguish between novel metaphors, expressions and underlying 'conceptual metaphors' (or what they first called 'protometaphors', in 1980), they do tend to see them all as part of a generic category of analogical processes. For this reason they will argue that most language is *metaphoric*. This argument is misleading: it appears absurdly daring and provocative until we come to understand that by 'metaphoric' they mean 'catachrestic' (reliant on lexical or dead metaphors). For example, Lakoff and Johnson will point to examples like 'the **leg** of the table' or 'time**table**' as evidence of the 'metaphoric' origins of expressions and composite words. Though what they are arguing is perfectly true, it is certainly not revolutionary. None of the linguists whom Cassirer relied upon would have contested this fact, and indeed, the catachrestic origins of concepts have long been shown by etymologists.

Nonetheless, by considering all language as metaphoric, Lakoff and Johnson were making an essential point: the division of language into one concrete literal form and another abstract intangible form is misleading. They refused the idea that conceptual language has a literal basis. Concepts do not exist without the linguistic constraints that create them, and those linguistic constraints are subject to the meaning we accord them as we use the language of bodily experience metaphorically to frame experience of a more abstract kind. Does this mean that our concepts have no basis in, and no relationship to reality? Not necessarily. Lakoff and Johnson would not argue, for example, that 'freedom' does not exist, but they would contend that the way we define it and the way we use and abuse that definition depends upon conceptual metaphors derived from bodily experience. Freedom is not a clear-cut product or property of the world 'out there'. And if we are to grasp it, we will have to define it, in language, in metaphors. We 'defend' freedom. We 'win' freedom.

# CHAPTER 3

# Metaphors We Live By

The explosion of work on metaphor in recent decades has its roots in the ground-breaking book *Metaphors We Live By*, written by Lakoff and Johnson in 1980. Though the two authors have modified their position in separate and co-written works since then, and though cognitive approaches have moved on to other fields of linguistics, semantics and epistemology, and though they have introduced new paradigms for analysing metaphor, it is worth quoting the fundamental claims made in this work, since these claims have influenced the terms of the debate that revolves around the representation of conceptual constructs in language. The pith of these fundamental claims can be summed up in seven points:

1. **Metaphors live.** Following in the footsteps of the French philosopher, Paul Ricœur, Lakoff and Johnson argued that the figurative language of everyday expressions could not be considered as 'dead metaphors', because they exerted a lively influence upon the ways we formulate our ideas and express them. Many people organise their lives around metaphors like **'time is money'**. Others find a poignant emotional content in the expression 'our relationship has **broken down**'. It is perfectly conceivable that the logic of the conceptual metaphor underlying the latter expression (Relationships are Machines) might induce the partners of a 'dysfunctional' relationship to

treat their love as they would a washing machine which breaks down: that is to say, by throwing it out. The consequences of metaphors for behaviour led Lakoff and Johnson to argue that metaphors were conceptual patterns that we follow, or, as they put it, that 'we live by'.

2.  **Metaphors form systematic constructs.** Metaphors and figurative language in general have traditionally been treated as isolated incidents, creative acts of expressive individuals who innovate in language by embellishing literal forms of expression. Lakoff and Johnson on the other hand explored a wide number of cases in which figurative expressions could be traced back to a common root, a 'conceptual metaphor' around which figurative expressions took form in an ordered and logical manner. For example, if time is money, someone can be 'wasting' your time. In the same way, you can refuse to 'invest' your time in a 'prof-itless venture'. 'Time is Money' is not a one-way metaphor. Money itself can be transfigured metaphorically. A spiritual experience can be 'enriching' and is therefore not a 'waste' of time, though it brings no material gain. In a word, metaphors are embedded in networks of underlying conceptual equations. Novel metaphors grow out of language as branches grow from the trunks of trees. These trunks function as clearly defined analogical points of reference. And the roots attached to those trunks reach deep into the language, and deep into our minds. Lakoff and Johnson were thus rejecting the idea of metaphors as random 'flights of fancy'. If metaphors could still be seen as creative endeavours, then the trajectories of those flights of fancy were at least to some extent mapped out along the flight plans that were already drawn up within the language itself. In contrast to romantic and modernist poetics, in which the individual writer creatively resists or rebels against language, the model of creativity which Lakoff and Johnson were moving towards was one in which the poet, or the expressive individual, reawakens language to its own inherently creative potential. That individual harnesses that potential and leads language along a new modified course.

3.  **Metaphors highlight and hide.** Metaphors highlight certain aspects of a concept while they may also hide other parts. The

oft-quoted conceptual metaphor 'Argument is War' highlights the competitive element present in many debates, but it can hide the fact that much debate is conducted in the endeavour to find a shared solution.

4. **Conceptual metaphors often contradict one another.** Though many metaphors may be attributable to one common core conceptual metaphor from which they are logically extended, conceptual metaphors themselves may be mutually exclusive. Time is often represented as moving through space, as in the expression 'time flies'. But this does not prevent us from using a contradictory metaphoric representation in which we are moving through time. Time is consequently represented as being static, as in the expression 'We're approaching the end of the year' (Lakoff and Johnson 1980: 44). To take another example, 'love' may be considered in terms of a journey, as when we say 'She really took me places'. But it may also be considered as an object fixed in time and space. We can look for love just as we can abandon it as we move on to new things. Thus, the person who one day finds themselves 'speeding down the highway of love' may, a few weeks later, find themselves complaining, 'It's not like it used to be. You left our love behind. You turned your back on our love.' Though at a deeper conceptual level these might be considered to be the equivalents of that stylistic faux pas, the 'mixed metaphor', they prove that various conceptual metaphors can form the basis of one single concept. Far from being regrettable, mutually incompatible metaphors allow us to use one conceptual metaphor to highlight aspects of a concept or experience which are hidden by another conceptual metaphor. For many people, for example, love has a dynamic moving element and a fixed unchanging aspect. This may seem like a paradox in logical terms, and it will no doubt perplex the philosopher who seeks to define the very 'essence' of 'love' as an unchanging concept which designates a permanent phenomenological given. Nevertheless, mutually exclusive metaphors do allow us to express the often contradictory nature of our emotional experiences, and in this sense, contradictory metaphors form an essential part of meaningful speech.

5. **Metaphors are grounded in experience.** Conceptual metaphors are often based upon bodily experience of the world.
   When we say someone 'swallowed' an idea, we conceive of
   ideas as objects which can be introduced into the mind as
   though it were a container, a stomach. This allows us to establish the conceptual metaphor 'Ideas are Food' (Lakoff and
   Johnson 1980: 147–8). The extensions derived from this bodily
   basis often seem to correspond to our experience of reality. If
   we say we are 'sickened by the idea' of exploitative child labour
   in developing countries, we are expressing ourselves figura-
   tively but we may have a corresponding physical reaction to
   the idea which seems to legitimise the metaphorical basis of our
   expression.

6. **Metaphors create similarity.** While Aristotle believed that
   the skill of manipulating metaphors could not be taught since
   it required an insight into the profound similarities between
   different things, Lakoff and Johnson argued that in many
   cases there was no correspondence or similarity between the
   source domain and the target domain of the metaphor. On the
   contrary, they argued that figurative language often created
   the similarity, or the illusion of similarity. They argued there
   was no particular reason why we should say 'the stock market
   is up today'. Nevertheless, we often experience metaphors as
   minor revelations. Intuition seems to be unveiling very real
   similarities in the world. If metaphors make immediate sense
   to people, Lakoff and Johnson argued, this was because they
   are grounded in the logic of the language. 'The stock market is
   up' makes sense to us because it activates a pervasive conceptual
   metaphor, 'More is Up'.

7. **Metaphor is the cardinal trope.** As has already been mentioned, the scope of metaphor, traditionally defined within the
   fields of rhetoric and poetics as a colourful or expressive use of
   language which departs from literal language, was widened to
   embrace other forms of comparison, the simile (for example,'
   pretty as a rose'), metonymy (for example, 'Can you give me
   a hand?') and personification (for example, 'Liberty *conquers*
   tyranny').

As has been said, these ideas have been criticised and adapted by other scholars, and the authors who advanced them have, to some extent, elaborated upon them and modified them. Nevertheless, these seven ideas continue to shape debate on metaphor in a wide number of fields, in various disciplines around the world.

CHAPTER 4

# Other Developments in Metaphor Theory

It would be a mistake to assume that cognitive linguists uncovered the secret power of metaphor. At least two reasons contradict such an idea: firstly, there has always been a great deal of work on metaphor, and, secondly, the concept of metaphor has itself been expanded in cognitive research to encompass questions and fields of study which up until recently had been investigated by scholars who did not consider metaphor to be their principle focus of interest. Indeed, a wide variety of disciplines from grammar to comparative linguistics have now entered into the metaphor debate. In contrast to this loose or all-embracing definition of metaphor adopted in cognitive linguistics, much of the research into metaphor that has been done throughout history and which has continued to develop parallel to cognitive research has proceeded by maintaining a restrained definition; for many approaches, metaphor remains a rhetorical trope. Four main approaches can be discerned among the diverse theories which attempt to account for metaphor as a trope: (1) philosophical investigations, (2) linguistic approaches, (3) the poetic tradition and (4) the rhetorical tradition.

## PHILOSOPHICAL INVESTIGATIONS

Let us begin with the philosophical account of metaphor. Philosophers, going back at least as far as Plato, have been intrigued by metaphor. This fact is, nonetheless, given a very biased treatment by cognitive scholars. Johnson, a philosopher at the University of Oregon, has steered the Lakoff and Johnson tandem from a linguistic towards an increasingly philosophical position as regards metaphor. But in both *The Body in the Mind* (1987), the expression of his individual stance, and in the expression of their joint position, *Philosophy in the Flesh* (1999), Johnson adopted a critical approach to philosophy. For both Johnson and Lakoff, metaphor represents a challenge to philosophy. To a certain extent, Johnson and Lakoff see themselves as thinkers who are taking up the challenge that philosophy has laid down to metaphor, since, according to them, metaphor has always been maligned and disparaged by philosophers.

Plato is the first arch-enemy of metaphor that Lakoff and Johnson set out to tackle. 'Plato, [they argued] viewed poetry and rhetoric with suspicion and banned poetry from his utopian republic because it gives no truth of its own, stirs up the emotions, and thereby blinds mankind to real truth.' This view, stated in 1980 (190) remained largely unchanged in 1999 when Lakoff and Johnson outlined the central tenets of the traditional theory of metaphor, the first three of which are:

> Metaphor is a matter of words, not thought. Metaphor occurs when a word is applied not to what it normally designates but to something else.
> Metaphorical language is not part of ordinary conventional language. Instead, it is novel and typically arises in poetry, rhetorical attempts at persuasion, and scientific discovery.
> Metaphorical language is deviant. In metaphor, words are not used in their proper senses. (1999: 119)

This prejudice against metaphor is, indeed, deeply entrenched in the university. The Lakoff–Johnson representation of the history of ideas in the West does, however, stand at odds with two essential facts, which both Lakoff and Johnson labour to downplay. Firstly, all the great philosophers have always expressed an interest in representation. The question is fundamental for both Plato and Aristotle, and Plato frequently makes use of allegories to expound his ideas. Secondly, a great deal of modern philosophy from Cassirer onwards has taken on board a concern for language and representation. This makes symbolic language and metaphor an inescapable part of their concerns.

Parallel to the work of cognitive linguists, the leading deconstructionists, Jacques Derrida in *La mythologie blanche* (1971) and Paul de Man in *Allegories of Reading* (1979) were arguing for a philosophy which could integrate the capacity to reflect upon its own process of reflection. Derrida argued that any definition of metaphor implied not only an underlying philosophical system, but also that philosophy itself depended upon the conceptual network which had constituted it.

Nonetheless, though Lakoff and Johnson certainly misrepresent Plato and overstate their case in defending metaphor against philosophy, it would indeed at times appear to be true that philosophers have expressed a certain hostility to metaphor. In the quest for an accurate or 'true' representation of reality, metaphor is considered to be a false form, a misrepresentation. In 1651, Hobbes, for example, declared that metaphor meant using words in a way they were not ordained to be used so as to deceive people (Hobbes 1985: 102). But Hobbes (to be fair to him) was thinking of rhetoric and propaganda. Like Thucydides, the historian of the Peloponnesian war (whom Hobbes translated into English from Greek), Hobbes was concerned with the ways propaganda tended to blur the meanings of words in order to make war, aggression, pillage and murder seem respectable. As we might imagine, Hobbes found that metaphors could contribute greatly to this process of *blurring*.

Moreover, it would be absurdly reductive to take the reflection of Hobbes as being representative of philosophy as a whole. In contrast to Hobbes's position, various philosophers have agreed with Nietzsche that many of the meanings of our words are metaphorical in origin. The controversy between philosophers in the romantic period centred not on the question of whether metaphor was fundamental for language, but rather consisted in a division into two camps contesting the origin and status of metaphor in language. One school of thought was championed by Nietzsche and claimed that language was initially concrete and literal in reference, while abstract vocabulary which is now considered to be literal is, in fact, metaphorical (Martin, in Preminger and Brogan 1993: 763). Another school of thought, which had its roots in the romantic tradition which preceded Nietzsche by over a century, was championed by Rousseau, Herder and later by Shelley. According to all three thinkers, the origins of language were to be found in poetry. In this romantic tradition, it was imagined that sense had generated out of sound. Music gave rise to meaning: chanting and rhythm were primary, primitive (and therefore all the more noble) forms of expression which were endowed with a vitality which modern poetry, so the argument went, should strive to emulate. For such writers, metaphors preceded literal forms of language.

In the twentieth century, many philosophers focused on the question of metaphor. In Wittgenstein's opinion, it was because the philosophical investigation of logic and ethics could not ground itself directly in reality that philosophers would always run up against the limits of language. For this reason, his investigations often involved the interpretation of metaphors, formulations on the frontiers of language-bound thought. His formulation of the question of unfulfilled wishes, for example, is strangely reminiscent of the approach espoused by Lakoff and Johnson:

§439. In wiefern kann man den Wunsch, die Erwartung, den Glauben, etc. 'unbefriedigt' nennen? Was ist unser Urbild der Unbefriedigung? Ist es ein Hohlraum? Und würde man von einem solchen sagen, er sei unbefriedigt? Wäre das nicht auch eine Metapher? – Ist es nicht ein Gefühl, was wir Unbefriedigung nennen, – etwa den Hunger?

In what sense can one call wishes, expectations, beliefs, etc. 'unsatisfied'? What is our prototype of nonsatisfaction? Is it a hollow space? And would one call that unsatisfied? Wouldn't this be a metaphor too? – Isn't what we call nonsatisfaction a feeling – say hunger? (Wittgenstein 2001: 109–10)

Wittgenstein's later philosophy of language was elaborated to a great extent using the metaphor of 'language games' in which 'players' learned the 'rules' necessary to allow them to communicate within given contexts. Wittgenstein's philosophical investigations had a considerable influence on linguistics as a whole, and semantics in particular (especially his critique of prototypical meaning). It would, therefore, be a mistake to consider linguistics and philosophy as clearly defined and mutually impermeable disciplines.

In recent years, the deconstructionist interpretations of the rhetorical strategies of the text can be seen as another chapter in philosophy's concern for the question of metaphor. And Nanine Charbonnel's thought-provoking work on metaphor situates her at the crossroads of philosophical, rhetorical, psychoanalytic and socio-cultural approaches to metaphor in that she explicates the conceptual foundations of Biblical imagery and allegories of the Catholic church, Freudian theory, as well as our ways of speaking about education, and hermeneutics. In analysing the transformation of the *Éducation Nationale*, the French state school system, for example, Charbonnel demonstrates the metaphoric consequences for post-revolutionary society when it replaced the parish priest with the school teacher. As she demonstrates, teaching colonised the founding metaphors used to define religion, the priest and his vocation. The teacher became a man 'illuminated' by 'enlightenment' whose 'vocation' it was to 'guide the flock' along 'the path to wisdom' (Charbonnel: 9–30). Charbonnel's study is revealing in that it shows how antagonistic and revolutionary movements invariably adopt the terms, concepts and underlying arguments of the bodies and the individuals they oppose: opposition is not only a breaking free, it is also, to some degree, a conceptual merging with the adversary. Her work demonstrates that above and beyond literature and philosophy, the study of metaphor can take us into concerns of a historical, political and sociological nature.

## LINGUISTIC APPROACHES

Linguistic approaches also reveal the ways distinct disciplines tend to overlap when it comes to defining metaphor. Among the linguistic approaches we can quote the research of the *Group Mu* which considered much of language to be figurative in nature while they reserved the term 'degree zero' for literal language from which much literary language and everyday language deviates. Ricœur's work situates him between linguistics and philosophy. One of his major contributions to the debate was to stress that metaphor cannot be explained in terms of words or even in terms of sentences; metaphors can only be understood in terms of discourse. This is an important stance to take, because lexicography (the study of words) tends to encourage us to examine language as a system of signs, and, as a result, linguistic approaches to metaphor often forget to take context into account. In the traditional framework, metaphor becomes a sign which is replaced or displaced by another sign. The literal meaning is cancelled out or transformed by the metaphorical meaning. Countering this, Ricœur stressed that words are by nature endowed with multiple significations and they take on their meanings only within the context of individual expression. Even at the most basic level, a sentence is not the sum of the meanings of the words within it: it is the sentence which determines the meaning of words by forging the links between them.

To formulate this in the terms of pragmatics, words mean what they are used to mean. If this is the case, metaphor does not necessarily entail a displacement of an initial meaning. Let us consider an example using an animal to describe a particular human character trait. In films like *West Side Story*, the concept of Man-as-a-Cat is established through multiple references to 'coolness'. Coolness is already a metaphor which assimilates lack of heat with lack of emotion, nonchalance, and the cat, the 'cool cat', is seen as incarnating this quality of admirable detachment. The young men of films like *West Side Story* wish to incarnate the virtue of the metaphorical cat, coolness, of course. Once this metaphorical link between nonchalance and cats has been established in the imagination, we leave phenomenological reality behind: real cats no longer come into the equation. Consequently, we can rely upon the *cool cat* as a concept unrelated to cats of the real world.

This is precisely what culture does time and time again, recycling established metaphoric paradigms. In Walt Disney's *The Aristocats*, for example, the cool cat folk theory makes it meaningful for a kitten to sing a blues song in which the refrain is 'Everybody wants to be a cat.' Obviously, it would be absurd to aspire to become what one already is. To this extent a kitten aspiring to become a cat is a meaningless pleonasm, and in this absurdity lies the humour of the Walt Disney song. But at a meaningful level, the kitten is simply making sense by activating a vibrant semantic link between coolness and cats which is so pervasive in the music tradition in which the song is written that it almost effaces the reality of cats as we know them. 'Cat', for Walt Disney's kitten, has displaced the real cat as a category of phenomenological reality. In order to follow the kitten's meaning, we are not forced to return to reality and to enact a metaphoric displacement. Metaphor has already eclipsed reality. Meaning, context-bound, is generated within the scope of established patterns of speech which do not require a return to literal meaning. The song Walt Disney's kitten sings makes sense, not by setting up parallels referring to the qualities of real cats, qualities which can be extracted from context and then applied to another object: the kitten makes sense by re-echoing a constructed similarity between coolness and cats, and by embracing that paradigm as a conceptual given and the ideal to which his own yearnings tend.

This example would seem to confirm Ricœur's intuition that metaphor acts within context, not (as is usually believed in philosophy and rhetoric) by importing one trait or quality from a literal to a figurative context. To this extent, at least, metaphor does not 'distort' the essential meaning of a concept, it harnesses the meaning attributed to a term within a given context. Metaphor does not pervert reality, it leaves concrete reality behind. This will seem like a failing, if we consider language as a tool for exploring reality and encompassing things which words are supposed to label. From the point of view of linguists such as Humboldt, Sapir, Whorf and Lakoff, and from the point of view of linguistically informed philosophers such as Cassirer and Ricœur, on the other hand, language consists in leaving concrete reality behind and in establishing networks of meaning which can serve as layers upon which further layers of meaning can be superimposed. Such layers can be conceived of as springboards from which we can jump to other dimensions by generating not 'real' connections but meaningful patterns within the language system.

Ricœur's work was being developed while one of the most influential linguistic accounts of metaphor in the second half of the twentieth century was taking root: Jakobson's opposition between metonymy and metaphor. Metonymy, Jakobson argued, was more typical of prose, while metaphor was more typical of poetry. Though uses of both could be found in both prose and poetry, each of the two tropes found greater or lesser expression in various literary movements and traditions. Jakobson found that realism tended to exploit metonymy more, while romanticism and symbolism were more inclined towards metaphor. Jakobson's opposition has often been criticised, and it would be difficult for cognitive linguists to take it on board, given their twofold tendency to see all language as basically metaphorical and to expand the definition of metaphor to include forms of metonymy. Cognitive linguists tend, for example, to consider synecdoche (replacing the whole by the part, for example, 'Can I give you a **hand**?') as a form of metaphor, in the wider sense they give to the term. However, the question of whether certain literary movements, styles and genres generate a creativity which relies on the tension implicit in inventing new modes of metaphorical expression or whether metonymic modes of expression rely more on association remains one which continues to fuel literary debates today.

One of the most intriguing contributions to metaphor theory made by a linguist was Christine Brooke-Rose's *A Grammar of Metaphor*, published in 1958. Brooke-Rose sought to set the balance straight, in a tradition which had interpreted metaphor primarily in semantic terms, by providing a formal approach. Contrary to expectation and counter to most traditional definitions of metaphor, which describe it as the replacement of one thing by another, Brooke-Rose established by statistical analysis that most metaphors do not concern 'things'. That is, in linguistic terms, most metaphors are not nominal: they are verbal or adjectival. And when metaphors do involve nouns they often make use of the genitive form. We do not say, for example, 'Her cheeks were red roses': we speak of 'the roses of her cheeks', attributing a rose's quality to the complexion of the girl (Brooke-Rose 1965: 146). In the same way, if we describe the dispensation of mercy in terms of a flowing fountain, we are more inclined to say of a woman that she is 'the fountain of mercy', rather than 'Her mercy was a flowing fountain'.

Brooke-Rose found verbal metaphors like 'The ship ploughs the waves' (206) to be far more common than nominal metaphors.

And she resisted the interpretation of such metaphors in terms of reference to an underlying nominal metaphor or equation in which a ship becomes a plough. This is the traditional logic, a logic which was adopted in the model of analysis for metaphor provided by Lakoff and Johnson. In contrast to this traditional logic which 'nominalises' metaphor, Brooke-Rose argued that verbal metaphors demonstrated our ability to intuitively perceive the similarity of two dissimilar actions.

Equally frequent, Brooke-Rose found, were adjectival metaphors like 'the visiting moon', which implies that the moon is to the world as the visitor is to a person (207). Some of the most interesting examples that Brooke-Rose interprets were metaphors which involve treating living things or people as objects. Such metaphors are usually referred to by the terms 'objectification' or 'reification'. This process of objectification forms the counterpart to personification. People are often implicitly described in terms of things. Brooke-Rose offered a verbal metaphor as an example: in Shakespeare's *Anthony and Cleopatra*, Agrippa, speaking of Cleopatra, tells us Julius Caesar 'plough'd her, and she cropp'd' (II, ii; Brooke-Rose 1965: 128). Procreation is represented as sowing seeds (a traditional conceptual metaphor). But though this example of reification is interesting in itself, it is in fact more complex than it appears in Brooke-Rose's account. If we return to Shakespeare, we find the full quote is:

> Royal wench!
> She made great Caesar lay his sword to bed:
> He plough'd her, and she cropp'd. (II, ii)

In making love not war, Caesar lays his sword to one side. Thus far, *sword* is a metonymy, a synecdoche, to be precise. But it is transformed into a metaphor for the penis when he lays this sword not to one side but uses it in bed. The penis becomes a sword which in turn becomes a plough. In this way, Shakespeare neatly transforms fierceness into lust and aggression into procreation, characterising Caesar's twofold nature as lover-conqueror with a maximum of rhetorical expression using a minimum of resources. Where Ricœur stressed that the meaning of words is context-bound and that metaphor does not transgress the denotative function of language by displacing meaning, Shakespeare demonstrates the way a single signifier can generate a complex meaningful polysemy by using 'sword' to evoke violence, peace, lust and breeding.

## THE POETIC TRADITION

Like many linguists of her generation, Brooke-Rose chose to focus on poetry in her study of metaphor. Though linguists of the Prague School such as the Russian, Roman Jakobson, and the Czech, Jan Mukařovský, were well aware that metaphor was a pervasive strategy of foregrounding found throughout language, until recently, linguists tended to accord a privileged status to poetic metaphor. The poetic approach itself has its roots in Aristotle's remarks on metaphor in *The Poetics* and *The Rhetoric*, but this approach was greatly refined in the nineteenth and twentieth centuries, in particular with the enormous volume of investigations into the use of metaphor in the works of individual authors which it would be impossible to try to cover here. Studies of imagery, symbolism and metaphor remain an important aspect of literary criticism today, and the school or university interpretation of texts is probably the form in which most people have encountered the study of metaphor.

It was in an attempt to build a bridge between this account of metaphor and cognitive linguistics that Mark Turner and George Lakoff wrote together *More Than Cool Reason: A Field Guide to Poetic Metaphor* (1989). That joint work introduced the idea of conceptual metaphor in exploring the creative imagination at work in fiction. In the poetic tradition, study of metaphor usually focuses upon startling rapprochements which fire the imagination and stimulate our perception of the world around us. To this extent, literary metaphors break into our worlds with a penetrating revelatory force. They force us to see the world anew. The allegoric systems which interest literary criticism are those worlds invented by authors: complex networks of meaning and patterns of extended metaphors which make a literary work a work of genius in contrast to the hackneyed allegories to be found in everyday speech and the flourishes of metaphoric creativity in the press and in advertising, for example.

The literary use of metaphor can be distinguished from other more pervasive uses of metaphor on two accounts: in terms of degree and in terms of function. Metaphor is used more fully and in more complex forms in literature. And literary metaphors should awaken us from our normal mode of conception and perception by facing us with a new expressive equation.

## THE RHETORICAL TRADITION

Running parallel to the tradition in poetics which involved the close reading of individual authors was the rhetorical tradition in which poetics often sought its concepts, categories and analytic strategies. The rhetorical tradition was, like the poetic tradition, initially derived from Aristotle's *Rhetoric*, but it was greatly developed throughout the Middle Ages and the Renaissance, and has continued to be refined and redefined throughout the modern period and in recent scholarship. Despite the wide range of work on rhetoric, the rhetorical tradition lost ground in academic circles in English-speaking countries in the second half of the twentieth century (despite revivals such as the Chicago school revolving around the work of Wayne Booth). This loss of prestige goes some way to explaining why Lakoff and Johnson seem to feel it necessary to come to the rescue of rhetoric. In France, in contrast, the rhetorical tradition has retained a central place among the academic disciplines, and from Pierre Fontanier's *Commentaire des tropes*, published in 1818, to Henri Morier's 1320-page *Dictionnaire de poétique et de rhétorique*, published in 1961, the French tradition tended to pursue an opposite path from the one taken by cognitive linguists in one important respect. While cognitive linguists opted for an inclusive all-embracing definition of metaphor, French rhetoricians saw their task as one of defining and refining categories and subcategories. They sought to do two things: (1) distinguish between metaphor and other tropes, and (2) identify and account for specific forms of rhetorical metaphor.

Morier (1989: 676–748), for example, defines metaphor in

terms of its function, efficiency, content and the means it uses to achieve its effects. While cognitive linguists have what might be called a *democratic* approach to metaphor which embraces all forms of figurative language, Morier maintains a hierarchical model of metaphor which places poetic metaphor at the summit and popular expressions at the bottom. Consequently, 'metaphor' is distinguished from 'popular cliché' by Morier (727): while metaphor is the expression of poetic genius in that it reveals the poet's ability to awaken the senses and the spirit to reality, a popular cliché such as the French expression *bavard comme une pie* ('talkative as a magpie') does not astound French-speakers, nor is it intended to.

In this respect, Morier is doing no more than reaffirming a traditional stance, one maintained in literary criticism. It is in the erudite subcategorisation of rhetorical metaphor that Morier excels as a modern scholar. In the same spirit as Aristotle distinguished between simile and metaphor, Morier offers his distinction between 'explicit' and 'elliptic' metaphors. 'Explicit metaphors' (*métaphores explicites*), which are also known as 'complete metaphors', name all three terms in the operation: the term compared, the means of comparison and the 'knot' (*noeud*) or the point of intersection (685). Morier offers the example *L'amour est un oiseau qui chante* ('Love is a bird that sings'). 'Elliptic metaphors', in contrast, dispense with one of the terms of the operation. The sun can be compared to a river in that the former beams down its rays (*jette ses rayons*) while the latter 'pours forth its waves' (*verse ses ondes*). This underlying comparison can be subtracted, however, in the metaphor which skips from the sun to the movement of the river without naming the river, as in the phrase *le soleil verse ses rayons* ('the sun pours down its rays') (688).

The connection between the term compared and the means of comparison can equally dispense with the *knot*, the point of intersection between the two terms. In the 'appositive metaphor' (*métaphore appositive*), the two terms are juxtaposed and the link between the two is replaced by a pause, or in writing, by a comma. The listener or reader is invited to determine the nature of the comparison. Morier offers the following example from Victor Hugo: '*Or tandis que les eaux fuyaient, mouvant mirrois . . .*' ('But while the waters fled, moving mirrors . . .') (708).

In what I will rename the 'boomerang metaphor' (*métaphore retournée*), we liken A, a real object, to B, an imagined object, but, paradoxically, it is B that is clarified or described in the process (718). This was another of Morier's erudite categories. In this form of metaphor, the poet delves into his contemplation, refining the term of comparison while the term compared is left unaltered. Morier quotes an example from the French poet, Saint-John Perse, in which 'turbulent sands' are compared to the 'sides of centuries' (*pans des siècles*). Instead of the centuries shedding light upon the sands, the metaphor returns like a boomerang to shed light upon centuries, allowing Perse to parody the history of civilisations and their fragility. Such metaphors are not simply curiosities which crop up from time to time: this process of representation is, in fact, widespread. Because mythology extrapolates the comparison of a scenario of an allegorical character in which the compared term participates only marginally, Morier suggests that myth can be considered as a network of boomerang metaphors (718).

In the 'reciprocal metaphor' (*métaphore réciproque*) (744), the term compared and the means of comparison are interchangeable: that is, A is described in terms of a metaphoric term, B, while B, in turn, is described in terms of a metaphorical term, A. In French, for example, the tube of the syringe is known as the 'cannon' while, in the language of artillery, the cannon is known as the 'syringe'. To take another example, while in French the compass is said to have two 'legs', the walker, in lengthening his stride, is said to widen his 'compass' (744). Like the boomerang metaphor, the reciprocal metaphor is a fairly widespread phenomenon. This fact goes some way to confirming the Lakoff and Johnson hypotheses that language is largely metaphorical in nature and that often no literal term can be found for the concepts we use in everyday life. It also confirms Ricœur's argument that literal meanings are not necessarily activated when metaphors are used. In terms of compasses and cannons, in French we have difficulty in establishing what the literal and the figurative meanings are. And far from obstructing meaning, metaphoric innovations would seem in this case to serve to make sense.

Poets exploit the potential of reciprocal metaphor. For example, in Lamartine's poetical universe, the starry skies become an 'ocean' while the ocean becomes a 'frothy sky'. The aptness of the comparison lies in the fact that the dual reflection is not only of a figurative nature, but the reflection of the starry skies in the sea at night lends a physical reality to contemplative reverie.

This is a fragmentary and elliptic account of an enormous volume of research covering wide-ranging concerns related to metaphor. It is no more than a brief overview which should enable us to disentangle some common threads from a colourful tapestry of approaches to the question of metaphor which have developed in various academic disciplines in various languages. From Aristotle to Ricœur, metaphor has tended to attract those who build bridges between academic disciplines. At times, however, disciplines have confused their own partial insight into metaphor with metaphor as a whole, with all its multiple facets. They have assumed that a definition and a methodology which serves the interests of their discipline are capable of revealing an exhaustive account of metaphor. The rudimentary quadripartite model proposed here, if it is to be of any use, should prevent the contribution made to metaphor by cognitive linguists in recent decades from eclipsing the wide variety of other approaches.

# CHAPTER 5

# Further Cognitive Contributions to Metaphor Theory

Cognitive approaches to metaphor show a great diversity in themselves, and this diversity is mirrored by the variety of strands within Lakoff's own work. In his individual work since 1990, Lakoff has concentrated a great deal of his energy on applying metaphor theory to politics. Adopting the role of the engaged intellectual, he has used the concepts of folk theories, narrative theory and conceptual metaphor to analyse the discourse of political rhetoric in studies such as his accounts of the two wars in Iraq. He offered a book-length account of the deficiencies of Democrat Party rhetoric in *Moral Politics*, published in 1996, in which he demonstrates that Democrats have often lost in rhetorical confrontations with Republicans because the latter manage to adopt a positive formulation – a pro-stance – and thereby oblige the Democrats to adopt negative formulation – an anti-stance. This is made all the more easy, Lakoff argues, since Democrats tend to embrace the negative formula because their party has deep roots in protest movements and has a tradition of dissent. Up until recently, as soon as Democrats were confronted with terms such as 'pro-life' by anti-abortionists and 'tax-relief' by right-wing critics of state spending and taxation, Democrats found their arguments powerless to sway public opinion. In a dramatic intensification of his role as engaged intellectual, Lakoff became a consultant to the Democratic think-tank in the period running up to the second election of George W. Bush, Jr.

## CRITICAL DISCOURSE ANALYSIS

Part of the success of metaphor theory in recent decades can be attributed to the way in which the study of conceptual metaphor has loaned itself to the analysis of economic and political discourse. Critical discourse analysis has been growing as a field of study over the last decade, and various researchers have formulated innovative ways of applying and adapting metaphor theory. One important contribution was made by Philip Eubanks with his *A War of Words in the Discourse of Trade: The Rhetorical Constitution of Metaphor*, published in 2000. To a certain extent, Eubanks can be placed within the cognitive school of metaphor in that he adopts the Lakoff–Johnson hypothesis which posits that much of our thought and language is structured using fundamental conceptual metaphors. The essential difference between his approach and the one adopted in *Metaphors We Live By* is one of scope and method, not of fundamental principle. Eubanks does not select commonplace expressions from language and analyse them without regarding the context that generates them (as generative linguistics did and as many cognitive scholars continue to do): Eubanks returns to speech. In this sense, he aligns himself more closely to Humboldt and Benveniste, for whom language does not 'exist' outside of speech or writing. Eubanks takes the cognitive study of metaphor back to the study of dialogue and discussion. This methodology conditions his conclusions. When he focused upon the way we handle metaphors in speech, the way we 'negotiate' them and colour them, investing them with our own political and philosophical associations, Eubanks was not led to abandon the idea that metaphors are things we 'live by', but his work made him reappraise what we mean by 'living by' something. In his study, we are forced to take into account not only the way metaphors mould our thought but also the way we remould metaphors with our thought. This takes us to the heart of the worldview debate. Just as Humboldt argued that world-conceiving both fashions thought and is refashioned by thought, as living thinking people reactivate and reaffirm or remodel the language system, Eubanks shows that not only do metaphors shape thought, thought in discourse carves anew the contours of our metaphors.

Eubanks devotes the whole of his book to the analysis of one single conceptual metaphor, 'Trade is War', to show the diversity of forms which it takes and the ways in which individual speakers endorse it, deny it or resist it. All English-speakers are familiar with the rhetoric of the trade war. We can 'conquer' markets, start a trade war, 'retaliate' with tariffs. All such 'manoeuvres' form part of our 'strategies' for 'marshalling' the resources in our 'arsenal' when we 'battle for economic supremacy'. In trade (the English language would seem to have us believe), there are winners and losers, and we strive to be the victors, not the vanquished. In his interviews, Eubanks found many people agreed that individuals often thought of trade as a war and acted accordingly (2000: 161). In other words, people were conscious that this metaphorical equation formed part of their worldview and influenced their choices.

To a certain extent, this is not surprising, since Trade-is-War is an age-old metaphor which forms part of our national and cultural traditions. According to Eubanks, this conceptual metaphor begins to take root in the English language towards the end of the medieval period, asserting itself increasingly with the beginning of the Renaissance. Throughout the Elizabethan period, the tariff was held to be a means by which to retaliate in a trade war declared by a rival nation (41). Consequently, it seemed perfectly natural for the novelist, Daniel Defoe, writing at the start of the eighteenth century, to praise Henry VII's trade policy aimed at securing a monopoly of wool exports, using the following terms: 'The King acted like a wise and **warlike prince, besieging a City**, who tho' he **attacks the Garrison**, and **batters the Out-works with the utmost Fury, yet spares the inhabitants** . . .' (42).

The fact that this conceptual metaphor affects thought (and therefore economic policy) would seem to be backed up by the controlled cognitive experiments carried out by the Belgian linguist, Frank Boers. Boers carried out a study of two groups of fifty participants in which he gave both groups an economic 'scenario about a European company that is confronted with a cheaper Taiwanese competitor' (Boers 1997: 236). There was one essential difference, however. One group was given a description which was framed in health, fitness and racing metaphors. The second group was given a scenario which was framed in combative and warfare metaphors.

The participants of the two groups were then given thirty minutes to find solutions for the company. Though the results of the two groups showed 'a fair degree of overlap' (237), health and fitness metaphors tended to predominate in the responses of participants in the first group: participants advocated 'surgery' and 'amputations' for the company. The participants of the second group were more inclined to harness aggressive or military metaphors and these conceptual constructs appeared to channel their thought to some extent. One participant suggested starting a 'price war'. Another suggested 'joining forces' with another European company in order to meet the opposition. A third suggested relocating the headquarters 'to confront the Taiwanese in their territory' (238).

Up to this point Boers and Eubanks reach similar conclusions concerning the influence of conceptual metaphor. One of the most interesting conclusions which Eubanks's study led him to, however, was that most people did not claim to believe that trade *is* war, or *should* be. Indeed, most of the people he interviewed denounced those who acted as though trade was war, though often they justified their own opinions and policies as 'retaliations' against aggressive trade-war postures. This led Eubanks to believe that metaphors do not 'direct' the way we think. Rather, he argued, metaphors are adopted as part of what he called our 'discursive strategy'. According to Eubanks, conceptual metaphors are frameworks of thought which we adopt and adapt to the needs of our own arguments at any given time.

One of the most common discourse strategies which Eubanks observed was what he called 'ascription'. The trade war metaphor was invoked but 'ascribed to', attributed to, another party, usually one the speaker considered to be an adversary. Eubanks cited the example of Lester Thurow, who epitomises the kind of rhetorical bad faith which consists in justifying one's own 'aggressively' competitive behaviour by ascribing the opening of hostilities to the other party (142–3). Thurow denounced the trade-war stance, in his book, *Head to Head: The Coming Economic Battle among Japan, Europe and America* (1993), but the book's title itself and the rhetoric which structures it reveal that Thurow is very much an exponent of Trade-is-War as a philosophy or unconscious mode of thought.

Ironically, such bad faith is not restricted to English-speakers, it can also structure cultural stereotypes found abroad. Trade-war metaphors can be found in other languages and they are often handled by speakers in ways that might be compared to Thurow's rhetoric. In French, the entry of Hyundai was described by the economic magazine, *Capital* (October 2003, qtd in Underhill 2007: 365) as an 'attack' on Europe. In *Le Nouvel Economiste* (16–22 April 2004, qtd in Underhill 2007: 365), banks were said to be waiting 'in ambush' (*en ambuscade*) in a bid to take control of the *Chunnel* (Channel Tunnel). Similarly, with their transition to the market economy, the Czechs increasingly appear to be adopting Trade-as-War rhetoric, though terms like 'tax war' (*celní válka*) and the concept of economics as part of war predate the 'velvet revolution' of 1989 (Underhill 2007: 366–8). Nevertheless, the Czechs and the French frequently 'ascribe' trade-war metaphors to the US and the global economy. In other words, they tend to see themselves as victims of an economic philosophy which they claim they would like to resist. The increasing frequency with which such metaphors can be found in both languages, however, reveals the Czechs and the French also participate in trade as gladiators in the arena, however much they see themselves as oppressed victims sacrificed at the altar of global commerce. This biased view of global trade, characteristic of economic debate in any country, simply serves to consolidate Eubanks's argument that metaphors are invoked and harnessed to fit our own personal purposes. This would appear to be true at a personal, political, geopolitical and cultural level. Metaphors are not conceptual limits we 'live within', they form part of the conceptual materials with which we build our representations of the world and of others, and which serve to structure our relationships to them.

Andrew Goatly's *Washing the Brain: Metaphor and Hidden Ideology* (2007) investigates the Lakoff–Johnson hypothesis in a similar manner by focusing upon metaphor in discourse. Like Boers and Eubanks, Goatly is concerned with the degree to which our cognitive representations, framed in conceptual metaphors, influence our behaviour and the social and political structures within which we think and act. Goatly's work widens the scope of metaphor theory. By assimilating modern French thinkers such as

Michel Foucault (1926–1984) and Pierre Bourdieu (1930–2002) to metaphor theory, Goatly builds bridges between cognitive research and political and cultural theory. By questioning the roots of conceptions of people and their 'worth', Goatly opens metaphor debate to a political, historical and moral dimension. And by comparing English with other languages, Goatly makes a significant contribution to worldview theory by allowing us to question to what degree conceptual metaphors can be claimed to be universal.

Goatly's research sets out from a position which is close to Lakoff's when he states, 'the lexicon of English is permeated by conventional metaphors that do not occur in isolation but belong to sets, variously known as conceptual metaphors, or metaphor themes' (2007: 35). While for Lakoff, conceptual metaphors can at times be adopted by political factions, Goatly contends that conceptual metaphors are invariably inherently political: 'most of these metaphor themes have ideological implications, in the sense that they are recruited and used by those exerting economic, scientific, political or personal power' (35). At a personal-political level, for example, Goatly is concerned with the degree to which sex is conceptually associated with violence. He quotes such expressions as 'shoots his load', 'fire blanks' and 'dressed to kill', juxtaposing these violent sexual expressions with figures of rape in different cultures. Rape statistics, it would appear, are four times higher in the USA than in Germany (84). Does this imply that many English-speaking men, at some unconscious level, assume that sex and violence are related? Confusing sex and violence conceptually may well go some way to making rape appear 'natural' to English-speakers.

At the level of ideology, Goatly examines the way representing political philosophies and regimes in terms of 'diseases' tends to coerce people by eliciting intended reactions. Goatly quotes Simon Leys, who spoke of 'the Maoist cancer that is gnawing away at the face of China' (139). As Goatly pointed out, such sweeping denunciations can be used to focus on restricted to political factions and individuals: the Gang of Four were also referred to as the 'cancer of China' (139). Post-colonial thinkers, filled with feelings of guilt, also fell prey to such conceptual metaphors: the contemporary culture critic, Susan Sontag, admits to having at one point believed that 'the white race is the cancer of human history' (139).

One of Goatly's strengths is his capacity to see contemporary linguistic expressions as reformulations of concepts within the ongoing history of ideas. In this respect, his work can be compared to that of Nanine Charbonnel. The historical scope of his meta-phor project allows him to uncover the origins and implications of expressions which appear to most of us innocent enough. Calling someone 'dear' or 'an asset' or 'a treasure', or saying you feel you are 'undervalued', may come naturally to us, but Goatly stressed that such expressions are manifestations of the conceptual meta-phor 'Life is a Commodity' (90–1). In his chapter on 'Capitalism and the development of ideological metaphors', Goatly quoted the seventeenth-century philosopher, Hobbes, who asserted that the monetary value of man was the only legitimate estimate that could be made of his intrinsic worth: 'The value or the worth of a man, is as of all other things, his price, that is to say, so much as would be given for the use of his power' (Hobbes, qtd in Goatly 2007: 367).

Goatly shows the way such a conception is currently structur-ing debate on procreation. We speak of 'sperm banks' and 'sperm donors' and 'stem-cell banks'. Subsequently, to a certain extent, it would seem likely that this historically encrusted and currently dominant metaphor which posits humans to be commodities of exchange is likely to shape the future of our society and our families not simply as representations but as lived realities. At this stage, however, it would appear that Eubanks was right in concluding that metaphors are always adopted and adapted as we negotiate with others and formulate our own discursive strategy: because we can resist the logic of concepts and metaphors. Indeed, the reduction of humans to commodities is frequently condemned. For example, the Archbishop of York denounced the sale of eggs and sperm (93). Speakers often appear to be lucid in exploring the logic that conceptual metaphors open up for us. The owner of one website suggested that 'We bid for everything else in society, so why not eggs' (Habgood, qtd in Goatly 2007: 94). Tom Shakespeare uncov-ered the logical consequences of commercialising babies when he argued that we should not receive children as though they were market products tailored to our needs and requirements: 'Children should be accepted for themselves, not to the extent that they fulfil our wishes and desires' (Shakespeare, qtd in Goatly 2007: 94).

Goatly's study of the history of conceptual metaphors and their political and ethical ramifications leads us to questions of a fundamentally spiritual order. Lakoff will consider the split self and self-possession in terms of one part of the self owning another part. This keeps us at an immediately conscious psychological level of being. Goatly, in contrast, forces metaphor debate to open up to the moral dimension of 'possessing' people. Quoting the famous distinction Eric Fromm made between the two philosophies of life, Having and Being, Goatly traces the way we seem to have sunk further into the reification of being, what he calls 'the commodification of humans' (93). We increasingly consider ourselves and others as commodities of exchange. We 'sell ourselves' at interviews. Meanwhile, kidnappers would seem to be using the same commercial logic in the current spread of human trafficking. Certainly, for citizens of ex-communist states, brought up to believe capitalism consists in the ruthless exploitation of others, and faced with massive unemployment, unbearable poverty and the collapse of state welfare system, selling young women to Western prostitute networks does not seem to contravene the conceptual metaphor that Hobbes was working with at the outset of modern capitalism: a girl is worth what men will pay for her.

To a large extent, Goatly's critical discourse analysis sets out to use metaphor theory as a means to face up to the moral and political problems of the contemporary world. For Goatly, conceptual metaphors have very real consequences. This differentiates Goatly's contribution to worldview theory from Humboldt's own project. Though Humboldt was himself a politician, a diplomat and one of the engineers of the modern German university, his linguistic thought was not ardently political. Although in philosophical terms Goatly remains much closer to Foucault and Bourdieu, in one respect, both Goatly's investigation into metaphor and his discourse analysis both reflect a capacity which Humboldt held to be central to language as a human faculty: Goatly shows a sensitivity for 'the sense of language' (*Sprachsinn*) (see Trabant 1992: 24–9). For Humboldt, *Sprachsinn* was the capacity of the mind to reflect upon language in speech and thereby open up the language system to new possibilities. Our *sense of language* is our ability to creatively renew language and remould it to suit our expressive capacities. Of course, to a certain extent all thought is language-bound in that we cannot escape language to penetrate a translingual plane of being and knowing, but language itself is the sum of our shared creative endeavours to perfect it as a means of expression and maintain it as a living and evolving worldview.

Much cognitive research has tended to take a synchronic view of language in the here and now and has bracketed diachronic questions. By looking at the origins of conceptual metaphors and asking where they will take us, Goatly is leading us towards a reappraisal of the fundamental concepts of our world-perceiving and world-conceiving and forcing us to question the legitimacy of our own personal worldview in the contemporary world. Following Bourdieu and Foucault, Goatly adopts the rhetoric of resistance. Critical discourse in French- and in English-speaking countries is radical: it unmasks and resists the discourse of elites which maintain their power by drawing citizens into the terms of their symbolic power. *Sprachsinn*, however, takes us over and beyond such fundamental political questions: with his concept of the *sense of language* Humboldt is reminding us that we are responsible for language, we create it, we maintain it; ultimately, language is the work of our shared endeavour as a linguistic community. It is, therefore, our responsibility. Thinking lucidly about the constraints different forms of discourse and conceptual metaphors impose upon the unreflecting individual is the only way to refine and reanimate the worldview we remake for ourselves.

This is not the only coordinate at which the trajectory of Goatly's thought intersects the direction Humboldt follows, however. Goatly is one of the few cognitive linguists to take on board other languages in his study of conceptual metaphors. No doubt the fact that Goatly is based in Hong Kong has preserved him from the Anglo-centric focus of much cognitive research. Interestingly, Goatly is sceptical about universal claims and the quest for universals themselves, a trend which he attributes to the Chomskyan heritage that cognitive scholars have found difficult to escape (2007: 276). This is not the place to go into this question in detail, but two points should be raised concerning Goatly's critique of the search for universals. Firstly, Goatly suggests that the search for language universals starts out with a naïve belief in a universally shared bodily experience of the world. This phenomenological given becomes questionable if we accept, as Goatly suggests we should, that our bodies are cultural constructs and that our concepts and feelings about our bodies and how they are used are subject to socialisation. Secondly, Goatly's examples from Chinese tend to prove that the equations upon which conceptual metaphors are based do not match up in the same way in different cultures. Goatly argued: 'The same target and source concepts exist in different cultures, but they are paired differently or paired in one language and not another' (265). Goatly found similar concepts for emotion and plant in Chinese and English but he argued that ' EMOTION IS PLANT comprises a much more important metaphor theme in Chinese' (265). For example, Goatly found no equivalents in English for the expressions in Chinese in Table 5.1.

The contribution of critical discourse analysis to metaphor theory should allow us to return to a broader approach to culture as a historically situated socio-political construct. Goatly and Eubanks both provide conceptual tools for categorising specific metaphorical strategies. In this sense, their work is compatible with Morier's rhetorical approach. However, by holding together economic, philosophical and ethical concerns, their analysis takes us beyond the rhetorical tradition of recent centuries and back to a conception of rhetoric which is closer to the one Aristotle described in *The Rhetoric*. For Aristotle, rhetoric was not simply a set of strategies used for the purposes of persuasion; it was a means of thinking clearly and moving others towards a more clearly defined and more

Table 5.1 Chinese expressions with no equivalents in English. (Source: selected from the list in Goatly 2007: 265)

| Chinese transcription | Literal meaning | Metaphorical meaning |
| --- | --- | --- |
| xin hua nu fang | heart flower in full bloom | be elated, be wild with joy |
| hua xin | flower heart | inconstancy in love, a change of heart |
| liu xing | the nature of the willow | carnal pleasure |

vividly animated version of truth. Rhetoric leads human beings
to a higher knowledge of themselves and of the world. For this
reason, Aristotle (the great master of scientific categories of understanding) did not fall into the trap of imprisoning rhetoric within
one closed-off discipline. In the Aristotelian concept of knowledge,
Rhetoric is part of Politics, just as Politics is part of Ethics, just as
Ethics is part of Philosophy, the quest for and love of knowledge
of the self and of the world. Each of the four approaches of the
preceding chapter (philosophical, linguistic, poetic and rhetoric)
tends to be seen by those that adopt each approach as the natural
and central mode of investigation. In contrast to this blinkered
or self-centred view, Aristotle did not see rhetoric as being at the
centre but as a dependant part of a greater, more fundamental
project. This can be portrayed using a rudimentary spatial diagram
(see Figure 5.1).

The mistake different approaches make (and this is an increasing
tendency in the modern university) is to take the dependence of
one's own discipline to other disciplines as evidence of the central
importance of one's own approach. If Goatly and Charbonnel
have something to teach us about metaphor, it is that linguistic,

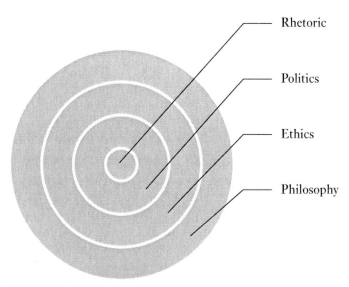

Figure 5.1 Rhetoric as a dependant part of a greater, more fundamental
project.

rhetorical, philosophical and cultural theories of metaphor, however interesting they may be, are ultimately inadequate in and of themselves. Metaphor theory requires a holistic approach, since metaphors are cultural in nature and therefore reach into various dimensions of life.

## TURNER'S CONTRIBUTION

In one sense, the exploration of discourse using metaphor theory was only one of the possible branches which sprouted from the work of Lakoff and Johnson. As we have seen, Lakoff himself made a contribution to discourse analysis with his *Moral Politics*. There is, moreover, a coherence and consistency in Lakoff's theory of language and his approach to philosophy and politics: starting from one central premise, the pervasive nature of conceptual metaphors as frameworks for thought, Lakoff branches out into other fields of study and action. Critical discourse analysis was only one avenue to be explored using metaphor theory. We have already considered the influence of Mark Johnson, who has tended to steer the Lakoff–Johnson tandem towards a metaphoric revaluation of philosophy. The diversity of cognitive study can be explained in part by the wide range of interests of cognitive researchers themselves, but it is also in part due to the number of tandems that have emerged in cognitive research. Cognitive linguists have often coupled up to pool their resources and penetrate the complex cognitive unconscious in pairs (Turner–Fauconnier, Sweetser–Fauconnier and Lakoff–Turner).

Mark Turner has greatly influenced the course of cognitive study and the development of Lakoff's own thought. Turner is representative of many cognitive linguists in that he has a background in science, but it is his concern for literature and the analysis of literary texts that has done much to mould what has become known as cognitive poetics. In his first major work, *Death is the Mother of Beauty* (1987), Turner analysed with remarkable conceptual rigour the network of metaphoric systems which underpinned the development of Milton's allegories in *Paradise Lost*. He found that the definitions of characters, their relations and actions were to a great extent framed in terms of an underlying framework of kinship metaphors. In studying kinship in *Paradise Lost*, Turner's aim was not merely to understand or aesthetically appraise the poem. Turner has always investigated language and literature in order to discover what both can tell us about the way the mind works. Creativity is considered to be partially constrained and it is the constraints of creativity which Turner subjects to scrutiny. 'Imagination [Turner argued] is not unfettered; it is governed by principles. These principles are automatic and below the level of consciousness. The job here is to show what some of these principles are' (1987: 16).

In the same way, Turner asked: What do we know about kinship? How does this knowledge give rise to basic kinship metaphors, and how do these metaphors combine with that knowledge and with each other to give rise to the basic inference patterns we use in inventing and understanding kinship metaphors? What answers did he find for these questions? Turner summarised his conclusions in the following manner:

> I wrote *Death is the Mother of Beauty* because I was intrigued that human beings seem to be able to put together very different concepts in ways that strike us as powerful and apt rather than exotic and surreal, and I wanted to explore this characteristic human ability. To do that, I thought it might be wise to choose a particular laboratory, and I settled on an exploration of the ways in which we connect concepts of kinship relations to other kinds of concepts. Kinship relations, after all, are a central conceptual domain for all human beings, although different cultures configure that conceptual domain quite differently. I found that, on the one hand, people can make very unusual connections involving kinship relations, and, on the other, there are some connections that are extremely familiar and continually expressed in the English language and other Western languages. One of the things I found that interested me most was that these connections followed constraints. For example, we connect the parent-child relation very widely to cause-effect relations in essentially any conceptual domain, and we do so according to constraints

rather than according to fixed linkages. We can say that 'age is the mother of wisdom' or that 'humility is the mother of wisdom.' Many things can be the mother of wisdom. But these connections seem to follow governing principles. For example, the scene of birth has certain kinds of elements and a certain event shape: first there is one thing, then there are two, and there is a sharp individuation between them, and the birth is relatively sudden even if the gestation is not, and both abide for a significant amount of time, and so on. When we connect progeneration to causation, we do so according to these topological features. We do not say 'She is the mother of the basket she just sank' or, if a cloud shifts slightly into a different form, 'That cloud is the mother of its present form.' There are very many such kinship expressions that would sound very weird to us because they contravene various governing principles. (Turner, in Underhill 2002: 704–5)

Two years after he wrote *Death is the Mother of Beauty*, Turner went on to co-write with Lakoff *More Than Cool Reason: A Field Guide to Poetic Metaphor*, which analysed 'generic-level connections that operate by constraints (an example is the familiar set of connections known as EVENTS ARE ACTIONS, as in "Death is stalking me"' (Turner in Underhill 2002: 705). This work also 'produced what came to be called the Invariance Hypothesis, which is essentially a claim that metaphoric connections follow a certain governing principle having to do with cognitive topology' (Underhill 2002: 705). If the work of Turner and Lakoff has helped to clarify the constraints of creativity, then cognitive poetics has already taken us forward. But Lakoff and Turner's analysis of the ways in which poetic metaphor departs from typical metaphor is also revealing. They defined this departure in the following terms:

The mode of metaphorical thought that poets use and invoke in their readers goes beyond ordinary metaphoric thought by including these elements:
• The novel extension of the metaphor to include elements otherwise not mapped, such as extending DEATH IS SLEEP to dreaming.

- The imaginative filling in of special cases, such as having the vehicle in DEATH IS DEPARTURE be a coach.
- The formation of composite metaphors in which two or more conventional metaphors are joined together in ways that they ordinarily would not be. Its effect is to produce a richer and more complex set of metaphorical connections, which gives inferences beyond those that follow from each of the metaphors alone.
- Explicit commentary of the limitations of conceptual metaphors, and the offering of an alternative. (Lakoff and Turner 1989: 71)

In other words, poets extend metaphors, they elaborate them, they compose assemblies of familiar metaphors, and they comment on the limits of metaphorical frameworks and offer alternatives.

Influenced by Fauconnier's *Mental Spaces* (initially written in French and published in English in 1985), Turner had already begun to work on what he and Fauconnier termed 'blending' when he wrote *The Literary Mind* (1996). The concept of blending reposes upon the idea that meaning involves the interaction of different conceptual frames. Thus far, Turner and Fauconnier seem to be working within the same interactive binary dynamics involving a source domain and a target domain that Lakoff and Johnson work with, a paradigm found throughout traditional metaphor theory from I. A. Richards to Max Black. What was innovative in the model of cognitive dynamics that Turner and Fauconnier put forward, however, was that they explained that the interaction of target and source domains gives rise to a third conceptual space, the blend.

## BLENDING

We typically conceive of concepts as packets of meaning such as 'marriage', 'birth', 'death', 'time' or 'tomorrow'. However, while these packets seem localised and stable, meaning is anything but stable. 'Meanings [Turner argued] are not mental objects bounded in conceptual places but rather complex operations of projection, binding, linking, blending, and integration over multiple spaces' (Turner 1996: 57). Analysing a parable in *A Thousand and One Nights*, Turner found that the 'talking donkey' involved not only the interaction between the donkey with its own characteristics and the man with his own (including the capacity of speech and the capacity to reason). The talking donkey took on a life of its own so to speak. It became a self-sufficient blend that could then be inserted into a story to form part of a meaningful allegory. As soon as we begin to follow the story and reason in terms of a donkey endowed with the capacity to speak (a scheming donkey who can be taken by surprise when his schemes turn out badly), we have moved beyond the interaction of two stable spheres of meaning and have taken the blend for a new distinct element in the interaction of conceptual spaces.

Because blends and metaphors are so widespread in literary texts, Turner concluded that meaning was literary (57). Consequently, thought proved that the mind itself was a 'literary mind'. Is this plausible, though? Such a conclusion may please literary scholars in search of defenders for their discipline, but this is a surprising slip-up for someone as rigorous as Turner. After all, to assume that all thought is literary because literary thought involves processes common to all thought is as logical as assuming a mammal is a dog because a dog is a mammal. Ultimately, if the 'literary person', the 'literary mind' and 'a literary sensitivity' are to have any significance in common parlance, then they must be restricted in scope and not applicable to humankind *per se*.

Since the mid-nineties, Turner's work has moved away from the analysis of literature and in his joint work with Fauconnier which gave rise to *The Way We Think* in 2002, he has tended to return to the more fundamental question of analysing creativity in language in particular with regards to blending. The scope of this work takes us beyond the study of metaphor. Indeed, there is something essentially 'universalistic' in the underlying desire to describe the mechanisms with which we think: because in this study of the way in which blending operates and way it is affected by language and identity, there is an attempt to formulate a definitive statement about the way *We* think. By 'We', Fauconnier and Turner would seem to mean we humans, mankind.

Though this attempt might shed some light on the workings of thought in general, it cannot take us any further in the Humboldtian project to get to grips with the different ways languages explore the world and fashion the material with which men and women of different cultures think and speak. Worldview theory sees the very formulation of a universal 'we' as the first stumbling block. While Turner and Fauconnier are working from the hypothesis that we all think essentially in the same manner, and then trying to analyse differences in terms of divergences, worldview theorists are far from convinced that we do in fact think in the same way.

## UNIVERSALISM

Turner and Fauconnier are not alone in returning to the universalist approach, and indeed there is a rising trend to move away from Lakoff's essentially relativistic starting point to seek out the fundamental, underlying thought processes of English and other languages. Linguistic diversity has remained upon the cognitive agenda. However, much cognitive research into metaphors in different languages remains dissatisfying for the comparative philologist, since the researchers involved in such inquiries invariably do not master the languages they are studying.

It would appear absurd for an English-speaker to describe the Italian worldview without mastering Italian, just as English-speakers would find it laughable that an Italian could gain a fair grasp of the English-speaker's worldview without learning to speak English fluently. Nevertheless, it is precisely this kind of approach that is found to be perfectly acceptable in contemporary comparative linguistics. The curious naïvety of this research can be partly explained by the success of English and the prestige of the USA in particular. Influential cultures tend to imagine they understand the cultures they dominate.

When the French dreamed of writing the encyclopaedia of human knowledge in the eighteenth century and set about the categorisation of languages, they were weighed down by the prestige of their own language. France, like modern English, had global pretensions. When Rivarol wrote his *Universalité de la langue française*, he truly believed that French was a universal language. On more careful study, French at the time could be said to be an important language within Europe, one which was widely used for diplomatic purposes and was thus learned by the upper classes of other European nations. In stark contrast to this, major linguistic communities living in France did not speak French, which explains why the *Droits de l'homme* of the French revolution had to be translated into dozens of dialects and local languages (such as Basque, Breton, Alsatian, etc. at the end of the eighteenth century). Despite this linguistic diversity within France itself, and faced with all the other major languages of Europe, learned French scholars, when they came to compare languages, seemed to have taken it for granted that the French language represented the natural logical order of the world. Any difference to French was consequently conceived of in terms of a disruption of that natural order. French followed the logic of rational thought. French reflected the crystallisation of reason. Other languages, when they diverted from the grammatical constructs and syntactic rules followed by French, fell into obscurity, confusion and irrationality. French, in contrast to such languages, it was believed, represented clarity; and indeed, even today, French grammarians speak of the syntactic structure of German which puts the modal verb at the end of the subordinate clause, in terms of an inversion.

American and British linguists often fall into a similar short-sightedness. Cognitive linguists have shown a sincere curiosity for linguistic diversity, but mainstream cognitive research has tended to fall into one of the three following categories:

1. Work which attempts to establish the universal existence of central conceptual metaphors (see Grady 1997).
2. Work carried out by English-speakers with the help of native speakers of other languages who answer the questions and comment on the hypotheses elaborated by English-speakers in English (for example, Emanatian's study of sex and lust metaphors in Chagga, a Bantu language of Tanzania [1995, 1999]).
3. Confirmations by speakers of foreign languages that similar conceptual metaphors can be found in their own languages (see Lakoff and Johnson 1999: 284–7).

These findings may provide interesting starting points, but linguists who are content to remain at this level of investigation are clearly planning to fit other languages into English, that is to say, they want to fit other worldviews into the concepts and categories which are conceivable within English. In contrast to this, studies of metaphor in different languages carried out on the periphery of cognitive linguistics by speakers of languages other than English have understandably declined to adopt the universal approach. Just as Goatly's research into Chinese revealed that conceptual terms do not match up in the same way in English as they do in Chinese, the work of researchers on the periphery sets out from the premise of diversity and works towards commonly shared linguistic traits where they arise in and of themselves, rather than trying to fit the foreign into categories developed within the frameworks of the English cognitive unconscious. This is an essential difference for Humboldt's worldview project. While cognitive scholars like Grady appear to adopt a traditional philosophical approach in assuming that the same concepts and categories (with a certain degree of difference) exist in different languages, studies of metaphor which are conducted outside of the English-language system tend to suggest that foreign languages force us to grapple with essentially different concepts, which only ever coincide to a certain degree. Contemporary cognitive linguists are still thinking in terms of supralingual semantic unity and variation; worldview thinkers, philologists and translators are thinking in terms of partial equivalence.

# CHAPTER 6

# Diversity on the Periphery

S tudies which approach the question of metaphor with a comparative approach include *The Ubiquity of Metaphor: Amsterdam Studies in the Theory and History of Linguistic Science* (1985) edited by Wolf Paprotté and René Dirven, the multilingual studies to be found on the *metaphorik.de* online journal, based in Hamburg, Germany, and work carried out by Czech and Polish scholars and published by Irena Vaňková in *The Picture of the World in Language* (*Obraz světa v jazyce*, 2001). Eve Sweetser, like Andrew Goatly, is somewhat of an exception in that she is one of the few prominent cognitive linguists to propose comparative work which steers clear of the universalistic approach.

## AN EARLY CONTRIBUTION

Dirven's work drew on the Lakoff and Johnson hypothesis, though Dirven found antecedents to cognitive linguists' claims in the work of the German post-Kantian philosopher, Ernst Cassirer, and the French anthropologist, Claude Lévi-Strauss. Indeed, Lakoff and Johnson would analyse such phrases as 'beyond our ken', and 'higher spheres' in the same way that Cassirer did: that is, as spatial metaphors. Back in 1923, Cassirer expressed himself in words that might have been found in *Philosophy in the Flesh:*

It is the intuition of *space* which most fully reveals this inter-penetration of sensuous and spiritual expression in language. The essential role of spatial representation is most clearly shown in the universal terms which language has devised for the designation of spiritual processes. Even in the most highly developed languages we encounter this 'metaphorical rendi-tion' of intellectual conceptions by spatial representations. (Cassirer, qtd in Dirven 1985: 86)

Cassirer (1953, 1968) found that myth and language as a whole shared the same fundamental basis and this led him to the same conclusion as Lakoff and Johnson, namely that thinking was very often 'metaphorical thinking' (qtd in Dirven 1985: 86). Following the same line of thought, Dirven sought confirmation for this hypothesis in the work of Lévi-Strauss, who confirmed that 'The mythical system and modes of representation it [a tribe] employs serve to establish homologies between natural and social condi-tions, or, more accurately, it makes it possible to equate significant contrasts found on different planes,' (Lévi-Strauss, qtd in Dirven 1985).

Dirven's own concern was to establish the role metaphor played in extending the lexicon, that is, for enlarging the number of ideas with which we think. What, he asked, is the relationship between morphology and metaphor? Dirven identified three motors for lexical extension: metonymy, metaphor and a third, less well-known one, 'synaesthesia', 'which denotes a process whereby one sensory stimulus may evoke a stimulus in a different sensory organ' (Dirven 1985: 99).

The power of metonymy for lexical extension is well known. A person's name can become a noun, as in the phrase 'Have you read John Knowles?' The name of a company can become a verb, as in 'Have you **hoovered** the dinning-room?' (96). One recent example of this process is the expression 'to do an Enron', which refers to the company charged with fiddling its figures to misrepresent its results in the period running up to the financial crash of 2001.

The German philologist who gave an enlightening account of the language of the Nazis, Victor Klemperer, notes a German verb derived from a metonymy and finds a parallel antecedent in

French: the Nazis claimed they were going to *Coventrieren* London ('to Coventry' it), by which they meant they were going to wipe it off the map by sending bombing raids, as they claimed to have done with Coventry. Klemperer noticed in this verb a lexical procedure which he had already observed in the French term *septembriser* ('to September'), which the *Daniel Sanders Dictionary* defined as follows: 'To commit political massacres of a kind perpetrated in September 1792 during the French revolution' (Klemperer 1975: 162, my translation).

Dirven argued that synaesthesia was a fundamental and pervasive phenomenon in language and that synaesthetic metaphors which involved the transfer of 'some feature or other from one domain of experience (or sense) to the other' were common. He quoted the example 'warm colours', which he interpreted as being associated with a fire, which is predominantly red and yellow (Dirven 1985: 99). Though language is often visual in its metaphors, synaesthesia often involves other senses (for example, 'loud colour'). For Dirven, synaesthesia occupied the middle ground between metonymy, which requires a relationship in the real world between the two terms compared, and metaphor, which implies the jumping from one field of experience to another. He argued that 'synaesthesia is an association process' (100); but it is different from metonymy 'in that the ground for the second stimulus is not immediately transparent and evident' (100). Indeed, if we look at historical examples of synaesthesia, we observe that this form of association can change over time, the link between the two terms becoming increasingly opaque. Take, for example, the French word *laid*, meaning 'ugly'. Though this word is almost uniquely reserved for describing the visual unattractiveness of something or someone, when it began to be used in the French language in the eleventh century, it originally meant 'odious'; it only acquired its present meaning later by extension (Picoche 1994: 312).

What Dirven's discussion of synaesthesia, metonymy and metaphor proves is a truth that philosophers from Nietzsche to Cassirer had often asserted: that much of our language is metaphorical in origin. Dirven listed the multiple meanings of 'cup' to show how, defined as a drinking container, it could be transformed into a part of the beverage it contained, which in turn would be used as a metaphor to designate a bitter experience (for example, 'take away this cup'). He showed how 'cup' could, when not related to drinking, be transformed into a prize ('the cup final'), and the way the cup's shape could be used to denote 'a hollow', while in golf, the cup designates not the hole itself but the metal container in the hole (1985: 102).

However, it is in his comparison of the different ways languages structure their lexical fields through the elaboration of metaphoric words and expressions that Dirven proves most interesting, because it is here that he introduces questions that an English-speaker would have found difficult to anticipate or even formulate. He found that in English the word 'heart' was active in expressions related to (1) the bodily organ, (2) the emotions, and (3) ideas unrelated to either physiological or psychological experience. It could refer to the blood vessel, 'the seat of life', the mind, the memory and the emotions. It could refer to courage, love, cordiality and tenderness. But it could also refer to the inmost and central part of a place (for example, 'the heart of the city'), the inmost and central part of time (for example, 'the heart of winter') or the vital part of something (for example, 'the heart of the matter').

Dirven did not find all of these metaphorically elaborated lexical innovations in Dutch. The Dutch language had followed similar paths to enable Dutch-speakers to use 'heart' to mean life, courage, love and the inmost part of a place, but there the similarity ended. What was particularly interesting in Dirven's findings was the way in which he showed how metaphor interacted with grammar. The element which interested him was the Dutch diminutive form: the suffix (1) used to imply smallness, (2) used to suggest an emotional – affective or derogatory – attitude, or (3) used as a mode of intensification. Of the uses of 'heart' in Dutch which paralleled English patterns, the diminutive form (*hartje*) was used only when referring to the inmost part of a place, while in other cases the non-diminutive form (*hart*) was used. Using *hartje* when speaking of love would presumably indicate affection. But using it for courage, as in the expression *met een klein hartje* ('with a small heart'), implied timidity or cowardliness. The obligatory use of the diminutive form in the expression 'in the heart of the city' (*in het hartje van de stad*), Dirven accounted for as a mode of intensification. And he offered similar uses of the diminutive form to back up this conclusion: *in het putje van de winter* ('in the little well of winter'), *zet de puntjes op de i's* ('dot your little "i"s').

These Dutch examples show that constraints other than those in operation in English affect the way meaning is generated by metaphor. By examining these constraints and the possibilities they open up for expressing thought, Dirven demonstrates that metaphor not only structures the lexicon, it structures the lexicon differently in different languages.

If, as would seem to be the case, metaphor as a mode of semantic expansion is subject to formal constraints, these constraints should not be understood as an obstacle to expression. English is relatively poor in diminutives and tends to employ a wealth of neologisms to expand its lexicon in order to express concepts which are logically derived from a small number of morphemes in Dutch, Italian and most Slavic languages. Formal linguistic constraints in these latter languages offer wide horizons to metaphoric innovation, and studying them should both widen the horizons of metaphor scholars and make their understanding of semantic creativity more flexible.

## THE ONLINE JOURNAL, *METAPHORIK.DE*

Since the late 1990s, the *metaphorik.de* online journal has given researchers a forum for work which explores the ways metaphors organise discourse in different languages. The project of the site is to establish the validity of the Lakoff and Johnson hypothesis, and to trace the various forms metaphor adopts and the cognitive patterns it explores. Because the researchers involved are often specialists of English, this language has become predominant, but because the website is the based in Hamburg, English and German are often compared. Other European languages have also formed the basis of rigorous corpus-based studies which focus on the discourse of fields such as science, politics and sport.

In Ralph Müller's article, 'Creative metaphors in political discourse: theoretical considerations on the basis of Swiss speeches' (2005), the author contrasts the use of metaphor in the speeches of two Swiss politicians. His study leads him to question two firmly established ideas. The first is that, since Aristotle, we have tended to consider metaphor as a useful tool of persuasion. Quoting Hagendoorn and Bosen, Müller posits that non-metaphorical speech is perhaps more persuasive (55). The second received idea he questions is one that has gained common currency since Orwell introduced it: the idea that political speech as a form of discourse abounds in 'stale metaphors, similes, and idioms' which save you from making 'much mental effort, at the cost of leaving your meaning vague, not only for your reader but for yourself' (Orwell 1968: 134). In contrast to this, Müller's study led him to believe that political speech was often creative; and part of the creativity of such speech consisted in questioning the very use of metaphor. Leuenberger, one politician quoted by Müller, highlighted the fact that concerning the issue of immigration, we sometimes feel we are 'at the mercy of events' (Müller 2005: 59) and that this sentiment was often expressed through the words we use: '*Da reden wir über die Süd-Nord-Migration wie von einer Naturgewalt: als "Flüchtlingswelle" oder "Flüchtlingsstrom"*' ('For instance we talk about the migration from the South to the North in terms of a force of nature: as "wave of refugees" or "stream of refugees") (59). As Müller pointed out, highlighting metaphor is often a strategy used to counter the argument of those who use it. To put this in Eubanks's terms, by ascribing a metaphor to an opponent we rob the metaphor of its power of persuasion.

In the May 2003 edition of *metaphorik.de*, Isabelle Collombat, a French Canadian researcher, proposed a comparative study of imagery in scientific discourse in French and English. She regretted the lack of corpus-based work on the translation of metaphor. In point of fact, there have been studies of translation within the scope of the metaphor debate. Peter Newmark contributed an article to Paprotté and Dirven's *Ubiquity of Metaphor* in 1985 in which he considered the different strategies which translators should adopt when confronted with creative metaphors and the figurative frameworks inherent in language, in particular the prepositions and suffixes which are active to different degrees in different languages.

Newmark's article contains many insights into the way metaphor works in language and one of them concerned the fact that certain words were more obviously metaphorical than their counterparts in other languages. He did not develop this idea but his insight can prove revealing if we test it out in comparing English with French and German. The reflexive nature of the prefix *ré-* is all-but forgotten in the French word, *réfléchir* (to reflect). This *dead metaphor* can still be reanimated, however, as Cocteau reanimated it when he said that mirrors should think twice before reflecting (*'Les miroirs feraient bien de réfléchir un peu plus avant de renvoyer les images'*) (Oster 1993: 684). But the success of this witticism depends upon French-speakers having half-forgotten that the word 'to reflect' (*réfléchir*) is formed using a reflexive suffix. The German word *überlegen* has a much more dynamic suffix which stresses the physical idea of *over*. This is lost in the English word by which it can be translated, 'consider' (derived from Latin), though the physical aspect is preserved in the expression of Germanic origin, 'to think over'. Indeed, phrasal verbs in both German and English retain a much more direct physicality. The fact that the preposition of the phrasal verb can be detached and moved to different places in the sentence also helps to highlight this physical dynamism of the expression. Highlighting physicality, in turn, opens doors to metaphorical innovation in German and English, where French will at times find it more difficult to reanimate the 'physical' or 'spatial' content of its prefixes.

The example of *überlegen* quoted by Newmark (in Paprotté and Dirven 1985: 300), which I have extended and developed here, is not an isolated example of thought on metaphor from the perspective of translators. Indeed, translation would seem to be the ideal context for comparing the metaphoric frameworks of different languages, and a great number of translators have commented on the subject. Nonetheless, the French Canadian, Collombat, is justified in claiming that commentary on metaphor by translators has on the whole been restricted to reflections on literary texts, and that translators have proved more interested in aesthetic evaluation than in describing the difference in the nature of the languages studied. Like Newmark's contribution, such work usually aims at finding pragmatic strategies for aiding translators to do their job better. Reflections upon fundamental differences in the language systems are usually limited to passing remarks. These in themselves may often be stimulating and richly informed by a wide practice of translation (that intellectual gymnastics that sends the translator somersaulting back and forth between worldviews), but they remain thought-provoking starting points rather than conclusive evidence about the workings of metaphor.

Collombat aims to set the balance straight somewhat by providing the preliminary results of a study of metaphors in the scientific press in French and English. Her study provides some intriguing examples: she shows, for example, how the universalistic discourse of human rights (so implicit to the constitutions of revolution-founded nations like the USA and France) can combine with the framework of gambling to represent the genetic fate of individuals in metaphoric terms: '*Châque être humain qui naît sur cette terre a le droit à son propre billet dans la grande loterie génétique*' ('Each human being born on this earth has the *right* to **his own ticket in the great genetic lottery**') (Collombat 2003: 42, my translation). Collombat also offers examples which allow us to confirm the existence of two metaphorical procedures which have become commonplace in scientific reviews in English:

1. Anthropomorphism or personification: for example, the molecules in the air we breathe are said to contain two *single* cells (50). (The French word *célibataire* employed here is used exclusively for unmarried individuals.)
2. Reification: for example, in one study, an adult, we are told, has recently been discovered to be 'a surprising reserve of progenitor cells' ('*une étonnante reserve de cellules souches*') (52, my translation).

Collombat's study also offers interesting statistical findings. Basing her findings upon 198 examples of imagery found in articles found in the scientific reviews *Découvrir*, *La Recherche*, *New Scientist* and *Scientific American* published in 2002, she found that both the articles in French and English showed a marked use of 'implicit metaphor' (what she calls *métaphores in absentia*). Around 50 per cent of images used were implicit (52 per cent in French and 49 per cent in English), while the remainder of the images divided up variously into explicit metaphors (26 per cent in

French and 16 per cent in English), similes and analogies. These statistics are interesting because while some multilingual studies highlight the different metaphorical patterns that emerge in languages, Collombat's study shows that languages often develop along roughly the same lines.

## EMBODIMENT

In the same edition of *metaphorik.de* as the one in which Müller published his work on Swiss speeches, Juliana Goschler published her appraisal of the concept of embodiment, *Embodiment and Body Metaphors*, basing her work on German and English examples. Goschler began by introducing Johnson's idea that conceptual metaphors related to the body constituted *image schemata* or *embodied schemata*, terms which Johnson used interchangeably (Johnson 1987: 23). She quoted Johnson's definition:

A recurrent pattern, shape, and regularity in, or of [. . .] ongoing ordering activities. These patterns emerge as meaningful structures for us chiefly at the level of our bodily movements through space, our manipulation of objects, and our perceptual interactions. (Johnson, qtd in Goschler 2005: 29)

This definition of embodiment remained largely unchanged in *Philosophy in the Flesh*, which Johnson published jointly with Lakoff twelve years later in 1999. According to Johnson and others who have adopted the embodiment concept, we tend to map ideas and experiences onto physical experiences in the real world. To be emotionally 'hungry' or 'unfulfilled' (the example from Wittgenstein which we have already seen) might be understood in this way. This idea dovetails with the theory of metaphor which suggests that abstract ideas or little-known fields of knowledge are explained by reference to more familiar frames of reference.

Goschler found much evidence to back up the theory of embodiment. However, she found the terms in which embodiment is framed to be unclear and ambiguous. Embodiment seems to affirm that unfamiliar things and experiences must be interpreted in terms of more familiar things, and it would seem, at first sight, that nothing is more familiar to us than our own bodies. For this reason, embodiment uses the body as the source domain. In contrast to this, however, Goschler found that bodily metaphors used the body for both target and source domains.

We can find a great many metaphors which refer to computers in terms of bodies in both German and English. Quoting Hänke, Goschler offered examples of the 'lifespan' (*Lebensdauer*) of the server hardware and the 'state of health' (*Gesundheitszustand*) of Windows (37). The body can be used as the target domain to describe something else, as in the case of illness. A country or population can be represented as an individual who is ill. The nation, conceived as a body afflicted by illness, has already been noted in Goatly's example of 'cancer'. Such examples are often used as a model to stigmatise the influences which are said to lead to its 'ill-health' (decadence, moral decay, rebellious youth movements, etc.).

This explains the logic of Nationalist parties whose spokespeople conceive of immigration as an infection. Such distasteful bodily metaphors are commonplace in Western countries, but they are by no means restricted to the West. The Algerian Nationalist Revolutionary Movement (*Mouvement Nationaliste-Révolutionnaire Algérien*) was presenting itself on the Internet in 2010 as the defender of an Algeria 'gnawed by the cancer of modernism' ('*rongée par le cancer du modernisme*'). The difference between Western racism and the kind found in Algeria is that pro-Arabic racism is fuelled in part by a sense of injustice caused by a history of colonial domination and foreign exploitation, and this feeling of injustice is carefully nurtured by certain groups and employed to defend policies which are said to be in the 'State's interest'. As we can see, however, though these forms of racism may have different roots, they proceed along the same conceptual and metaphoric lines as propaganda in Western democracies.

In each of the examples given above in Goschler's study, the source domain is mapped onto the target domain of the body: computer software, a nation, a culture. Even a group of people are conceived of in terms of a body which is healthy or unhealthy, pure or infected. In this way, rhetoric invites computer programmers to see themselves as 'doctors' who can perpetuate the 'lifespan' of software, while self-righteous (and well-intentioned) statesmen dealing with epidemics set about policy-making as though they were curing or inoculating the nation against an infection. If I have introduced the Algerian example to the discussion of Goschler's findings, it is to render her commentary on embodiment all the more poignant by placing us, as Westerners, in the uncomfortable position of having to play the 'disease' that must be cured in order to purify the Algerian nation.

Goschler also found that the body can be transformed into the source domain of other conceptual metaphors related to disease and illness. Sontag (1988, in Goschler 2005: 40) and Nerlich, Hamilton and Rowe (2002) have all analysed the way in which disease is mapped onto war. Nerlich et al. show how fighting a disease can come to be conceived as 'combat' involving 'battle groups' and 'spies' that have 'to be defeated', 'exterminated' and 'wiped out'. Stibbe speaks of illness as 'a powerful *enemy* . . . (whose) *foot soldiers* are beyond number' (Goschler 2005: 40). These examples of body metaphors would seem to undermine the claim that embodiment maps lesser known concepts onto the body and contradicts Traugott, Dasher and Sweetser who claim that meanings are not mapped in the opposite direction (Sweetser 1990: 19).

Goschler's study also provided peculiar examples in which one part of the body was represented in terms of the interaction between bodies: the brain was described in terms of people. Parts of the body, neurons, were represented as bodies which could 'communicate with each other' ('*miteinander kommunizieren*') and 'work together' ('*zusammenarbeiten*') (42). In other examples, such as the English expression studied by Kövecses, 'my **blood boiled**', Goschler claimed it often proved difficult to analyse such expressions in terms of source and target domains (43). Here, anger, an emotion, is described in terms of a physical sensation (boiling) which, if it had any real physical basis, would entail the death of the individual and the inevitable end to all sensory perception. The bodily metaphor is itself, it would seem, already partially abstract.

These considerations do not bring into question the usefulness of embodiment as a tool of analysis, but they do indicate that some refinement is needed in order for us to be able to explain the direction in which bodily metaphors tend to project between target and source domains. Are bodily metaphors primarily target oriented, source oriented, or are they, to adopt Morier's term, 'reciprocal'? That is to say, do metaphors work in both directions? Do bodily metaphors project back and forth symmetrically like the 'legs' of the *compas* in French? And is embodiment a universal phenomenon? Or to what extent does the relationship between bodily functioning and symbolic language vary from language to language?

If we are to understand bodily metaphors in different languages, Goschler claimed it was necessary to take into account something she claimed that Lakoff and Johnson had forgotten, that is to say, that the body is to a large extent a cultural construction. In questioning embodiment, Goschler was questioning the naïve assumption that there is nothing we know better than our own bodies. If, argued Goschler, as some people claim, 'the body is not the ultimate grounding of experience, but rather a complicated construction that emerges from bodily and cultural practices' (48) then the Lakoff and Johnson position in which 'the body is taken as given' (48) appears to rest upon shaky foundations.

Here, Goschler is being somewhat unfair: Lakoff and Johnson repeatedly insist that the concept of the body differs from culture to culture. Lakoff and Johnson do, on the other hand, argue that certain aspects of bodily experience would appear to be universal: we consider things as being above and below us, in front of us and behind us. Some things can be seen, others remain invisible. And our language tends to reflect these basic experiential frames of understanding in the way different languages allow the same metaphors to develop.

So how do the varying constructions of the body affect the way conceptual metaphors evolve? Goschler restricts herself to a corpus of German and English metaphors, but if we look at the way the body is defined in Czech, even at a very basic lexical level, then we can see that the specificity of the Czech lexical structure will influence the metaphorical expressions that this language will allow, as the following examples should demonstrate.

In US politics, speakers tend to associate different roles with different parts of the body. The heart, in conjunction with everyday associations, tends to be reserved for feelings like caring, sympathy and patriotism. You can take the plight of illegal immigrants 'to heart' without seeing yourself as a 'bleeding heart'. If a politician instigates or supports a policy, on the other hand, then 'he takes things into hand'. Obama would obviously like his citizens to feel that the USA is 'safe in his hands' (a belief Bush worked hard to encourage during his own two terms in office). Bush would no doubt have made a similar claim about Iraq. And few Americans, however critical of the occupation of Iraq they may be, would support a withdrawal of US troops if this were to be represented by the opposition as 'the USA washing its hands of the destiny of Iraq'. Hands must be used for getting the job done. The Americans like to see themselves as a 'hands-on' nation.

'Hands' and 'heart' seem to be such straightforward bodily metaphors that it is difficult to see what is to be gained by analysing them any further. But what happens when we translate them? Though translating 'heart' as *srdce* into Czech may prove difficult in certain metaphorical extensions, the basic analogy between the heart and the emotions is mirrored in both languages (as it is in Dutch, as we have seen). But what about 'hand'? In Czech, no lexical distinction is made between the hand and the arm: only one word is used, *ruka*. But is 'to hold something in your hands', the same expression as 'to hold something in your arms'? Hardly. We may be said to hold our destiny in our hands. We hold our loved ones in our arms. This does not prevent Czech from forming many of its expressions along the same lines used by English. In Czech, for example, we can say someone acts in a manner which is 'underhand' (*pod rukou*). In other expressions, it is irrelevant whether we distinguish between arms and hands. If we say 'Hands up!' (*ruce vzhůru!*), it matters little that we do not indicate that the arms must be raised along with the hands: they must be since they are connected. Nevertheless, distinctions in the ways we divide the body up will influence the creation of different concepts and metaphorical expressions related to hands and arms, and, in the translation from Czech to English, certain ambiguities in Czech can lead to embarrassing misunderstandings. If I say I took someone 'by the arm' (*za ruku*) across the road, one might reasonably suppose I am speaking about my grandmother. If I use the same phrase to say that Jitka takes me 'by the hand' (*za ruku*) across the road, one might suppose I am talking about my girlfriend.

How do all of these *metaphorik.de* studies contribute to the metaphor debate? How do they tie in to the question of world-view? They show ways the cognitive unconscious can sprout off in different branches. If they do that, then they not only explore the expressive possibilities of different languages, they also trace the epistemological paths a language clears as it navigates its way through human experience. As the discussion of embodiment shows, that experience of the world includes our relationship to the world, our relationship to ourselves and our relationship to our own bodies. This is 'our' world. The 'world we live in' is not the unified, totalised world of philosophical models, models which can be surveyed, grasped, defined and divided up into sections which can be labelled. That 'world' is a concept, and though it may have meaning for philosophy as such, it says very little about the way we experience reality and the way we speak about it. For this reason, though grammar and metaphor may seem to offer limited insight into the world as a whole, they offer small revelations about the way we form order out of the chaotic fragments of everyday experience, building skyscrapers out of a few fragments of brick and broken glass. Metaphor helps us form 'models' of the world, worldviews.

Research of the kind that Dirven and the *metaphorik.de* website are carrying out contributes to the study of the relationship between metaphor and thought in three important ways:

1. It allows us:

    a. to define the different paths that metaphor takes in framing the way we speak about reality;
    b. to uncover analogous frames that are shared by different languages (though it would be presumptuous to speak of universal frames at this stage).

2. It serves as a testing ground to enable us to verify the validity and usefulness of concepts proposed by cognitive linguists (such as embodiment), and thereby to refine them.

3. It encourages us to consider the different formal constraints of other languages, and forces us thereby to invent new questions about the ways in which metaphors are shaped and the way they shape the concepts with which we think.

## THE SLAVIC CONTRIBUTION

Among the other forums inspired by the Lakoff and Johnson hypothesis, one noteworthy example is the work on 'world-picture' (*obraz světa*) carried out by Czech and Polish scholars. In her own article published in a collection of articles, the editor, Irena Vaňková (2001), stresses that the picture of the world and the related cognitive and cultural aspects of language are essential for the mother tongue. The mother tongue is thus conceived of as a kind of 'home in speech' (24). If we are to understand how we come to 'make our homes' within the world, it therefore becomes essential to study language.

This is precisely what the Czech and Polish researchers set about doing. In *Colours in Czech Sign Language*, Myslivečková, Hudáková and Vysuček consider the symbolism of colour as it is elaborated throughout speech in Czech and in the Czech Sign Language (CSL). They found that the two languages elaborated the colour system in a broadly similar way. In both, the colour system is divided up into eleven prototypical colours. And both the associations with the colours themselves and the expressions in which the colours were used appeared to coincide to a great degree.

Red (*červená*), for example was 'felt to be a very expressive colour: it is connected with strong emotion, love, passion but also danger, blood and fire' (Myslivečková et al., in Vaňková 2001: 69, my translation). There were, however, some noteworthy exceptions: red was also associated with lips. This might be considered an original innovative metonymy in spoken Czech, but it is fundamental to the term in the CSL which uses the gesture of two movements of the fingers towards the lips to form the sign for 'red'. In general, the semantic formation of signs within the CSL was often 'visually motivated' (75): that is to say, signs were more clearly physical than in the spoken language. Coffee (*káva*), for example, was used as a prototype for the colour brown (*hněda*). Myslivečková et al. also found similarities between associated signs when they compared, for example, 'black', 'night' and 'dark', or compared 'grey' with 'ash'. In spoken Czech, however, these words show no such similarities (and it will be noticed that neither do the English translations I have given for them). Whether this provides evidence for the CSL being a more primitive language system, and whether it can be inferred that physicality and spatial metaphors belong to the origins of language more than to sophisticated forms of cognitive thought (Nietzsche's hypothesis), remains to be seen. It would be interesting to establish whether sign languages reflect expressions derived from sound metaphors adopted from the spoken mother tongue. Since a lot of our metaphors are 'dead' to us, in that their metaphorical content is not immediately apparent, there is no reason to suppose that metaphors derived from sound (or forms of synaesthesia such as 'loud colour') could not survive in a language designed for, and kept alive by, the deaf. Likewise, it would be interesting to question blind readers as to the way they experience visual metaphors when they read Braille. Unfortunately, neither Myslivečková et al. nor anyone else seems to have studied these questions to date.

In another study edited by Vaňková, Jasňa Slědrová studies the trajectories of two synonyms, *mělký* and *plytký*, in Czech usage. Slědrová considers the definitions given by numerous Czech dictionaries, but it will suffice for our needs to replace them here by the definitions of the two terms given by Poldauf's *Czech–English Dictionary* (1986): while *mělký* is defined as 'shallow', 'commonplace' and 'superficial', *plytký* is defined in terms of the first and the last but not the middle meaning ('commonplace'). This would seem to bear out the claim that the two words can, nevertheless, be considered synonyms.

Slědrová brings to light one intriguing point concerning the elaboration of metaphorical meanings, sprouting from these two terms with a shared physical definition: the metaphoric patterns generated by the two words do not appear to resemble each other. *Mělký* has retained its primary meaning related to physical form. In the Czech National Corpus (created in 1993) that served as the resource for Slědrová's study, 75 per cent of expressions used *mělký* with its initial meaning (as in expressions related to water, sea, streams and lakes). Only 25 per cent of expressions involved a metaphorical usage (as in a superficial idea, story or document).

The metaphorical usage of *plytký*, on the other hand, was overwhelming (95.4 per cent). Slědrová's study demonstrated two things:

1. For one reason or another, synonyms do not seem to have the same propensity for metaphorical extension.
2. Metaphorical extensions are not static but develop over time, thereby altering the status of the *primary* meaning. *Plytký*, for example, would seem to be losing its spatial dimension (85).

One further point raised in Šlědrová's study was the fact that despite the weakening of the spatial dimension of the word *plytký*, this word continued to be used in certain non-figurative expressions in specific dialects, such as in the Moravian expression *plytký talíř*, for example. Cognitive studies have yet to incorporate an account of metaphorical expressions in dialects. On the whole, Lakoff and Johnson's corpus of examples tends to restrict itself to standard American usage, and because of its universalistic bent, the second-generation cognitive linguistics is unlikely to make headway on the way metaphors change and develop within dialects.

In the same way, cognitive studies have shown little sensitivity to questions of register, social class, gender and personality. If we are to speak of the trajectories of metaphors which structure the language we live by, these are important questions to take on board. There is, after all, no reason to suppose that an unemployed woman living on a council estate in Glasgow will feel at ease with the same conceptual metaphors and metaphorical expressions as a US congressman. Indeed, studies of slang in French have stressed that various professions tend to generate complex patterns of analogies in order to speak about life in general. A shopkeeper, for example, will speak, about 'handing in your balance sheet' when someone dies.

## SWEETSER'S CONTRIBUTION

The contribution of cognitive linguists is a considerable one, and, judging from their influence on linguistics in other countries, it is likely to be a lasting one. The work inspired by the Lakoff and Johnson hypothesis certainly does not preclude a concern for questions of alterity and linguistic difference, and many researchers have branched out to investigate other languages using this hypothesis.

Eve Sweetser has given greater philological depth to the question of conceptual metaphors by studying their etymological derivation, the way one language remodels its concepts from the clay moulds borrowed from foreign tongues. She shows, for example, that the verb *in-sist* originally meant 'to stand on' or 'to stand one's ground', while the verb to *pro-pose* meant 'to put forward' (Sweetser 1990: 20). Both verbs, Sweetser concluded, tended to confirm the idea that argument is conceived of in terms of war and battle in English (as Lakoff and Johnson had argued in 1980).

Sweetser's comparison of Greek, Latin, Old English, German, French and English terms has taken cognitive linguistics into another dimension, and has helped clarify the relationship between etymology and semantic structure. Sweetser has also investigated both the way polysemy and metaphors act within the semantic structure and the way they evolve over time. What she hopes to provide is 'a motivated account of the relationships between the senses of a single morpheme or word, and of the relationships between historically earlier and later senses of a morpheme and word' (3). For Sweetser, words do not randomly acquire new senses: new senses are acquired by cognitive structuring (9). They are created by following analogical associations along logical paths. Vision is associated with knowing, which entails complex (but logical) metaphorical extensions within the lexicon in which the verb to see (*weid-*, in Indo-European and *eidon* in Greek) will give rise to 'idea', 'wise' and 'wit' in English. Sweetser observed the same semantic change take place again and again throughout widely different Indo-European languages. This led her to conclude that the relationship between prototypical meaning and metaphorical meaning was 'directional'. In order to understand the direction of semantic development, it is necessary, therefore, to understand the metaphoric basis of the etymology of words. Conversely, considering metaphoric extension as a fundamental linguistic process allowed Sweetser to provide an interpretation of the origin of a word like 'any**way**', which does not appear to us at first sight to have much to do with 'paths'. Sweetser's explanation goes as follows: 'logical structures and conversational structures are at least partly understood in terms of physical travelling and motion'. Consequently, we can conceive of 'anyway' as meaning 'by any mental or conversational path we take, we reach this conclusion' (46).

The concern for the transformation of prototypical meaning into metaphorical meaning, and the transformation of metaphorical meaning into prototypical meaning, aligns Sweetser with Slĕdrová. Both linguists share a passion for uncovering a motivated account of metaphorical meaning. Such an account would certainly prove useful to Slĕdrová in her attempt to explain the different courses of transformation undergone by synonyms.

Sweetser goes on to analyse the physicality of words in a way similar to the way we analysed phrasal verbs in discussing the importance of metaphor in translation. But while we limited our analysis of prepositions and prefixes to a synchronic cross-linguistic approach, Sweetser shows the advantage of bringing to bear a diachronic analysis. In her analysis of the metaphorical extensions of knowing = seeing, she distinguishes between 'ambiguous forms' and new prototypical forms. As an example, she offers, 'to look down on' (33), which might be used in 'to look down on the city from the Eiffel Tower, or to look down on your neighbours'. Over time, expressions become independent and often shed their original metaphoric meaning. This is the stage at which terms like 'foresight' and 'overseer' emerge. The word as a lexical unit is strengthened as the metaphoric origins of the words which compose it are weakened. Sweetser shows that words like 'foresight' and 'overseer' are not arbitrary innovations, and, in fact, the word 'overseer' merely re-enacts a transformation that had already followed the same logic in Latin (*super-visor*) and, before that, in Greek (*epi-skopos*).

## REACHING BEYOND A *LANGUAGELESS* LINGUISTICS

Sweetser's work is certainly one that can help us build bridges between languages in order to explore the worldview question. It may also help to bridge the growing divide between European and American scholarship. Developments in metaphor theory in the USA in recent decades show a desire to reach out beyond the limitations of the generative formalist paradigm in order to allow us to explore the generation of alternative metaphoric patterning and to investigate foreign worldviews. Cognitive linguistics, in its American form, has drawn scholars from throughout the world to come to study within the framework of the themes and questions that have emerged from the study of metaphor. Nevertheless, the question of linguistic difference has inevitably been recast in the light of concerns of English-speaking researchers. And it is difficult to comprehend other worldviews when we observe them through the prism of our own language-bound, conceptually-structured worldview.

On the whole, though cognitive linguistics has set itself up as a challenge to Chomsky's generativist approach, a latent universalistic tendency has come to manifest itself more and more in recent years. If language is to be analysed as the gateway through which we are to gain access to the way 'we' think, then cognitive linguistics will have to bring the question of linguistic difference to the forefront of the debate, because, though we all think with language, we do not all speak the same language. The conclusion this would seem to lead us towards is that we do not all think alike. Consequently, Fauconnier and Turner's explanation of *The Way We Think* might well have to be seriously modified once the question of different languages is taken on board.

If comparing different languages opens up new worlds to us as Humboldt suggested it did, then the study of the different nature of those languages should help us understand the courses that the mind can take in charting the world we live in. Work which is being carried out on the periphery of the cognitive debate leads us to focus on fundamental aspects of language. The reader's patience may have been taxed by the list of work that has been going on concerning metaphor, especially since the scope of this chapter will not allow us more than a glimpse of the principal findings of such research. However, the diversity of approaches and findings should prevent us from bracketing off essential questions and from confining the question of symbolic representation within one single approach. Most of all, it should help us generate a multilingual approach to metaphor, a language-inspired approach: the antidote to what Jürgen Trabant warned against, 'a languageless linguistics' (2007).

The questions raised by German, Czech and Polish scholars, like the questions raised by Sweetser's language-based approach and Goatly's comparison of the pairing of concepts in Chinese and English, force us to confront formal questions. But these questions are not simply 'formal' in nature, or if they are so, then they are 'formal' in the sense in which Humboldt understood 'form'. Structures and associations were, for Humboldt, the different layers of language which were laid down by thinking individuals as they struggled to formulate thought in expression. All form was content-forming, he believed. In this sense, Humboldt's concept of *Sprache* (language) coincides to a large extent with what has come to be called the *cognitive unconscious*. It is the map of terms, associations and interactive connections we assimilate after learning to find our way around in the world of words. At first, our steps are hesitant and we need guidance, but fairly soon we find it easy to walk along language's streets and avenues. Soon we can explore unknown side streets by creating new linguistic innovations of our own based upon the structure and possibilities of the language system we have assimilated.

If language systems are different, then those differences will inevitably colour and shape the cognitive unconscious to some extent. In Humboldt's terms, the worldview (*Weltansicht*) *we* inherit as we assimilate the language system contributes to the shaping of our own worldview (*Weltanschauung*). The short list of philologists and linguists we have looked at hardly begins to enumerate the different ways language structure might interact with expression and cognition, but this brief overview does open the door to questions which will remain closed to us so long as we content ourselves with the study of English alone.

If metaphor can contribute to expanding the lexicon, then the question of synonyms should be taken into account in order to observe the reasons why one word is especially fertile for bearing metaphorical fruit. The different ways of categorising the world and our bodies should not be forgotten. Grammatical questions such as the question of diminutives should not be ignored. And comparing the grammatical structure of phrasal verbs with their semantic equivalents in other languages should contribute to helping us understand why certain languages seem to ground their expressions more in physical reality while the structures of other languages tend to resist this by remaining abstract. This question will take us way beyond a simple comparison of the prepositions in English phrasal verbs with prefixes in French. How, for example, should we compare both French and English with languages which would not have recourse to prepositions or prefixes? Slavic languages and Finnish, for example, would opt for declination and suffixes where prepositions would be used in English. Were such suffixes originally symbolic? To what extent can their metaphorical nature be awakened in creative speech? Understanding the symbolism of individual languages might help us understand the nature of their sign languages more fully, and comparing sign languages with the spoken language might open up new horizons for understanding the way we perceive of and conceive the world.

That makes for a lot of 'perhapses'. Wading our way towards new hypotheses might make heavy going. The questions comparative philology opens up to us might be perplexing in that they force us to reappraise the 'givens' of our own conceptual ordering of the world. They force us to question our language, and the relationship between language and world.

Our findings might be slight, fragmentary, and for those looking for short cuts to exotic foreign worldviews, they might appear disappointing. Scholars celebrating linguistic diversity and defenders of dying languages are often in the habit of making rather cavalier claims about the alterity of foreign worldviews, providing slim evidence in support of their arguments. Ultimately, however, sweeping generalisations and dramatic oppositions which situate different languages at opposite poles belong to the rhetoric of tourist-agency brochures promising day tours to exotic destinations. In the worldview debate, such oppositions are of little interest to serious scholars. As Humboldt rightly pointed out, it will require an enormous amount of painstaking work to provide even the most tenuous and limited of hypotheses.

It is now time to begin this painstaking work, as we leave behind the discussion of the conceptualisation of metaphor to return to discourse analysis. This will take the form of what I will call 'cross-lingual discourse analysis', the comparison of equivalent and divergent patterns of symbolic representation in multilingual studies. In the following section of this study, the relationship between metaphor and worldview will be investigated in individual case studies focusing on specific questions. This will take us on an arduous tour of two foreign languages, Czech and German. And we will indeed be entering a different worldview when we enter these languages. But two dimensions of worldview must be distinguished in this investigation: worldview at the level of the language system itself and at the level of ideological linguistic constructs. We must suspend our own conceptual patterning, the bearings our own language system provides us with, in order to come to grips with the ways in which fundamental concepts are defined, delineated, grouped together and interactively opposed in these languages. This may seem to imply that Czech and German are rigid constructions which condition thought, but though there is unquestionably a degree of constancy in the definition of the fundamental concepts of understanding within each of those two languages, both of them prove to be as flexible and as subject to change as English does for English-speakers. Entering into these languages will not only involve learning what 'the State' and what 'the People' means for Germans and for Czechs, it will involve trying to understand how these concepts became caught up, harnessed and perverted in the discourse disseminated by reigning ideologies. To this extent, entering into the worldviews of these case studies will involve entering into strange and disturbing worlds, the foreign conceptual worlds which reigning ideologies set up within the language system and which they seek to impose upon the speakers of a language at a given time in history.

Metaphor will prove to be an essential force in the patterning of language, a force which shapes worldviews at both the fundamental level of perception and conception, and at the level of ideologies. The third case study will take us beyond ideology to a reflection upon the 'nature' of language itself. But the very 'nature' of language will turn out to be a construction. Studying the metaphoric construction of French should enable us to stand back from language and to reflect upon the limits of language as a concept. This is what language enables us to do: to reflect upon the products of our understanding, to redefine them and refine them. In this sense, though they are essentially critical, all three case studies should contribute to realising something of that great potential which is inalienable in language, the work of the mind. These studies should help us to discern more clearly the limits of language and of thought, in order to aid us to move on (within language and by the force of our thinking) beyond those limits.

# Part II  Case Studies in Metaphor

# Introduction to Part II

The following three case studies will explore the relationship between speech and metaphor in the construction of ideological worldviews and in the very construction of our concept of language itself. In the first and second case studies, we will discuss the role played by metaphor in constructing ideological worldviews, or what we will increasingly call cultural mindsets. Two unfashionable mindsets have been selected deliberately, in order to upset readers and force them to leave behind their own convictions and concepts, and to enter into an unfamiliar and probably 'unsavoury' vision of the world. The first study will investigate the function of metaphor in constructing Czechoslovak communism. The second will investigate the Nazi worldview and the role metaphors play in what Viktor Klemperer has named *Hitlerdeutsch*.

The third case study will turn the methodology of the other two on its head: rather than studying the metaphors we find in language, we will consider the metaphors we use to construct our concept of 'language'. Metaphoric models used to conceptualise French and English will be compared and contrasted within particular socio-historical situations. The study will then consider the ways in which lyrical ecological metaphoric paradigms are being used to defend the concept of linguistic diversity in recent scholarship in French and in English.

In all three of the case studies, the material we will be investigating should challenge readers and should force them to consider the ways in which perception and conception are affected by language at different levels. The concepts of the language will be shown to organise the way speakers conceive the world and society, and the way they perceive their place within them. At the same time, language will be considered in terms of discourse, and the individual will be considered as the active speaker who participates in the construction of his or her world. World-perceiving and world-conceiving may legitimately be considered to be over-arching shaping forms and patterns of thought: and to this extent it may be argued that language influences thought.

Nevertheless, the individual always interacts with the shaping forces of language, and the worldviews which language engenders cannot be sustained or perpetuated without the participation of individual speakers. The term 'cultural mindset' will be reserved for those competing, conflicting and often mutually exclusive ideologies which arise in any given language. World-perceiving and world-conceiving belong to the more fundamental sensory and conceptual level of cognitive organisation in language. Both terms would be understood by Humboldt as parts of the *Weltansicht*, the worldview of the language into which we enter when we begin to master a foreign tongue. Cultural mindset will be reserved for the concept of 'worldview' as it is understood by philosophers, sociologists and cultural theorists.

These definitions have already been discussed in Chapter 1 of this book, but it is important to stress that neither the concepts of world-perceiving and world-conceiving, nor the concept of cultural mindset, can account for the degree to which individuals remodel ideas and transform their own language. Both the linguistic concept of worldview and its philosophical counterpart, on the contrary, tend to encourage us to consider the relationship of speakers to language in a deterministic manner. Because it is essential to debunk this reductive and misleading paradigm, it is important to consider worldview from the perspective of the personal world, the fairly constant and coherent space which each one of us opens up for himself or herself in language. At the same time, the flexibility and fluidity of experience and impressions makes it important to bear in mind that our perspective of the world is constantly changing. The permanent substructures are always being reinforced and challenged, consolidated and effaced as speech unfolds. Permanence, paradoxically, exists only within flux. Rigid linguistic norms are unthinkable outwith dialogue and discussion, which constantly introduces transgression, innovation and linguistic playfulness (in jokes, irony, poetry and wordplay, for example).

Perspective and personal world should serve as concepts to remind us that language is fundamentally discourse, whether it is speech or writing or any other form of medium. Discourse evolves in space and time. Language can only ever be kept alive in the expression of different perspectives as individuals bind together in communication, exchanging their views and juxtaposing their personal worlds and negotiating their cultural mindsets. This negotiation brings them into union, but also into opposition and confusion. However, understanding and miscomprehension both require a certain degree of exchange and complicity, and this complicity is made possible by the language system and the shared structures of world-perceiving and world-conceiving which language alone can open up to us. Marxists and neo-liberals may disagree fundamentally, but their disagreements must be based upon varying interpretations of shared concepts (relating to the State, to history and to individual responsibility, for example). In the same way, religious confrontations between Protestants and Catholics take place, at a conceptual level, within the sphere of shared concepts encompassing God, love, fate and Creation.

Metaphor will be shown to be a shaping form of conceptual patterning, one which is active at all five levels of worldview. Language itself cannot escape metaphor. So how can we hope to escape it? The aim of these three case studies is neither to denounce metaphor as some philosophers have done, nor to celebrate it, as cognitive scholars such as Lakoff and Johnson have done in recent decades. The aim is to trace the way the speakers of different languages negotiate metaphors as they go on shaping the worlds they live in. Entering into foreign worldviews should, it is hoped, encourage us to think more deeply about the way we ourselves are caught up both in metaphor and in worldviews. It should also serve to remind us that we cannot complacently surrender to the shaping forces of language, but must assume our own responsibility for the worldviews we accept to live within and perpetuate.

# CHAPTER 7

# The Language of Czechoslovak Communist Power

*'Jsme jiný svět.'*
'We are another world.'

(Kliment 1979, qtd in Fidelius 1998: 167)

## DOES IT MAKE ANY SENSE?

Critics of communism have never been rare, but during the Cold War, critics were obliged to find arguments to defend the West, the American way of life, and democracy as we understood it and enjoyed it in Europe. Since the breakdown of the Soviet model, the Western press and public opinion have on the whole tended to conclude that the failure of the USSR and its satellite states logically reflects our own success. 'We won the Cold War,' we like to tell ourselves. The Western press hurried to bury Marxism with slogans like 'Communism is dead!' And the euphoria of victory whipped up a din of celebration as the iron curtain opened up to us and our way of living, working, consuming and organising the State and the economy. In all that excitement, the aspirations and objectives of communism were often dismissed or forgotten. Since the end of the Cold War, intelligent comment on alternatives to the market economy has become rare. It seems that opposition forces us to sharpen our wits: lack of opposition enfeebles the critical, creative and speculative faculties of the mind.

Self-satisfaction induces intellectual and political apathy. To many people today it appears odd, if not absurd, that Karl Marx could have inspired millions of people in nations throughout the world to transform their societies in the hope of creating a humanitarian world community in which would reign the guiding principle of the greatest good for the greatest number. To the vast majority of young adults born in the 1980s, the idea is all but inconceivable. Individualism for this generation does not represent so much an option, as a self-evident fact of existence. We might as well defy gravity or try breathing underwater, as go against the sovereign right of the individual to seek his or her happiness where and however it can be found. Does this imply an intellectual complacency? Or does it not simply show how comfortable most of us feel (intellectually speaking) within the limits of our own worldview, now that no alternative ideology questions or menaces it?

At any rate, it requires an effort for us to enter the world-view of a communist country. Many will no doubt find that the attempt is not worth the effort. Why walk back into the past, especially when that past was, from the Western point of view, perverted by the communist perspective of the world? Certainly, most Czechs and Slovaks today are unlikely to find it a very enticing trip to step back into the past of the *Československá socialistická republika* from which their two countries seceded after the country's division in 1992. But this shows only too clearly the desire to sweep away the concepts of the past and to relax back unthinkingly into the ones that the new market economy has generated for Czech and Slovak citizens, concepts that we (in what used to be known as 'Western Europe') have been brought up with and within.

In the early 1990s, a radical post-velvet revolutionary spring-cleaning began in the Czech and Slovak Republics: libraries could not give away many of the books which had up till then formed the required reading of schools and universities. And so began a whole new chapter in the destruction of past documents, and with it a rewriting of history for the *Česká republika*. The question of who managed to take the step into the future and who remained with one foot in the past depended upon personality, past affiliations and education but, most of all, upon age. Many adopted the ironic smile of those who know their newly adopted catchwords and slogans sound odd to friends and family.

Those who were still adolescents at the time of the 'Velvet Revolution' in 1989 find the language of communism not only uninteresting but also 'unreal'. They find it impossible to fathom. Czech adolescents cannot find their bearings in the conceptual world of communism. Those who were over twenty at the time of the revolution are what might be called 'ideologically bilingual', and throughout the 1990s such people acted as the 'translators of capitalism' for older generations who resigned themselves (often unwillingly) to the fate of having to find their way around the conceptual world of the market economy.

The pain and anxiety of waking up to a capitalist world was not merely caused by the very real impoverishment that the transition brought to the vast majority of those over fifty. It was also caused by those citizens being forced to think differently, or rather by their being forced to think. Because communism, like any ideological mindset, did not require people 'to think'. Communism did not induce most people to think through its premises and its aspirations, its logic and its arguments. All that the State hoped for or required was that citizens simply accept its arguments and obey its laws.

Far from embracing communist ideals and endorsing the State's rhetoric, far from approving of its logic and accepting its arguments, by the mid-1970s most Czechs seem to have adopted an attitude of resignation towards communist rhetoric. The Party line was endured. The general state of apathy was apolitical to the extent that the Party began to worry about the lack dialogue between itself and citizens. The Party even tried to provoke criticism from citizens (albeit within the limits the Party circumscribed itself). The Czechs' equivalent of Russia's *Pravda*, the daily paper *Rudé Právo*, was dismissed by many people as 'nonsense' (*nesmysl*) or 'bullshit' (*hovno*). Curiously, this did not make it impossible for readers to follow the logic of the Party's arguments, and, more importantly, hostility and scorn for those arguments did not make it any easier for those who dismissed the Party's nonsense to make any sense of the arguments of Václav Klaus, the new Prime Minister, when he began adapting the economy to the free market with the 'liberation' of prices (*liberalizace ceny*). Distrust, resentment and dissent, the malaise of communism, did not prepare people conceptually for capitalism.

What does this suggest? It would seem that contempt and irony did not prevent most people from living their lives in accordance with the ideological and conceptual precepts upon which the Czechoslovak communist system was based. However great the widening gap between the Party's worldview and the mindset of the Czech and Slovak citizens, those citizens continued to coexist with the State and its institutions – if not in harmony, then at least in accordance with the State's dictates; and if they managed to do this, it was thanks to their capacity to share the State's conception of the world. But what exactly was that shared conception based upon? Critics argued that communism and its rhetoric was nonsense. But does nonsense have a basis? Can we live in accord with nonsense and obey its laws? Does absurdity have the coherence to structure a society?

The Czech thinker, Petr Fidelius, assigned himself a curious task when he decided to take the rhetoric and the logic of *Rudé Právo* seriously. He realised that in taking the Party's main organ of propaganda seriously, he was going against the grain of his generation. What he wanted to learn though was 'whether all those terribly bizarre linguistic expressions offered by *Rudé Právo* make any sense' (Fidelius 1998: 11, my translation). On analysing in depth the articles of the paper, he found, to his surprise, that a logic did transpire. He concluded:

> it is really a language about some kind of world, albeit an 'imaginary world', that is to say, a certain ideological *world picture* [*obraz světa*] [. . .] And so I started to explore the content of the fundamental principles upon which that language [*řeč*] reposes, as well as the relations which link them to one another, the language's 'building principles' [*stavební principy*]. (11)

With a wry sense of humour, Fidelius found himself forced to admit that 'in its own language, the communist regime gave a wholly truthful [*pravdivý*] image of its character' (11).

What is to be gained by following Fidelius on his analysis of the conceptual architecture of a worn-out communist discourse? A study of communist rhetoric of the 1970s will not provide us with a display of linguistic virtuosity. It will not show us the way concepts can, almost overnight, be radically destabilised, as we saw in the case of *war* in the propaganda related to the invasion of Iraq in 2003 or the neo-conservative discourse of the 'War on Terror'. Communist rhetoric of the 1970s neither had the creativity of Nazi rhetoric, nor did it hold the macabre charm that *Hitlerdeutsch* held for Germans, as the Nazis whipped up hate for Jews and resentment against the world powers. On the other hand, following Fidelius might show us how the mindset of millions was modelled around certain fundamental principles which, though they might not have been embraced enthusiastically, nevertheless did manage to order and organise the way people perceived and conceived the world, and, consequently, influenced the way those people acted in that world. The interest for our study of metaphor and worldview will lie in examining the role metaphors played in constructing and maintaining those fundamental principles in the ongoing expression of communist discourse by the Party.

## CONCEPTUAL CLUSTERS

Often, when asked why they left a job or a partner, people will sigh and say, 'Where should I begin?' Explaining the different interlinked roles and relations that structure a given situation seems all but impossible. Explaining communist concepts entails a bafflingly similar task. To define a concept, we have to disentangle it from the web of relations which structure the meaning it takes on in everyday life for people. And this process of disentanglement in turn entangles us with other concepts which must themselves be explained, but which can only be explained by referring back to the concept we began by trying to explain. At least four inextricable concepts are fundamental for the organisation of the communist worldview and the mindset that it cultivated in its citizens. These four concepts were:

1. *Historie* (history)
2. *Lidé* (people)
3. *Strana* (Party)
4. *Stát* (State).

As we shall see, these concepts are defined in largely metaphorical terms. The relations between them are structured metaphorically. Moreover, the relations between citizens and these four concepts will give rise to a flourishing abundance of metaphors which will be used to impose the Party line and consolidate its political hold upon the citizen and its conceptual hold upon his or her mindset by coercing the citizen's mind along the logic of its language to conclusions which correspond to the Party's worldview. These four concepts – *history*, *people*, *Party* and *State* – form what we might call a 'conceptual cluster'. The relations between the parts of this conceptual cluster are, as we shall see, paradoxical. They are rigid in that they impose the inflexible Party will upon the individual, while at the same time, they are flexible in that the definition of these terms, the relations between the terms and what they can refer to, evolves over time and changes from situation to situation. Let us begin at the beginning by tracing the outlines of *historie* in the discourse of *Rudé Právo*.

## Historie

Everywhere in communist discourse, history is a trajectory, a path. This is saying no more than that socialism, as a form of positivism, adopts the progressive conceptual metaphors common to other ideologies, metaphors which have been shared by both the sciences and the social sciences in many Western languages and cultures for at least two centuries. Nineteenth-century man advances along the path of history from his origin to his ultimate destiny. This entails steps, stages in a logical development. Various historians have contested this representation of the past as one single evolutionary trajectory. Moreover, this representation has the added disadvantage of implying that what went before is leading us to an inevitable and necessary conclusion: man will realise himself by moving forward through history to his historically defined goal. His role is to recognise that goal and realise it. Such a view is fundamental to the worldview of socialism, but this conception is a construct which socialism shares with many other worldviews, worldviews which continued to flourish throughout the twentieth century and which show no signs of flagging in the twenty-first century.

In the Czech version of this positivism, 'the masses of the people' ('*lidové masy*') were called upon to 'create history' ('*tvořit dějiny*') (Fidelius 1998: 30). *Tvořit* is the generic word for 'to make', 'to create' or 'to fabricate' in Czech. But in socialist discourse, which celebrates the working man of industrial society (the very man that Marx claimed had been 'brutalised' by capitalism and had thereby been rendered 'brutish', inhuman or dehumanised), *tvořit* takes on an industrial, mechanical meaning. For this reason, metaphors which portray history as constructive, mechanistic process are common in Czech communist discourse. People in the Czechoslovak State are expected to 'actively take part in the building [*budování*] of a developed socialist society' (41).

The future is conditioned by the past and man's role is defined in terms of his obligation to fulfil his own personal destiny by conforming to his historical role of realising history's destiny. This implies both a metaphysics of man and historical destiny. But socialist metaphysics remain shaped by the conceptual metaphors which had their origins in the industrial age and which championed the transformation of life and nature by machinery. Newtonian physics and mechanistic analytic formulas shape this metaphysics. History is a machine. It works. And it works in only one way. For this reason, *Rudé Právo* speaks of the 'universal historical process' ('*celkový historický proces*') (34).

We can oil the works of this process or we can get in its way. 'Going against history' ('*jít proti dějinám*') (53) might be compared to sticking a spanner in the works. Socialism was a vehicle. Consequently, the bourgeoisie became a group which 'put the brakes on history' (29). Anyone who undermines the people's fulfilment of its destiny will, as the first Communist Prime Minister, Klement Gottwald, put it, inevitably 'end up on the rubbish dump of history' ('*skončí na smetišti dějin*') (178). Who actually throws them upon the rubbish dump becomes of secondary importance.

History will take care of them. Dissenters are responsible for their
own destiny, or rather, they are incapable of realising their destiny
because they refuse to recognise their historical role. By pursuing
'other goals', 'other ideals', goals and ideals contrary to the interests of the people, they themselves are responsible for estranging
themselves from 'the people' (45). This implies an unsustainable
contradiction which cannot fail to destroy those that enter into
opposition with history itself. By opposing the Party, dissenters
oppose history. In doing so, they oppose the people and thereby fail
to serve their own interests (since they should recognise themselves
as part of the people and recognise that their own interests are the
people's interests). Opposition becomes, according to this logic,
a perverse form of self-serving individualism which ultimately
cannot even serve the individual's interests. Crushing opposition
becomes an inevitable historical necessity. For all the celebration of
the conquest over the forces of capitalism, in the eyes of the Party,
there is nothing glorious in crushing individuals who oppose the
deterministic dialectic of history. Their destruction is regrettable.
But can its opponents blame the Party? As one journalist from
*Rudé Právo* put it: 'Can someone who lays himself down upon the
railway lines to stop the movement of history, blame the train that
cuts his legs off?' (53).

This mechanistic definition might seem to go a long way to
objectifying man within the context of the unfeeling inhuman
machinery of the historical process. And to a large extent this metaphoric conceptualisation of history may have estranged communist
States from Marx's humanistic conception of man. Man was not
entirely reified by communist rhetoric, however. Man remained
a form of 'elemental living' energy (*živelná energie*). This living
energy was, nevertheless, conceived of as a form of 'carburant'
which would fuel the journey to socialism. In order to fuel it, this
living energy had to be channelled (*kanalizovaná*) in the right
direction by the Party. This would allow the Party to 'exploit' this
energy fully without wasting any of it. The thrifty metaphors of
penny-pinching household economics which structured capitalist
economics seem to have survived the transition to the communist
worldview here.

## *Lidé*

Fidelius sums up the role of the 'people' in his own analysis of communist discourse in the following way: '*"lid" otevírá bránu do "světa socialismus"*' ('"people" opens the gateway to the "socialist world"') (18). 'People' is both a key concept, a cornerstone upon which socialist rhetoric is constructed, and a source of confusion and dispute which will engage the Party in a relentless struggle to maintain its grasp over the term whenever it claims to manifest the will of the people to act in the people's interests. The people's destiny is to realise history's destiny. The people must walk with history towards the predestined goal to which the universal historical process tends.

This implies an inclusive and essentialist understanding of the concept of 'the people', however. After all, even the Party (or especially the Party) knew that not all people walked with 'the people'. In order to account for this, one *Rudé Právo* journalist distinguished between 'honest' and 'dishonest' people. According to him: 'All honest people of integrity of this land of ours walk with the Party, working towards the development of a socialist society' ('*Všichni poctiví, čestní lidé této země jdou se stranou, pracující pro rozvoj socialistické společnosti*') (22). History needs honesty and people of integrity. These will be the catalysts of history. It transpires, however, that this unfolding of history is of a paradoxical nature: history is both a destination and a process, a journey. The role of the people consists in helping history to unfold: but this is an ongoing activity, an activity which, by definition, cannot be achieved, because if the people were to reach socialism, they would thereby lose their historical role. For this reason, socialism and history remain precarious conceptual constructs defined in a contradictory formulation: each one is both a trajectory and the destination of that trajectory.

The division of the people into honest people who build the socialist society and dishonest people who obstruct it and disrupt it, led Fidelius in his quest to understand the rhetoric of *Rudé Právo* to conclude that two definitions of 'the people' were at work. 'The people' could be used as a restrictive or a global term of reference (19). He traced the formulations of definitions of 'the people' in dictionaries with a mixture of sardonic irony and naïve disbelief. He found that 'the people' referred to 'working people', which had the disadvantage of excluding the elderly, the sick and all children. But the rhetoric of *Rudé Právo* often coupled 'the people' with other bodies of working people, which implied that such groups did not belong to 'the people'. Artists were required to reflect and promote socialist ideals during the communist chapter of Czech history, and in praise of those that did so, a *Rudé Právo* journalist claimed: 'Our artists walk with the people, and the people walk with them' (21). This would seem to disqualify artists from the ranks of the people. Such a schizophrenia is pervasive in the structure of socialist discourse. A part is said to adhere to the whole without a clear spatial metaphoric conception of the identity of the part or its relations with other parts of the whole being rendered possible.

This, of course, is one of the central contradictions of communist rhetoric. Like the leaders of most parties which reach power, the political leader of the Communist Party, Klement Gottwald, had claimed in 1948: 'Your will, the will of the people will be the law of this land' (*'Vaše vůle, vůle lidu, bude v této zemi zákonem'*) (qtd in Fidelius 1998: 23). The sole justification of the State, the system and the Party thereby became the serving of the interests of the people. Obviously, demagogical and totalitarian rhetoric is intended to persuade the majority by persuading it that it is the whole, or at least the essential part of the whole. This permitted Gottwald to identify non-communists as 'enemies' (*nepřítele*) of the people.

It is important to situate the concept of enemies (*nepřítele*) in the context of post-war Czechoslovakia. The Czechoslovak Republic had been born in 1918 with the support of the allied nations who were interested in both weakening Prussia and dismantling the Austro-Hungarian Empire. Twenty years later, the Republic had been consumed as part of Hitler's *Lebensraum* project to enlarge Germany's eastern frontiers. In such a context, the enemies of the Czechs were perceived to be the 'foreign invaders' who came from without the nation's boundaries. These 'enemy invaders' ironically included the three million German-speakers who had been annexed within the frontiers of Czechoslovakia in 1918, however, a fact which outraged Hitler and which Churchill and even the Czech Prime Minister Beneš both admitted was intolerable. With the restoration of the Czechoslovak Republic in 1945, these German-speakers (a minority of whom had collaborated with the Nazi occupying government) were tarred as 'enemies' and expelled from the Republic.

How does this concept of 'enemies' influence the definition of 'the People'? '*Lidé*' ('the people') turns out to be a concept with a changing history. It is the emotive call to national identity during the Czech revival of the nineteenth century, a movement which indulges in post-romantic notions of the nobleness of the national character and the glorification of the peasantry. Such romanticism is inspired by nostalgia, and by a superficial reading of Rousseau. However, as kitschy as such neo-romantic notions may now appear, they exerted a powerful pull on the Czech imagination. The German-speakers (in Germany, Austria and in the Czechoslovak Republic) become the opposite of the Czech ideal of a wholesome, community-centred people with its roots struck deep into the earth of the homeland of which the Czech people had been unfairly deprived. Hostility to progress is evident in all reactionary movements which celebrate the land, the homeland and traditional values in contrast to the perceived decadence of the city and the depravity of its dwellers. Czech neo-romanticism does not escape this, and it taints the ideal of the Czech identity and shapes the idea of its enemies, but in addition to this reactionary neo-romantic ideal, we have the wholly understandable resentment against the occupying Nazi government. Many members of the resistance and freedom fighters were not only ardent patriots inspired by a love of their homeland and often an idealistic image of its people, they were also communists who perceived all German-speakers as enemies, and all those who resisted communism (the victory of the people) as 'class enemies'.

## *Strana*

Communists from Klement Gottwald to Gustav Husak, the Prime Minister of the seventies and eighties (and himself a resistance hero), perceived the protection of Czechoslovakia to be an urgent fight, a fight against the Germans, against forces willing to collaborate with them, against the bourgeoisie which would make the nation into a slave of international capital. For such men, the nation's struggle was a struggle against all forces which became obstacles to the consolidation of a strong Party which would be able to protect the destiny of the Czech nation and its people. Men whose characters were forged by fighting the Nazis and assuring the communist revolution were hardly likely to be flexible and tolerant. And indeed the Party had no time for those among its citizens who obstructed its will. As a *Rudé Právo* journalist put it: 'The Party will discuss nothing with anyone' ('*Srana nebude s nikým diskutovat*') (44).

Such a refusal of dialogue would seem to be a supreme contradiction of democracy. Democracy is, after all, usually defined by us as the rule of the people by the people. However, in a socialist society the State would have us believe that their democracy had reached a higher stage of evolution. This argument entails a distinction between 'traditional democracy' and the 'new democracy'. Under capitalism, various interested parties struggle with one another to assure their own interests. This is a period of individualism. Socialism is fundamentally hostile to individualism, as can be seen in the definition the *Concise Dictionary of Political Terms* (*Stručný politický slovník*) published in Prague in 1962, in which *Individualismus* is defined in the following terms: 'holding individual interests above the interests of the collective or of society as a whole' (Fingl et al. 1962: 105). Inevitably, hostility to individualism – equated with selfishness – spills over into hostility to 'the individual' as a concept, and hostility to tangible individuals who refuse to conform to the collective will (which is difficult to distinguish in communist discourse from the will of the State).

The Czechoslovak Communist Party would have us believe that revolution had allowed socialist society to transcend the period of individualism in which the conflict of a plurality of interests had some justification. Socialism had brought history, as a Hegelian process, forwards towards its final destination, resolving oppositions and transcending them to form a harmonious whole society in which plurality no longer had any function or raison d'être.

The Party thereafter protected the people's interests. There was, therefore, no logical reason for protecting any opinion other than that of the benevolent Party.

The Party consequently had no reason to discuss things with people. It *was* the people. And if it was the people, with whom could it speak? Presumably, only to enemies. And the State would waste no time with those enemies who had chosen to lose themselves on the path towards history's final destiny. The Party would leave those enemies where they belonged, on the 'rubbish dump of history'.

'The Party makes all classes and layers of society one in its interests' (Husak, qtd in Fidelius 1998: 51). In this role, the Marxist–Leninist Party plays a crucial historical role: it alone can allow 'the working class to accomplish its historical vocation as the gravedigger of capitalism and the creator of the communist society' (*'splnit své historické poslání hrobaře kapitalismu a tvůrce komunistické společnosti'*) (František Havlíček, *Rudé Právo*, qtd in Fidelius 1998: 37). The Party can even be said to transcend history since it anticipates the unfolding of the universal historical process. This transcendental role is captured, once more in metaphor. In a pastiche of a Biblical metaphor, the leaders of the working class and their Party are said to be 'the alpha and the omega'. If the Party is the beginning and the end, it cannot be confined to one period in history. It is both the origin and the destiny of history. To contest it would be absurd.

This implies not only a conception of politics and of political life but a conception of life in general. Life is activity, or 'dynamic movement', and at its head is the Party as 'the natural and acknowledged leading power of society' (*'přirozená a uznávaná vedoucí síla společnosti'*) (75). Thus, the Party is not defined within society, and society does not take its place within nature: the Party defines both life and nature. It therefore goes without saying that it defines and organises society. To refuse the Party would be to go against nature and to go against life itself.

In describing the nature of the Party and its insight into life, society and history, the words 'natural' and 'objective' become synonyms. 'Objective' is set up against 'subjective'. 'Subjective' belongs to individualism and individuals. In any conflict between the subjective perspectives and interests of individuals on the one hand and the State's objective perspective and its role of safeguarding of the people's interests on the other, 'subjective' would seem to rhyme with 'subversive'.

Communist rhetoric takes it as a given that the Party's leaders have understood the nature of society and history. Its universal process holds no secret for them. Citizens may not fully understand this universal process and may fail to grasp the necessity of the Party's decisions in directing society: they may fail to perceive the essential role that they themselves must play within the unfolding of history and the construction of socialism. The Party is there to provide enlightenment, however. As Dalibor Hanes explained, only the State holds the key 'to the resources of objective understanding' ('*zdrojům objektivního poznání*') (qtd in Fidelius 1998: 76). The Party has the remarkable capacity of synthesising and condensing the whole of 'the people', society, nature and history within its 'nucleus', and this in turn permits it to envelop education and science within the scope of politics. In order to understand science and the objects of science, we must stand with the Party and see things through the eyes of the Party. This gives a whole new scope to the concept of 'political science'.

In this auto-celebration there is an invitation (and an implicit obligation) to celebrate the Party. But who should celebrate the Party? The people, presumably. This entails some confusion, since the Party claims to be the people. This confusion can be escaped, though, if we understand that the Party is the 'nucleus'. This was the argument advanced by Ladislav Hrzal (Fidelius 1998: 26–8). The nucleus controls the cell. By analogy, the 'Party as Nucleus' controls the people. The people, in such a metaphoric construct, are no longer people (and certainly not individuals), they are the assembled parts of the social body. They are transformed into the masses, a material form deprived of activity, motivation or consciousness. The masses are essential for the worker's struggle. Nonetheless, as Lenin tells us, sometimes the masses appear 'to be sleeping' (qtd in Fidelius 1998: 28). This entails a curious paradoxical process. People are objectified; they become material, then the objectified assembly of people is conversely personified. This strange metaphorical process deserves a name but there seems to be none available at present. For this reason, I will christen it as the 'personified reification'.

The personified reification is a complex and contradictory construct. Nevertheless, its logic clearly transpires: the role of the Party, the nucleus of the working class, the essence and directing force of that class, is invested with the task of 'awakening the masses'. Waking them will involve animating the inanimate, transforming inert matter into energy. The Party will activate them, humanise them and motivate them, thereby enabling them to liberate themselves from their slavery under capitalism. This will transform those workers into 'the people'. Despite all the brutal aspects of socialist society, this allegoric reasoning retains something that is reminiscent of the fairy tale, *Sleeping Beauty*.

## *Stát*

If the Party is the alpha and the omega, the guarantee of the accomplishment of history, and the protector of socialism and the people's interests, then the State would seem to be superfluous. But, as the logic of socialist rhetoric would have it, all organs of the State have their place. All parts of socialist society serve a function. So what is the function of the State? And how does it differ from the Party?

The answer to these questions is provided by two *Rudé Právo* journalists, Fojtík and Tomášek: the State is 'the organ of power of the working people' ('*mocenský orgán pracující lidu*') (qtd in Fidelius 1998: 69). As Dalibor Hanes put it, the State 'programmes our goals and organises and inspires the masses to realise those goals' (qtd in Fidelius 1998: 68). Nonetheless, though the State is the founding principle of socialist life, and the safeguard of the destiny of the people, socialist politics requires a separation of powers. This is not required for the same reason that democratic powers separate, for example, the judiciary, the executive and the legislative functions of government, following the precepts laid down by Montesquieu in the *De l'esprit des lois* in 1748. Such a separation is designed to safeguard the interests of society from each of the State's bodies which might (unless inhibited) take on too much power and misuse it. However, since it is inconceivable that a part of the State should act otherwise than in the interests of the people, the safeguard that Montesquieu prescribed for monarchic government and which was adopted by modern capitalist democracies becomes superfluous in communist society, according to the logic of the State.

In communist society, this division of power is of a pragmatic nature. The State inspires the goals, the State implements them. It fulfils an 'operational function'. The orientation of the State is directed by the Party, but the Party requires the State to assure that society moves in the designated direction according to its will. Society can, indeed, lose its way, and the State is there to make sure it sticks to the correct course. For this reason, Fidelius argues the State is to the Party what the secretary is to her boss (72). Fidelius is obviously giving way to his sardonic sense of humour here though, since it is highly unlikely that the Party would describe its relationship to the State in these terms. The State is not there simply to carry out the Party's orders (*příkazy*), as Fidelius suggests. The State is independent. Nonetheless, this independence shows certain limits.

Like the Christian of Augustine's *Confessions* who is 'free' to obey His Creator, the State is 'free' to carry out the plans inspired by the Party. This freedom does not leave any place for opposition, because since the Party is the essence of the people, its 'nucleus', and since the State is the 'organ of power of the working people', to oppose the Party would be like opposing oneself. To use a simile, it would be like a man slapping his own face. The Party reserves the role of surveying and controlling the way in which the State 'freely' carries out its plans and objectives, as Tomášek pointed out in clear terms: 'The Party marks out and controls the lines of state policy with the aim of deepening its democratic character' (qtd in Fidelius 1998: 58). Tomášek admits that the State functions as a 'dependent operative organ of the working people': but far from this 'dependence' weakening the State's 'independence', it assures it and consolidates it. The Party, Tomášek argues, 'does not replace it [the State], neither does it reduplicate it, it leads it towards its creative independence' (58). How exactly it does this is not clear. Fidelius underlines the tortuous nature of Tomášek's rhetoric according to which 'the State assures the independent functioning of power and the efficient functioning of the State' (*sic*) (58). The independence of the State would seem to depend upon some mysterious form of self-regulation. As Tomášek's rhetoric would seem to prove, however, the inseparable nature of the relationship of the Party and the State is such that even the most ardent and sincere advocates of socialism were not always able to avoid mixing one up with the other.

### Historie and Doba

Since the Party holds the resources of objective understanding of life, society and history, it alone understands the role of 'the People' in creating that life, that society and the historical destiny of that life and society. This is because, according to the fundamental logic of communist rhetoric, the Party inspires, directs and controls the State's activity in assuring that the 'democratically independent' organs and groups of socialist society do not lose their way. For this reason, it would seem that the Party is infallible. This, however, would seem to be in contradiction with two facts.

Firstly, the State is constantly 'reforming itself' and 'reforming society'. But if the Party has regulated society correctly after having led it to socialism, then what need is there for reform? Reform implies that the socialism that the Party has inspired and directed is somehow defective. For similar reasons, Fidelius treats with irony Gorbatchev's policy of trying to discover 'the humane face of socialism' (197). As Fidelius points out, Gorbatchev is implying socialism, the people's state, thus far, has displayed an inhuman face (*nelidská tvář*), something which would of course have been unthinkable for party members.

Secondly, on top of this ongoing process of reform, the Party is from time to time forced to admit that the State, in the course of its activities, has made mistakes (*omyly*). Since the Party is infallible, it goes without saying that the Party is not to blame for these mistakes. In fact, their origin is not always clarified, but, nevertheless, these mistakes have arisen, and the Party desires to resolve them. This clearly does not contradict the Party's essential functioning as a 'reforming principle', it rather gives evidence of the Party's efficiency and goodwill, as Fidelius explains:

The often-asked question of whether 'socialism' can be reformed derives from a rather embarrassing misunderstanding: in truth, no system is so easy to reform as 'socialism', doubtless because its identity and continuity are guaranteed by the unchanged and unchangeable 'nucleus' which cannot be affected by any of those changes in 'form' however revolutionary they might be. (194)

Socialism not only can 'reform' itself, it must 'reform' itself. This constant reproduction of its will and this constant renewal of its form are part of its definition and function. None of its reforms affects its essential inner form, however. These mutations are mere 'changes in form'. Though at times the State may have strayed from the path of socialism, this cannot be considered a 'deformation' of the essential nature and purpose of the Party. To suspect as much would be to question the Party and to oppose history itself which legitimates the Party: any doubt concerning the Party line would be considered as 'enemy propaganda' (78).

All societies change with time and states try to change with the times. At first glance, the Communist Party would also seem to follow this general rule. This truism proves inconceivable, however, within the framework of the Party's logic. Being above time and being both the scientific explanation of the universal historical process and the final destiny to which all history tends, the Party's essential nature cannot be touched by time, nor can it be out of synch with time. The Party does not run after the times, trying to keep up. It does find itself, nevertheless, obliged to admit that changes must be made, and that past mistakes have made those changes necessary. This contradiction is explained in two ways. Firstly, what today might appear to be a mistake can be explained in terms of 'changes in historical conditions'. 'In its time' ('*Ve své době*') (78) it was 'the only appropriate approach' ('*jediným správným postupem*'). The Party could not have made the mistake since the Party never makes mistakes. What is more, it goes without saying that since the Party is infallible, only the Party can repair the mistake.

The second argument used to explain away mistakes is that these mistakes are merely passing issues which affect a certain 'time' (*doba*) or 'period' (*období*). 'History', however, would appear to transcend time and periods and (like the Party itself) remains untouched by them. Here we find ourselves at the heart of communist metaphysics: the forms and phenomena of reality would appear to have no bearing on the essence of the Party, the destiny of history and the unity of the two with 'the people.' The words 'concrete' (*konkrétní*) and 'concretely' (*konkrétně*) are pillars of communist discourse, but they should not be confused with 'real' or 'practical' or with 'in reality' or 'in practice': these words open the doors to 'transcendence'. Though no communist would accept such a word, it is clear that the true and transcendental nature of the Party, its essence, like the essence of 'the people', is inalterable. A concept of the Party has supplanted the acting Party, a concept of 'the people' has supplanted the sum total of citizens, and a concept of society has supplanted the social world in which those citizens live.

## *Boj*

The relations between the socialist and the world are defined in terms of *boj*, a word which in Czech signifies both 'conflict' and 'struggle'. 'Class conflict' and 'class struggle' are terms fundamental to the Marxist–Leninist worldviews that emerged in various language systems. These terms migrate between languages. Yet each language, and indeed each period, will shade the concept of conflict differently, and it is the exact shading of the Czech term which concerns us here. Like Fidelius himself, our aim is not to struggle against communist discourse, but to enter into its world in order to unveil its logic and its strategies in order to understand how people thought with and within the conceptual world of the communist mindset.

Marx himself would have argued that most wars are economic. The bourgeoisie and imperialists struggle among themselves, and their struggles often break out in war. Embargoes, and 'trade wars' are only milder expressions of 'economic wars' which aim to deprive a country of the means of defending itself against the economic power of a rival or rivals. We hardly need to consult the Czech *Concise Dictionary of Political Terms* to be told 'The working class and its revolutionary Party fundamentally fight [*zásadně bojují*] against imperialist war [*imperialistická válka*]' (Fingl et al. 1962: 104). The universalism inherent in Marxist dialectic with its international message is all too clear here. The workers of the world must unite to fight class oppression throughout the world. The struggle against external imperialist powers finds its internal reflection and parallel within society in class conflict in which the workers struggle against the power of the bourgeoisie in order to free themselves from exploitation. The 'struggle' against the bourgeoisie widens its scope as a concept to swallow up all international struggles which must (from the communist perspective) be reinterpreted as a struggle of the workers of the world against the forces of imperialism. The enthusiasm which warmed the hearts and fired the imagination of many of the heroes of the resistance during the Nazi occupation (not only in Czechoslovakia but in France and other countries) was the faith in communism which, it was believed, was bound to vanquish the forces of international capitalism.

However, the Nazi occupation of Czechoslovakia introduces a third form of struggle which itself is double in nature: this was a struggle against both the Germans (who were portrayed as the oppressors of the Czech nation which had wandered homeless for centuries) and against the National Socialists (who annexed the country and imposed their rule upon the Czech people). Distinguishing between the Germans and the fascists proved difficult enough for the Czechs. As enemies, the Nazis formed part of the allied fascist forces. However, the question of opposition was rendered considerably more difficult by the presence of three million German-speakers who had become the inhabitants of the Czechoslovak Republic since its creation in 1918. In retrospect, these people can be seen as the victims of the Versailles Treaty, the people who are forced to shift alliances and adapt with the redrawing of national boundaries. Throughout the1920s and 1930s, though, they represented an implicit threat to the sovereignty of the Czechoslovak nation, and they would become the lever which Hitler would use to justify annexing the Czech nation, in his expansionist military surge to the east. In such a historical context, the concept of *boj* ('conflict/struggle') and the verb which means 'to fight' or 'to struggle' (*bojovat*) developed to take on a quadruple justification: the Czech socialist was fighting for his or her class, against the bourgeoisie, against imperialist powers, against the fascists and against the German nation who had resisted the renaissance of the Czech nation.

The character of those engaged in this struggle should not be misrepresented by clichés of commissars manufactured by Western films during the Cold War, clichés which have been recycled in recent decades. These men and women were often ardent idealists and pragmatic revolutionaries. That did not prevent them, however, from entertaining the kitschy naïve ideal of the Czech homeland that was popular at the end of the nineteenth century and at the beginning of the twentieth century: that of an idyllically wholesome nation of noble peasants living close to the land and in harmony with one another. This image dovetailed with the destiny reserved by history for the Czech communists who would, once socialism had been constructed, live in peace, since the reason for war (imperialist rivalry) would have been removed. Paradoxically, with socialism, the fight would lead to peace. This fairy tale does, however, leave two questions unanswered:

1.  What role will the revolutionary play once we reach socialism?
2.  How are we to account for protest and power struggle within socialist societies?

The first question haunts all revolutionary movements which by nature inevitably render themselves redundant with their own success and deprive themselves of any further justification. Like any such movements, the Party which took power in the Czechoslovak Republic struggled to remain a 'movement'. This explains in part the Party's predilection for regular reforms. Unless it kept on moving, 'moving beyond', 'moving towards', it would lose all momentum: its elan would cease to exist. Stagnation would mean death. Stopping would mean suicide. The spatial metaphor of the movement, however appealing it first seems to its converts, reveals itself to be a trap. Once entered, it cannot be escaped. A movement which promotes itself as a 'way out' turns out to be a 'container', an endless dead-end. This contradiction and the forced enthusiasm of a second and a third generation of communists who had forgotten (or never known) the struggle against the occupants and the revolution of 1948 was probably one of the major factors which contributed to the decline of faith in communism. An inevitable malaise sets in as stagnation takes up residence in a rhetoric that cannot escape the confines of movement.

Another major factor for the declining appeal of communism was without doubt the Party's incapacity to tolerate dissent or even the concept of dissent. In the early years of Czechoslovak communism, all dissent was condemned as the 'counter-revolutionary activity' of 'class enemies'. After around thirty years of communism, though, by the 1970s, in the decade after the invasion of Prague by Soviet troops in 1968, it had become clear to the Party and to the journalists of *Rudé Právo* that cynicism and dissent were beginning to take hold of the country. In order to avoid a head-on collision with this brooding force, the journalists of *Rudé Právo* took it upon themselves to educate their readers and help them return to the fold. The majority of cynics and dissenters were described by the paper as citizens who had 'lost their way'. The journalists affirmed, however, that: 'The majority of those people will sooner or later find their way back to the path towards society, towards their country, towards their socialist homeland' (*'cesta ke společnosti, ke své zemi, ke své socialistické vlasti'*) (qtd in Fidelius 1998: 94). Curiously, though communist discourse maintained the path-to-destiny metaphor here, it exploited it in a different way by making the destination the existing society. This was not only unattractive to dissenters, it also revealed the truly stagnant moribund nature of the so-called 'path-towards-communism'.

Those who remained resolute in their resistance to the Party were reserved another destiny. Of course, though they were struggling against the Party, they were not engaged in a *boj* (struggle). The Party had a monopoly upon 'struggle': struggle against the Party was inconceivable. That is to say, the spatial metaphor of an internal conflict could not enter into the mindset of the communist powers. Conflict structured the character of the Party, the revolutionary and his or her relationship to history and society. However, this essential struggle did not allow for actual struggle against the Party. Though dissenters did physically exist within society, they could not be tolerated by the communist mind, and they were conceptually expelled outside of the frontiers of the homeland. 'Those dissenters and traitors [. . .] no longer have their homeland – because in our land [*u nás*] there will never be anything other than our socialist homeland' (Fidelius 1998: 94). Dissenters and traitors became 'citizens without a homeland' ('*občané bez vlasti*') (95). Such people, a journalist of *Rudé Právo* claimed, 'do not live the life of this country' (95).

This refusal to represent conflict affects language at a grammatical level: socialist discourse is unwilling to attribute an active role to people who enter into conflict with the Party. Activity belongs to the Party, which acts supremely when it struggles. Dissenters are confined to the realm of negation. They do not belong. They do not stand with the people. They do not live with and within their homeland. But they do not 'struggle' against it either: they simply take up a position. Position relegates them to a passive role, a post: they engage in passive resistance to the obligation to fight as part of the people. Dissent is thus conceived of in terms of reactionary resistance. Dissenters refuse to move with the Movement. Their refusal becomes stagnation. Dissent displays the desire to paralyse the Party and the people's progress towards its historical destiny.

Consequently, dissenters are excluded from 'the people' (in the Party's definition of the term). Of course, the Party is not responsible for this exclusion: neither is the Party portrayed as struggling against dissenters at this stage in Czechoslovak history. Dissenters do not belong within the country and they themselves are responsible for cutting themselves off from society: 'they stand elsewhere than where we are, because they have divided themselves from our society' (94). This marks the culmination of an argument with four steps:

1. Dissenters are condemned, and they are indeed condemnable because they dissent.
2. They are expelled metaphorically from society and from the homeland.
3. The Party attributes the responsibility for this expulsion to the dissenters themselves.
4. Finally, the dissenters are linguistically excluded from their

homeland. They have become a 'they' who no longer belong to 'our' homeland.

This last step reveals to what extent pronouns define our relations in spatial metaphors of inclusion, exclusion, proximity and distance.

## AN ABC OF CZECHOSLOVAK COMMUNIST TERMINOLOGY

In the film version of Kundera's *The Unbearable Lightness of Being*, directed by Philip Kaufman and starring Daniel Day Lewis, Lena Olin and Juliette Binoche, a long chapter failed to make its way into the scenario. Admittedly, it would have been difficult to put it to a film which, thanks to the love intrigue, involving the faithful wife, the libertine doctor and his artist-mistress, set against the romantic decor of Prague's Old Town, could legitimately hope to make a commercial success. The chapter concerned incomprehension and the impossibility of communicating between worlds. Sabrina, the Czech artist-lover of Tomas, begins a new affair with Franz, a Swiss academic based in Zurich.

The short glossary of incomprehensible terms which Kundera (2000b) provides is important to the story in that it shows the difficulties the new lovers experience when trying to explain why everyday terms such as beauty, light, fidelity and betrayal, and political terms such as solidarity and protest marches, become incomprehensible when used by someone who has been exposed to an entirely different worldview. Even a visit to a church for Sabrina and Franz becomes a minefield of incoherence. On another occasion, when she is invited to take part in a demonstration protesting against the invasion of Prague, Sabrina finds it impossible to express her repulsion and malaise, facing mass manifestations of unitary will, which remind her of a regime which crushes individual will in order to enslave it to collective, party-directed aims. The words which excited, animated and inspired a generation of Western protest in the sixties and seventies terrify and disgust Sabrina.

Sabrina's lover, Franz, a handsome, intelligent and sensitive individual, comes off the worst when Kundera contrasts the two lovers' worldviews. Franz is ridiculed by a cruel authorial irony as he commits himself to a romantic image of his Czech exiled-artist-mistress: even when she abandons him, he remains faithful to the caricature which he has imposed upon her. In a sense, Franz is ideologically and emotionally 'castrated' by Kundera: he can make love to his artist-mistress but he cannot 'penetrate' her worldview. He remains outside of Sabrina's intellectual and emotional space, enclosed within his own condescending and complacent Cold War clichés.

In the same spirit, Table 7.1 is a list of words and definitions which should allow us to take a glimpse into the gulf that separates worldviews. It is worth simply juxtaposing concepts as they were understood and defined by Czech encyclopaedias with an almost word-for-word translation. The terms defined have been selected from three works:

- *Stručný politický slovník* (*Concise Dictionary of Political Terms*), ed. J. Fingl et al., Prague: Nakladatelsví Politické Literatury, 1962 [SPS]
- *Filozofický slovník (O–Z)* (*A Philosophical Dictionary*), Prague: Svoboda, 1985 [FS]
- *Malá Československá Encyklopeie (I–L)* (*The Shorter Czechoslovak Dictionary*), vol. III, ed. Miroslav Štěpánek, Prague: Akademia, 1986 [MČE].

The words chosen are not restricted to the key concepts of the socialist worldview which structured Czech consciousness in the post-war period: they include a variety of everyday concepts. Nonetheless, as it will transpire, those concepts are swallowed up, consumed and digested by socialism. An impressive internal logic will yoke and harness various everyday concepts and ideas, demonstrating the overwhelming logic which washes over society and transforms all over which it passes like the rising tide. English-speakers will experience difficulty and ill-ease in trying to 'get their minds around' concepts which have been transformed in order to bring them into line with Party doctrine and the metaphysics of the communist worldview. But in struggling to get to grips with them, we should gain insight into the concepts of society, history and social relations which the dominant discourse of that period was generating and propagating. This is the challenge that faces us when we seek to enter into foreign worldviews, the cultural mind-sets that take root in other languages and which simultaneously grow within and transform the consciousness of peoples and eras other than our own.

Table 7.1 Words from another world

| Czech word and definition | English translation |
| --- | --- |
| **Buržoazní ideologie** soustava názorů a teorií, kterých používá buržoazie k obhájení svého postavení a svých cílů, k udržení vlastní moci. Buržoazní ideologie je 'falešným vědomím', nepravdivá a nevědecká. (SPS: 40) | **Bourgeois ideology** system of opinions and theories used by the bourgeoisie to defend its status, its aims and to uphold its power. Bourgeois ideology is 'false consciousness', untrue and unscientific. |
| **Bytí** filosofický termín označující *objektivní realitu* nezávislou na lidském vědomí. Pojmem bytí je rovnocenný s pojem hmota. Dialektický materialismus učí, že bytí (hmota) je prvotní, vědomí (myšlení) druhotné – je odrazem hmotného světa. (. . . SPS: 41) | **Existence** philosophical term designating objective reality independent of human consciousness. The concept of existence is synonymous with matter/substance. Dialectical materialism teaches [us] that existence (matter) is primary, and consciousness (thinking) is secondary – a reflection of the material world. |
| **Imperialistická válka** válka vedená imperialisty za *účel*em dobytí cizích území, zotročení nebo olupování národů. Je to nejkrajnější prostředek k prosazení zájmů imperialistické buržoazie. I. v. byla 1. svět. válka a také 2. svět. válka začala jako imperialistická. (SPS: 104) | **Imperialist war** war carried out by imperialists with the objective of conquering foreign territory, the enslavement or the looting of nations. It is the most extreme manner of asserting interests for bourgeois imperialists. WWI was an imperialist war, and WW2 also began as an imperialist war. |

**Kafka** *František*, 3.7.1883–3.6.1924, pražský žid. prozaik píšící něm. V jeho díle se spojuje human. cítění a myšlení s krizovými pocity nejistoty a s těžkým rozčarováním z kap. reality. (MČE: 256)

**Kafka** *František*, 3.7.1883–3.6.1924, Prague-born Jewish prose writer, writing in German. His work links humanistic feeling and thinking with the feeling of crisis and uncertainty and with the deep disenchantment with capitalist reality.

**Komunistická kultura** kult. odpovídající kom. fázi spol. vývoje; jejím zákl. je nebývale vysoký stupeň vývoje výr. sil a jim odpovídajících výr. a spol. vztahů. (MČE: 470)

**Communist culture** the culture corresponding to the communist phase in societal development, whose basis is the unprecedented level of development in productive power and the corresponding productive and social relations.

**Kultura** souhrn materiálních i duchovních hodnot vytvářených ve společenské výrobě, hospodářství, politice, vědě, umění, výchově, aj. (a v jim odpovídajících institucích) v jejich dějinném vývoji. (SPS: 136)

**Culture** the totality of material and spiritual values produced in collective production, economic activity, politics, science, art and education (and in the institutions which belong to them) in their historical development.

**Osoba** v průběhu staletí prošel pojem 'osoba' mnohými změnami. [. . .] Z historického hlediska vyjadřuje pojem osoba z politické, právní a etické stránky stále odtržení jedince od společnosti a absolutizování lidského rozumu. (FS: 31)

**Person/Individual** in the course of centuries, the concept of the 'person/individual' has undergone many changes. [. . .] From a historical point of view, the concept of the 'person/individual' expresses in terms of politics, law and ethics, the separation of the individual from society and the absolutisation of human reason.

**Pojem jedinečný** pojem, který odráží jedno individuum a vztahuje se pouze k němu. (FS: 70)

**Concept of the individual** a concept which designates the single individual and which relates to that individual alone.

**Pojem kolektivní** pojem, který odráží uspořádaný celek stejnorodých předmětů. [. . .] Jednoznačným

**Concept of the collective** a concept which designates an ordered whole consisting of homogeneous subjects.

kolektivním pojmem je 'lidstvo'. [. . .]
Vztah mezi kolektivním pojmem a
individui, která pod něj spadají, je
intenzionální a náleží proto do oboru
dialektické logiky. (FS: 68)

[. . .] 'Humanity' is a clear example of
a collective concept. [. . .] The
relationship between the individual
and the collective into which he falls
is an intentional opposition which
pertains by necessity to the domain of
dialectical logic.

**Politika** spoločenská činnost
zaměřená k obhajobě třídních zájmů,
k vybojování, uchování a upevnění
vlády a státní moci určité třídy nebo
k vytvoření příznivých podmínek pro
boj a moc ve státě. (. . . SPS: 195)

**Politics** social activity to defend class
interests, to secure, to defend and
consolidate the control of state power
by one class, or the creation of
favourable conditions for struggle and
power within the State.

**Politologie** (řec., lat.) buržoazní
společensko-vědní disciplína, která je
těsně spjata s politickou ideologií
monopolistické buržoazie a je
rozhodujícím teoretickým základem
procesu politického rozhodování, čímž
přímo ovlivňuje buržoazní strategii a
taktiku. (FS: 81)

**Politology** (Gk and Lat. derivation) a
bourgeois social science which is
closely linked to the political ideology
of the monopolistic bourgeoisie and
which constitutes a decisive
theoretical foundation for the process
of political decision-making, by which
it directly influences bourgeois
strategies and tactics.

**Pokrok** historický vyšší vývoj lidské
společnosti, příp. jednotlivých oblastí
spoločenského života. Myšlenka
historického pokroku je relativně
pozdní produkt historického vývoje.
Dějiny myšlenky pokroku začínají
teprve s raně buržoazním osvícenstvím
[. . .] Marxisticko-leninské pojetí
spoločenského pokroku [. . .] se
osvědčilo jako jediné pojetí problému,
které obsahuje nejen vědecké
objasnění pokroku, ale i vědecky
zdůvodněnou koncepci praktického
utváření pokroku v zájmu dělnické
třídy a lidu. (FS: 92–3)

**Progress** historically higher
development of human society in the
various fields of social life. The idea of
historical progress is a relatively late
product of historical development.
The history of the idea of progress
begins only with the dawn of the
bourgeois Enlightenment. The
Marxist–Leninist conception of social
progress proved itself to be the sole
conception adequate for handling this
problem, since it includes not only a
scientific explication of progress but
also provides a reasoned account of
the conception of the practical
shaping of progress in the interests of
the workers' class and the people.

**Teorie umění** teorie o specifických formách estetické aktivity člověka, ve kterých si obraznou formou všestranně přivlastňuje sám sebe jako rodovou podstatu, svůj život, totalitu svých vztahů k realitě. Jde o podstatnou součást estetiky. Marxův výrok, že člověk přisuzuje předmětu vždy inherentní míru a tím ho formuluje podle zákonů krásy, platí i pro člověka samotného. (FS: 318)

**Art theory** the theory concerning the specific forms of man's aesthetic activity, in which a symbolic form broadly reflects the way he has appropriated for himself for the basis of his life, the totality of his relations with reality. This is a fundamental part of aesthetics. Marx's affirmation that man adjudges an object to an inherent degree, and that he forms an idea of it according to the laws of beauty, also holds true for individual men.

**Vědomí** specifický lidský myšlenkový odraz objektivní reality pomocí centrálního nervového systému. Vědomí zahrnuje celek smyslových a racionálních forem odrazu i oblast lidských emocí a vůle, tj. celou psychickou činnost člověka. [. . .] Dialektickomaterialistické pojetí vědomí spočívá na zobecnění odpovídajících přírodovědných poznatků, praktických zkušeností lidí a kritického zpracování dějin filosofického myšlení. Vědomí je nejvyšším vývojovým produktem hmoty. 'Hmota je prvotní. Počitek, myšlení, vědomí je vyšší produkt hmoty organizované zvláštním způsobem. Takové jsou názory materialismu vůbec a Marxe a Engelse zvláště.' (V. I. Lenin, 14. s. 54) (FS: 359)

**Conscience** a specific human conceptual reflection of reality by means of the central nervous system. Conscience embraces the entire range of sensual and rational forms of reflection as well as the domain of human emotions and the will, that is, the whole psychic activity of man. [. . .] The Dialectical materialistic concept of conscience is rooted in the generalisation of knowledge related to natural history, practical human experience and the critical appraisal of the history of philosophical thought. Conscience is the highest, most developed product of matter. 'Matter is primary. Sensation, thought, conscience is a higher product of matter organised in a specific way. That is the belief of materialism and especially of Marx and Engels.' (V. I. Lenin, 14, p. 54)

That political terms will take on a biased, political shading in the Socialist worldview hardly comes as any surprise. But that politics itself and the study of it, political science, are critically reappraised, takes somewhat more patience to understand. The Czechoslovak socialist sees clearly his goal of 'objective truth' (*objektivní pravda*). But everywhere, the forces of obscurantism abound, deceiving and seducing us, confusing and distracting us. Escapist literature and films, from such a perspective, are seen as the 'bread and circus strategies' by which Roman emperors sought to keep the people occupied and to keep them from revolting against their social status and objecting to their poor treatment. *Obskurantismus*, within the communist worldview, was a resilient and deeply enrooted movement which countered enlightened progress and the road to socialism.

Liberalism formed part of this obscurantism. The stress on the individual's role as the motor of progress is believed by communists to be characteristic of bourgeois society, in that it hides the fact that, in truth, most living individuals have little scope to influence society and history because of their limited material means and their dependency upon the job market. Maintaining the belief that each one of us can change the world (or at least play a part in changing it), and explaining history in terms of the acts of individuals imposing their will upon society, are no more than 'fairy tales' told to us in order to keep us calmly producing wealth for the ruling classes, the communist believes. Utilitarianism, for the Czechoslovak socialist, is a form of reactionary bourgeois ethics which persists in encouraging us to believe that industrial capitalism is capable of producing a universal harmony despite the inherent class conflict which the media persistently attempt to downplay, deny or obscure.

War is imperialist war for Czechoslovak socialists. Indeed, it must be admitted that such a perspective seems largely justified in certain cases. The Czechs themselves experienced the appropriation of their land by the Nazis of the *Wehrmacht*, who considered the Slavic peoples as little better than degenerate beings, only fit for slaves, and who considered their territory as *Lebensraum* for the inheritors of the Aryan race. More recently, the two wars in Iraq can be accounted for as the struggle between the USA and post-colonial nations (Britain and France) to gain control over the natural resources of the Middle East. And indeed reading the *Rudé Právo* newspapers of the fifties, sixties and seventies reveals revolting images and reports on the atrocities of wars perpetrated by the

USA in Korea and Vietnam, images and reports which (though now largely corroborated) were not revealed by Western media at the time. Internet now enables people to access the different TV representations of war that are being fed to US citizens in one highly stylised form, to French citizens in a slightly less adulterated form, and to citizens of Arab nations in shockingly brutal form. Juxtaposing such forms of representation confuses and perplexes us. This should not serve as an apology for the Czechoslovak socialist conception of 'imperialist war', but it should force us to stop and think: it should serve to delineate more clearly the contours of the world we are being presented by our media, and the limits of the concepts with which we are being asked to understand the world of modern geopolitics.

Few English-speakers will find the Czechoslovak socialist world easy to relate to or to understand. Indeed, many Czechs today will find the terms of my short ABC obscure and absurd. But this shows only that Czech society has moved on. As Fidelius affirms, the Czechoslovak socialist world was not a nonsensical world but one which was logically expounded. Communism was defined as the goal of society and history. The State and the future were both defined and deployed in terms of the charting of that course towards the logical outcome of historical evolution. What will upset most 'free-thinking' English-speakers about such a philosophy, is that everything that contradicts the 'objective truth' of socialist reality is conceived of in terms of an aberration of nature and a refusal of the rational unfolding of progress.

Art and the human conscience must find their place in the constellation of this communist cosmos. Art theory inevitably becomes the cultivation of an imagination attuned to Party doctrine. The 'inner world', and the division of the 'private' and the 'public', are disparaged as a perversion of capitalist individualism which, because it leaves little scope for individuals to realise themselves authentically in society, encourages them to turn from the world and seek solace in their own private fantasy worlds. Hollywood is the archetype of 'inauthentic escapism', from this perspective. Kafka is only one case among many of the tortured individuals fleeing 'inauthentic existence' in late capitalism.

One thing is striking in the various presentations which Kafka has undergone. The Western version makes reference to 'modern society' but cuts that society off from the economic mode of production, as though work, money and status were irrelevant to life. This gives a universal nature to 'modern' society. Post-modern accounts of Kafka playfully portray him as a prophet of absurdity. Kafka's insight into the absurdity of bureaucracy was scrutinised by the socialists, but it is now being blithely marketed by the tourist industry of Prague. Czechoslovak socialists would have seen this as one more chapter in obscurantism. For their part, Kafka remains a historical individual, and above all a Czech, which explains their insistence on the Czech form of his Christian name (*František*), which was certainly used by his Czech acquaintances.

What is interesting for our study of worldviews is the way that Kafka is appropriated by each generation and portrayed according to the interests of the ruling ideology. There is one Kafka for post-modern American undergraduates seeking *Mittel-Europa* absurdity. There is another for Parisian intellectuals. And there is a very serious one for defenders of art, not for art's sake but for society's sake. For Marxists who intend to transform the conscience of the people, Kafka's characters are the incarnation of a very real alienation which is far from laughable and which will find no remedy in capitalist society.

The social origins and the social goals of art were essential and meaningful for the communists. Dvořák and Janáček, for the Czechoslovak socialists, are the defenders of a people's music. This is not a perverted misinterpretation. This refers to a very real strand in the inspiration which animated their work. But how are we to understand it? We English-speakers have so thoroughly divorced the culture of the people from any real animated tradition that we must consider it in terms of 'folk culture' and 'folk music': it is nostalgic, quaint, twee and kitsch. These are hardly adjectives which come to mind when we hear Dvořák and Janáček. A very vibrant, real and immediate pulse moves in their work, and it continues to move many Czechs today as it moved Czechs of the socialist period. For the Czechs of the fifties and sixties, the folk and the people were one, and both were meaningful concepts. For us, the former belongs to nostalgia and the second rings with the hollow hope of the hippies. For this reason, we should be cautious about dismissing other worldviews. Have we not lost the words to express something that remains audible and expressible in another language within another time?

## CONCLUSIONS

The fact that the symbolic structure of communist discourse takes root at the fundamental grammatical basis of Czech by harnessing pronouns to create inclusive and exclusive space shows to what extent the communist mindset took hold of the Czech language. 'With us' (*u nás*) means also 'by us', 'alongside of us', 'on our side'. It also means 'in our country'. The struggle for power and the struggle to maintain power required the expulsion of class enemies. Dissenters were said to resist the Movement, or to lead others astray from the path to socialism. In semantic terms, they were stigmatised, and in grammatical terms, they were deprived of agency and increasingly dispossessed of their part of the communal 'we'. The worst traitors began counter-revolutionary activities, which implied dragging people back against the tug of history and marching in the opposite direction from progress. At best, such dissenters were 'deactivated', they simply stood elsewhere. They had cut themselves off.

In communist rhetoric, many things remain confusing or confused, but two things are clear. Firstly, we can only understand each of the concepts history, the Party, the State and the people in terms of one another. The definition of each of these terms is linked. Secondly, it transpires that these concepts and the relations between them are defined metaphorically. Exactly how metaphorical their definition is, is not always easy to say. To what extent does 'war' become 'class war'? To what extent can we call a political 'movement' a metaphor? All representations of political movements and of the movement of history itself are spatial and dynamic, and dynamism and space are used as symbolic representations not only in Czech socialism but in many European languages and in many ideologies. As Ernst Cassirer (following Humboldt) was already arguing in the 1920s, these conceptual constructs are dependent upon *symbolic forms*. Far from being perversions of reality, it is by virtue of the symbolic forms that we are enabled to embrace reality within the scope of consciousness. Nevertheless, a distinction must be made between a movement as a universal concept and the manner by which that universal concept regenerates itself within a given culture and society within a socio-historical context. There is nothing particularly innocent about the French President's handling of the concept of 'movement' in his own UMP movement (*Union pour un Mouvement Populaire*). Nicolas Sarkozy's 'movement' inevitably promises transformation and radical revitalisation of the State's bodies. It becomes clear, however, that we are dealing with a radically different concept of movement and entering a whole new worldview when we enter into the communist world. In saying this, we can wholeheartedly agree with the opening quotation from Jan Kliment, the *Rudé Právo* journalist: truly he and his colleagues did belong to 'another world'.

This forces us, nonetheless, to face once more the inadequacy of the term 'worldview'. After all, is it the communist world which is foreign to us? Or is it the Czech language itself? Certainly, Czech has embraced other worldviews, and throughout the communist period other ideologies were present within the Czechoslovak Republic, whether they were confined to minority groups or the convictions of individual citizens. Here it becomes necessary to distinguish between those concepts and frameworks of thought found in the Czech language as a mode of perceiving and conceiving the world, and the linguistic construction of the mindset of communism.

That mindset introduced and defined its own concepts and symbolically elaborated the relations between bodies of people and institutions, between the origins of its principles and the objectives and destiny of its ideology. But it did this using the concepts and relations between those concepts as they existed within the Czech language. Czech communists perceived and conceived the universal historical process of international socialism from within the neo-romantic nostalgia of a Czech nation which had struggled to gain independence in 1918, which had lost that independence once more to the occupying forces of fascism, and which had won it back once more after the liberation of the country by Soviet and allied forces. Nostalgia and euphoria helped to herald communism into power and allowed it to enter the language of the homeland. The ideal of folksy traditional values gave a vibrant elan to the word 'people'.

Going against the homeland and against the people in such a fragile world might well have seemed like suicide for the nation. The need for unity and cohesion must have exerted a strong pressure upon the imagination of a people whose destiny seemed precarious. The charm of a rational objective historical process which promised to guarantee a glorious destiny for the people is understandable in such a period. Thus far, we are contrasting the *Weltanschauung* of the period with the *Weltansicht* of Czech; the ideology with the worldview which a language's concepts open up for the mind. But the *Weltansicht* of Czech, at a very fundamental level, often corresponds closely to the worldview found in German, French and English, and it is for this very reason that it is so simple to translate many of the expressions used by Czechoslovak communists to explain their vision of the world. Our own modern view of movements and of history, and even to a large extent our concept of law-breakers whom we 'exclude' from society or 'remove' from it, are all structured along the lines of the same shared conceptual metaphors. In this sense, much that is fundamental to Czech is fundamental to our own world-perceiving and world-conceiving. This should have helped us understand how Czech communists arrived at conclusions that, at first sight, appeared to us to be completely illogical. To this extent, we have managed to enter the worldview of communism.

Part of world-perceiving and world-conceiving in Czechoslovak communist discourse, even when it appears to us unfounded, is 'founded' upon symbolism and conceptual frameworks we can ourselves understand. Part of the mindset of communism is enrooted in concepts we can recognise ('homeland', 'people', 'traitor', for example). These concepts take on a different colour and meaning for the Czech imagination, however, and part of Czechoslovak communism remains fundamentally foreign to us. Its concepts and the relations between those concepts baffle us. Understanding them requires a considerable effort of imagination.

Nevertheless, though many of the arguments of Czechoslovak

communists may well appear absurd to us, they do remain 'arguments' and as such they are structured along logical lines. They may be based upon premises which are unfounded. They may harness concepts together in an unconvincing manner. Those concepts themselves may be ill-defined. One concept might merge into another as the Party and the State merge into one another, while other concepts might break up and divide (as 'the people' divides itself up to exclude many of the people living within the frontiers of the Czechoslovak Republic). Nevertheless, communist writers and thinkers regarded themselves as enlightened people, and they strove to understand and explain society and its destiny in rational and logical terms. Though communist discourse has been dismissed as simple nonsense by many of our contemporaries, as it was dismissed by many of the contemporaries of Fidelius himself in the 1970s, the communist worldview made a kind of sense. It logically elaborated its concepts and its arguments and 'gave sense to its world'. For that reason, Fidelius argued that communist discourse was 'a real language which spoke of a kind of world albeit an imaginary world' (Fidelius 1998: 11). It was 'an ideological world picture' ('*ideologický obraz světa*') (11). If we have understood something fundamental about that foreign worldview, the curious mindset of the Czechoslovak communist, and if, in turn, that has helped us understand more fully the way ideology influences language and the way language shades and structures ideology, then we must thank Petr Fidelius for this tour of the thought-world he found himself forced to live within.

# CHAPTER 8

# *Hitlerdeutsch*: Klemperer and the Language of the Third Reich

## MINDSET AND PERSONAL WORLD

In the last chapter we considered the way metaphor helped to shape and structure the worldview of Czech communists in the 1970s. We were, however, forced to accept that we were often dealing with three different kinds of worldview. The Czech language itself, as a network of concepts, conceptual links and linguistic habits, had been remodelled by the forces of the Marxist–Leninist worldview. This was by no means a one-way process: on the contrary, the concepts of 'people', 'folk' and 'nation' which were fundamental to the communist worldview were modelled using the plastic material of the Czech imagination, an imagination shaped by the revival of the Czech people, the fight for independence from the Austro-Hungarian Empire and the liberation of the Czech lands by the Soviets in 1945. Within the framework of this dynamic struggle between tradition, on the one hand, with its concepts for history, society and for progress, and the communist *Weltanschauung*, on the other, with its worldview-transforming concepts and political agenda, Czechs perceived and conceived the world around them. This world-perceiving and world-conceiving (which no Czech speakers could escape whether they resisted it or not) contributed to the construction of a shared organised worldview which over-arched the division into political camps. Dissent, opposition and political hostility, however antagonistic, however radical, all suppose a shared basis of fundamental concepts, principles, arguments and ideals, which form the basis and the framework for dialogue, dispute and the positioning of alternative philosophies.

The Czech language allowed different cultural mindsets. Democrats and dissidents resisted and criticised Gottwald and his Communist Party. Liberals emerged in the 1960s to contest the established order, but such debates and confrontations took place within the context of a worldview which remained framed in the concepts of 'people', 'folk' and 'nation' which were shared by the different sides in those debates and confrontations. The worldview of each person was coloured by the concepts offered up by the language, the same concepts which were harnessed by the Party and remodelled by those who resisted the Party. In this way, though it is necessary to distinguish between the mindsets at work in a culture at a given time and the personal world (the worldview of the individual), the personal world cannot be clearly divided from the cultural mindsets of philosophies, ideologies and movements which vie to assert themselves in society. Nor can those mindsets or personal worlds extract themselves from the language system in which they are rooted and which they continue to invigorate and perpetuate by the reactivation and transformation of concepts, conceptual links and linguistic habits.

Distinguishing between world-perceiving, world-conceiving, cultural mindsets and personal worlds is difficult because they take place not only in society but within the mind: they are negotiated and redefined in conversations. Nevertheless, we must bear in mind that these interlinking and interacting forces are fundamentally different in nature and should not be confused. The language system does not condition and determine the means of individual expression. The individual is not the slave of the Party's concepts. Resistance and creative and original thought are possible at all times. Fidelius's own attempt to escape both the mechanics of Party doctrine and the non-conceptual or anti-conceptual irony of the dissenters who disparaged it bears witness to such creativity, but so does a whole tradition of dissident literature and cinema. Nonetheless, though Czech individuals of the 1970s could both criticise the Party and stand back from the language system, they could not extract themselves from the sphere of influence of the Party or stand outside the linguistic system of their own mother tongue to assert a phenomenologically, philosophically transcendental position of their own. Individuals remain a part of the society which socialises them, and a part of the language and culture which introduce them to conceptual thought. People cannot, however, be considered the 'products' of their culture any more than they can be considered as culture's 'artisans': individuals contribute to their culture just as their culture allows them to take their place in society and in language, to define themselves, and to take position in relation to others.

The relationship between ideology and language would seem to be subtle and complex, then. This, at least, would seem to be the lesson which Fidelius has to teach us. Entering into a foreign worldview (now very much a worldview of the past) helped us to understand that universal cross-cultural models of ideological manipulation are reductive and simplistic. When we find ourselves confronted with a given concrete historico-cultural situation, we cannot hope to grasp it without a wider angle of approach, an approach with a scope which is capable of taking on board the particularities of languages, cultures and individuals. Czech communism remains Czech because of its people's culture, its history and, above all, its language, which acts as the vector of its cultural and historical identity.

So what will we find if we enter another language, another era? Will we find that metaphors contribute to the shaping of worldviews at a conceptual-linguistic level, at the level of ideologies and at the personal level? In the transformation of the German language by the rhetoric and the worldview of Hitler's Nazi party, we will find many parallels to the ways metaphor shaped worldview in Czech. We will find conceptual clusters in which radical new definitions begin to shape one another. We will observe the infiltration of the personal world by political concepts. We will see the way the grammar of the language itself begins to shape itself to conform to the contours of the mindset of the Party by inventing nouns and verbs, and privileging the use of certain prefixes and suffixes.

Nonetheless, we should be wary of hasty comparisons between Nazi and communist rhetoric. Fidelius insisted that the communist rhetoric of the 1970s (though largely discredited at the time he was writing) *did* actually 'make sense'. That is to say, those who wrote and spoke the language of communism saw themselves as enlightened individuals who were politically and historically aware of what had happened to their land and who sought to convince others by reasoned argument that they knew how to guide their nation down the road to progress. Communism was a movement shaped by Marx, a major philosopher. Communism was put into practice by political thinkers and adroit political activists. Its propaganda resembles that of the Church in the Middle Ages. Though its representatives and bodies sought to move and persuade the people, they did so in order to draw the people closer to their version of truth. Priests and popes certainly did not see themselves as trying 'to dupe the masses'. The Church sought to inform, to enlighten and to uplift people. Similarly, Czech communism sought to promote its own ideology with its solutions and its benefits: and it must not be forgotten that the socialist movement successfully convinced a sizeable part of the Czech community (notably the intellectual and ruling class) for more than one generation, using discussion, debate and education.

The roots of the Nazi regime are very different in kind. The Nazis were hostile to the Enlightenment and inspired by neoromantic notions of the greatness of the Germanic nation and the 'purity' of its people. They were the children of sentiment; and the sentiment which most invigorated them, the will to power, was frustrated by the defeat of 1918. Frustrated by that defeat, humiliated by the Versailles Treaty, fearful of communism, and crushed by the traumatic post-war poverty of the 1920s which was exacerbated when it was followed by the crisis of capitalism in 1929, a strong proud people were faced with a national situation which was almost intolerable and a world situation which made people throughout the Western nations wonder whether society could go on functioning in the way it had up till then. What would such an explosive cocktail herald for the German people? How would those forces find expression in the Nazi movement? And how would that movement express itself linguistically? How would the metaphors born of that movement contribute to the reshaping of the German that was spoken at work, in the streets and at home?

## *HITLERDEUTSCH*

The language of the Third Reich offers a fascinating example of the way in which metaphor can be harnessed in perverting the way we understand the world. This chapter deals with the 'construction' of that perverted worldview. This poses a curious philosophical problem, however: because the term 'worldview' itself implies a certain relativism which makes value judgements precarious. Indeed, it is because of the implicit relativism in the term that existentialists such as the modern German thinker, Karl Jaspers, find it serves their purposes. For the same reason, contemporary Christian scholars such as the American, David K. Naugle, see 'worldview' as a challenge, a challenge that Christian thought must address if it is to assert its idea of one single Truth, the truth that belongs to God and that is upheld by the Church.

If various worldviews coexist, and if the very definition of 'worldview' itself is subject to controversy, can we speak about a 'perverted worldview'? Surely, if we accept that each culture has its worldview, then no one worldview can be considered more authentic or more perverted than the next. This conclusion appears, at first sight, unavoidable. If we look at the way certain mindsets are organised, though, we uncover the internal contradictions and inconsistencies which make them untenable as philosophies, as versions of truth. Foreign cultures invariably appear to us strange and incomprehensible at first, but as we familiarise ourselves with them, the secret organisation of interwoven ideas, ideals, narratives and practices transpires more and more. With patience we cannot hope to understand or grasp the 'truth' of what remains foreign to us, but patience rewards us with precious insights. We begin to intuit that though things may often remain obscure to us, they do indeed appear to make sense to the members of that foreign culture. Words, concepts and arguments, past stories and ideals combine to weave a meaningful version of the cosmos and that people's place within it. This helps maintain the framework within which a people can understand events, actions and projects.

Can we enter into the Nazi worldview, though? Can we understand it with an effort of will, as Fidelius sought to understand the logic of the Communist world? This not only brings into question the object of study but also the view of the observer: it obliges us to question the basis and the legitimacy of our own perspective. We ourselves can only observe this spectacle of perversity from without. Time, space and language all separate us from the Nazis as living, breathing people. This is frustrating, though, because from without we know that all alternative worldviews appear absurd and perverse. From within, on the other hand, our own vision of the world, our way of thinking, our way of speaking, our ways of acting in relation to one another, all appear normal and natural. This is true to such an extent that it hardly occurs to us to question our fundamental ideas, opinions, prejudices or everyday actions. Our actions follow custom as much as they follow the dictates of personal choice informed by reason. In thought, speech and action, all of us follow (more than we lead) the culture we live within.

For this reason, the insight of the insider is precious: the records of someone who lived through (or survived, rather) the Nazi regime are invaluable to us. The German-Jewish philologist, Victor Klemperer, worked day after day to collect his impressions of the transformation of the spoken and written German language from 1933 to 1945. Like Orwell, Klemperer was wary of the metaphorical expressions which individual people adopted without thinking, and which both reflected and contributed to the transformation of their perspective of politics and history, and which affected the way those individuals behaved with one another.

Without wishing to denigrate Orwell in any way, his engagement is overshadowed by that of Klemperer, though. Orwell represented the Western twentieth-century intellectual who observed political strife from afar. Ironically, though he has become the icon of all those who condemn propaganda, Orwell was in fact involved in diffusing propaganda during the war. And when he was critical of propaganda – as in his essay, 'Propaganda and demotic speech', first published under the title 'Persuasion' in the summer of 1944 (1968: 135) – he condemned it not for political or moral reasons, but for pragmatic reasons: the propaganda of his time was not effective enough for Orwell. He dismissed 'the bloodless dialect of government spokesmen', who presented their ideas in a 'stilted bookish language' typical of the radio and the BBC. Such a form of expression, characteristic of the upper classes of the Home Counties, would never, Orwell felt, tap into the current of working-class sentiment in other parts of the UK (135–56). No doubt Orwell was right, but that hardly makes him a free-thinking radical, an antagonist of the powers that be. During the war, Orwell worked for the government. As the Cold War began to set in, Orwell once more found himself providing the Information Research Department with the names of his acquaintances who, because of their left-wing sympathies, were to be kept out of positions of influence in the government and in the media which were being set up by the new order that was to reign throughout the Cold War.

None of this lessens the greatness of Orwell's writing or the poignancy his ideas might retain for us today, of course, but it does somewhat cut down to size the role he played as an engaged writer. Klemperer was an altogether different kind of man. Klemperer was an eminently 'political' figure in that he took up a position in relation to the powers in whose grip he found himself. He was a man who meditated upon unfolding events and thought through his position and role within the *polis*, the social sphere. Rather than accepting the passive state that victimisation attributed to him, he rose to take on an active role as a linguistic subject. For him, that involved taking the stance of the thinking man who carefully recorded his own intellectual resistance to forces which were shaping the discourse and the mindsets of all those around him. Those in search of a hero of free-thinking, integrity and unflinching intellectual honesty need look no further. Not only did Klemperer risk being sent to Buchenwald or Auschwitz if his diaries were discovered, he forced himself, day by day, with a rare discipline, to face up to what he abhorred and to reflect upon the object of his horror with an unswerving lucidity.

The philologist is by definition 'he who loves language' (from the Greek, *philo-logos*). Klemperer, for his own part, loved French. And the more he heard the discourse of the Nazis resounding in the streets, the more he began to hide away in the language he loved. He pored over the writings of French eighteenth-century thinkers. Those thinkers of the Enlightenment brought some light into his sombre hours. But Klemperer also loved his mother tongue, German, and that is precisely why, in the end, he refused to allow the Germans to take it away from him and deform it as a means of expression. Here we have a clear-cut example of the resistance of the individual to an ideology which seeks to invade his consciousness and encompass it. One personal world took a stance against an emerging cultural mindset.

Klemperer soon realised that his love of French was 'seducing' him and turning his eyes away from the world around him. He came to understand that his project to write a book on the thinkers of the French Enlightenment was partly an act of moral and intellectual evasion: and at that point, he decided to patiently and lucidly employ his analytic powers and his erudition as a philologist in tracing the influence of *Hitlerdeutsch* upon the German language.

The great scope of Klemperer's culture was the culture of the philologist, not that of the linguist. Klemperer did not do a corpus study as we might do today. Klemperer listened and he took note. The sensitivity and the intuition which his wide reading of literature had cultivated in him made him all the more perspicacious when it came to analysing the phrases and metaphors of the language of the Third Reich which began to spread throughout everyday speech. When we speak of 'everyday speech', this is not merely an expression. Klemperer was listening to the way people expressed themselves over dinner, at work and in the shops. In his research, he would compare the number of persons who said *Heil Hitler* on entering the butcher's shop with those who said *Guten Tag*. He analysed the pompously archaic Gothic Christian names which parents chose when christening their children.

Most of all, he strove to understand the concepts which structured the discourse of the Nazis. This research led him to consider both the roots and the implications of metaphors. As a literary scholar, Klemperer was highly sensitive to the expressive force of metaphor, but in contrast to his Nazi contemporaries, Klemperer knew in which linguistic and literary tradition the metaphors which animated *Hitlerdeutsch* were rooted. He also knew to what extent those metaphors had been perverted from their original usage by the Nazis.

This chapter has one simple aim: to bear witness to the heroism of a thinker who resisted a certain form of language, and who refused to be seduced by metaphors which became a menace to society, as they were adopted by unthinking, fervently fanatical 'sentimentalists'. Looking through the eyes of Klemperer, we shall see how his personal world resisted the mindset of the Nazis, and resisted the transformation of the world-perceiving and world-conceiving of the German language which began to be eaten away by the Nazi mindset. This will allow us to give some degree of form and order to the way in which metaphors worked within the Nazis' propaganda. If that allows us to understand (to some degree) their mindset and the way metaphors embodied it and orchestrated Nazi rhetoric and logic, then this chapter will have served its purpose.

## SEVEN PERVERSIONS

We can observe at least seven forms of perversion in the metaphors cherished by the Nazis. These forms concern the ways Nazi concepts are partly defined metaphorically, set in opposition by metaphoric reasoning, the way metaphors themselves are recycled by the Nazis and transformed in the process, and the way metaphors are employed in an incomprehensible or inconsistent manner. The following questions will be addressed:

1. conceptual clusters
2. binary definition
3. *essentialisation* and exclusion
4. adoption and inversion
5. instability
6. contradiction
7. absurdity.

## CONCEPTUAL CLUSTERS

The language of the Third Reich was baptised the *Lingua Tertii Imperii* (LTI) by Klemperer because of the classical Roman pretensions which it cultivated. When we enter this language, we begin to understand the way concepts are linked and confused. But what is confusion? At what stage does fusion become confusion?

And to what extent is conceptual blurring a result of the wilful propagandist's attempt to dupe his audience? To what extent is the demagogue carried away with his furious confusion, losing himself as he draws others into the whirlwind of his own uncomprehending intellect? Is it possible to tell to what extent Goebbels and Hitler were lucid manipulators, and to what extent they were the playthings of their own unbridled and unfocused ravings? This remains unclear, but it is certain that their lack of conceptual rigour served the purposes of Nazi propaganda.

Throughout this propaganda, concepts remain vague and indeterminate. We move from one concept to another to reach the strangest of conclusions. Let us take, for example, the definitions attributed to 'the German', 'the Jew', 'the people (*Volk*)' and to 'race'. The interdependence (or rather the confusion) of these four concepts can be represented by the model in Figure 8.1.

Today, it may seem strange today to confuse a people with a race, but at the beginning of the last century, the two were coupled often enough. Colonial powers were flattered to see themselves as the rightful masters of the world. They ascribed their success to nature. They attributed their financial, military and technological supremacy to an implicit superiority of race. In a perverse misreading of Darwin's *Origin of the Species*, the dominance of the European nations was attributed to the natural expression of the force of our races in an international context which was analysed

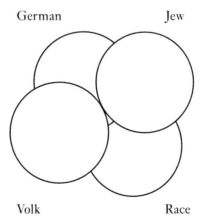

Figure 8.1 The confusion of four cardinal concepts

through the prism of 'the survival of the fittest'. According to the Social Darwinism of the period, our races were the predestined or preordained regents of the world. From the nineteenth century onwards, attempts had been made to define the nature of 'the character of nations' and races, which were then compared and contrasted in order to allow us to establish hierarchies which attributed a transcendental justice to transient reigns of power and spheres of influence (see Messling 2010).

Viewed through the prism of Social Darwinism, who were the German people? Friedrich Stieve, the author of the *History of the German People* published in 1934, provided an answer that suited the tastes of the times. Consolidating the prejudices of his era and the wistful nostalgia which transformed patriotism into Nazi nationalism, Stieve argued that the principle virtue of the German people as a race was its feeling (*das Gefühl*). This cliché has its roots in the poems and novels of the German Romantics who opposed feeling and sentiment to reason, in an emotionally charged rejection of the modern world. The Romantics and neo-romantics drew their inspiration (rightly or wrongly) from Rousseau and his concept of the 'noble savage', man unperverted by the enslaving shackles of society. Nazis found such an ideal invigorating and life-affirming.

It may seem curious that this supposed essence of the German race owes so much to a French Swiss thinker, but history shows us again and again that nationalism never tires of finding foreign inspiration for its supposedly culture-specific identity. Rousseau also inspired, for example, the romantic primitivism of the 'Russian soul', the cherished ideal of writers from Tolstoy to Alexander Solzhenitsyn. And it was the celebration of feeling and intuition (at the cost of reason) which animated the 'romanticism' of German nationalism in the 1930s.

According to Stieve, 'Feeling endows the Teuton with imagination and a religious inclination' ('*Das Gefühl verleiht dem Germanen Phantasie, verlieht ihm religiöse Veranlagung*') (qtd in Klemperer 2006: 246; 1975: 337). 'Feeling propels him towards the infinite' ('*Das Gefühl treibt ihn ins Grenzenlose*') (2006: 246; 1975: 338). The German people is animated by a '*Furor teutonicus*, that inspires him to take up battle against the *Great All*. 'Feeling makes a conqueror out of him, furnishes him with the Germanic faith in his own calling to world domination' ('*Das Gefühl macht ihn zum Eroberer, schenkt ihm den deutschen Glauben an den eigenen Beruf zur Weltherrschaft*') (2006: 246; 1975: 338). The use of Luther's term *Beruf* ('calling/vocation') is not incidental here. Stieve was addressing the German soul and demanding its participation in the world. To a people humiliated by the defeat of their armies in 1918, and facing a traumatic post-war economic recession which was to intensify after the Wall Street Crash, this praise of a great, glorious and potentially victorious race can hardly have fallen on deaf ears.

According to such rhetoric, a people must respond; it must answer to its calling, answer to the call of its race. Each one must follow the destiny of his people. Of course, since the Teuton was combative by nature, this destiny would inevitably be bloody, gloriously bloody. In this period the concept of the soldier as a 'warrior' (*Krieger*) was gradually replaced by the concept of the *Kämpfer* (fighter). This is misleading, as it seems to soften the word. On the contrary, the replacement in fact evokes *Mein Kampf*, thereby furnishing the soldier with a political function. The patriot defends the nation, the Fatherland, the National Socialist becomes the defender of the Party; and the Party must be protected from enemies both without and within.

The bloody glory of battle would not only wash away the humiliation of 1918, it would realise the potential and the vocation of the German people: because blood is what makes a race a race. In the 1930s, that blood was calling to its people to realise itself.

Multiple perversions are at work here. The People and the nation are confused; the people are confused with a single and unique race. Yet, for all the pseudo-science which was invented by the National Socialists in the field of racial and medical categorisation in order to reassure the meticulous bureaucrats who wished to perform their duties with the utmost respect for well-established norms and procedures, no attempt was made to clearly define race. After all, would definition be desirable for the Nazis? Were vagaries not more comfortable, more suited to the Nazis' needs, whether those needs be political, administrative or emotional? Nazi propaganda aims to reassure its people; it invites Germans to lie back and complacently offer themselves up to a series of clichés and unquestioned prejudices concerning the greatness of the German people.

These clichés would have been less to the taste of the great Germans themselves, who were in part 'great' because they refused to stoop to petty prejudice and facile unquestioned clichés. Would Goethe, the poet, the scientist, the erudite scholar who read and wrote both English and French fluently, have found such clichés to his taste? If the Romantics (and Nietzsche himself) were great Germans, it was in part because they were learned and open to the world, because they were capable of giving a new and immediate sense to foreign ideas and culture. They did not seek to find greatness in destroying what was foreign. On the contrary, the Romantics considered it their vocation to cultivate their *schöne Seele* ('beautiful soul'), and the soul they cultivated was capable of accepting, appropriating and assimilating what was foreign. The translation of Shakespeare and the impact his translations had on German culture is only one obvious example of their open-minded relationship to foreign culture.

And yet, with their cult of sensibility and their hostility to Reason, with their nostalgia for the Middle Ages and their hero-worship of the great blond beast, savage, noble and heroic, the Romantics did pave the way towards some of the Nazis' most cherished ideals. The Nazi vision of the blond beast was a brutish vulgarised version (one every drunken barroom brawler and storm trooper could identify with). It nonetheless retained some of its neo-romantic glamour for those who sought in violence a noble and heroic justification.

This was no longer the noble ideal of the soldier willing to make the greatest sacrifice for his regiment, his family and his Fatherland. This was a far cry from the notion of *die blonde Bestie* introduced by Nietzsche (Nietzsche 1989: 40–3, 86), a primitive but spiritually rejuvenating force. The blond beast did, nevertheless, form the focal point around which stereotypes revolved and to which clichés clung, and it exerted a significant tug on the German imagination by lending an elevated and inspired air to the expression of sadism, cruelty and the venting of frustration upon scapegoats.

How did Nazi rhetoric work? Let us, for an instant, stop judging those who were seduced by this rhetoric, and let us try to put ourselves in the shoes of those who heard 'the call of the race'. Race presents itself as a personification. It constitutes our very essence, our soul. Paradoxically, it speaks to us (like the soul) from both without and within. Race calls us back to ourselves. At the same time, race calls upon us, calls us on, inviting us to become ourselves, by realising our full potential. This metaphorical conception of space in which a force draws us backwards in order to project us forwards into the future is difficult to seize, and yet, it is one which has structured philosophy and religion from the beginnings of Western culture. We find precisely the same dynamic in the Greek concept of *telos*, the idea that the essence of a thing is expressed in its development towards a given goal. The acorn must become the oak. In the same way, both Augustine and Bonaventure were working with the notion of the soul as something endowed with a mission to realise itself, beyond itself, and in God by working back and reaching deeply into itself. Within a Christian culture, the idea that the race wished to draw us out of ourselves in order to allow us to find ourselves once more takes on a much greater significance and coherence. It resonates in harmony with tradition. Our destiny belongs within us and breathes within us. All we have to do is reach within ourselves. In this way, race leads us on. We were adrift, lost, but our race has found us, our race will save us, our most inner, most essential nature will assert itself in the expression of our race.

Of course, we can resist our race. But resisting our race means resisting ourselves. Within the logic of the Nazis, such resistance was absurd. Dolfuß and his Austrian government resisted the Nazis, but in doing so, he was seen as turning against 'the call of the blood' ('*die Stimme des Blutes*') (Klemperer 2006: 245; 1975: 336). The invasion of Austria consequently became 'the hour of blood' ('*die Stunde des Blutes*') (2006: 245; 1975: 336).

Here we see a people metaphorically defined in terms of blood. This implies a metonymy: the body is reduced to the blood. The people are then transformed into a body. In one abstract ideal body, the identity and the desires of the whole nation are supposed to be represented. Once established, this powerfully emotive representation will then offer a framework within which to understand all that is done by the nation-person, represented by its blood (and within which to understand all that is done to it). Since (according to this logic) Dolfuß should listen to the call of his inner nature, his soul, his blood, and join with the Nazis to realise their mission on earth as world-saving world-conquerors, his act of resistance appears as an insane defiance in the face of history and destiny, a betrayal of his own race and of his very nature.

## Purification

Another metaphor which actively participates in structuring Nazi rhetoric is the metaphor of purity and purification: such metaphors are rarely innocent. This is the metaphoric framework within which the Nazis will enclose the Jews and which they will employ to stigmatise them because according to their metaphorical under-standing of the healthy nation-person, the *Volk*, the Jew becomes the epitome of 'impurity'. If the Jew became the focal point of Nazi discourse, it is not simply because the Germans institution-alised the ancient Christian antipathy for the Jews or because anti-Semitism was on the rise in Eastern and Western Europe, it was because the Jew served to define the German by opposition, in a binary definition.

Purity implies poison; purity is construed as being constantly menaced by a polluting force. The diseased body serves as a con-trast to the perfection it menaces. All spheres of Jewish life and activity are held up in Nazi rhetoric as forms of a grotesque threat to the purity of the German lifestyle, culture, race and idealism. Hitler's use of such rhetoric is unrelenting in *Mein Kampf*: 'In every "tumour of cultural life" he inevitably finds "a little Jew {*Jüdlein*} ... like a maggot in a rotting corpse"' (Klemperer's quotes of Hitler, translated by Brady, 2006: 162). The most diverse fields of activity of the Jews are regarded by Hitler as a pestilence, 'worse than the Black Death of old' (*'schlimmer als der schwarze Tod von einst'*) (Klemperer 2006: 162; 1975: 220). The Black Death was no ordinary disease, it was the plague, the catastrophic epidemic that descended upon Christendom and risked annihilating God's work on earth by exterminating the Christians of Europe. Eradicating the disease therefore became a religious necessity, a moral project, and it was all too easy to awaken latent prejudices by invoking images of a Jewish corrupting influence upon Christendom and Christian states, images that had been used again and again since the times of Luther.

Such metaphors also have the advantage (from the Nazi perspective) of transforming the relationship between the German and the Jew into a relationship between man and beast. The Jew becomes the parasitic rat which pollutes the society it profits from. Alternatively, as in the quote above, the *Jüdlein* ('little Jew') was represented as the maggot feeding off a rotting corpse (2006: 162). This reactivates a metaphor used by Luther. When he found his hopes that the Jews would convert to his reformed Christianity dashed, he described them as worms, in a memorable invective.

It is hardly surprising, therefore, that the verb *ausrotten* ('exterminate') is used frequently in Nazi discourse when it comes to treating the Jews in the Third Reich. What can such notions as 'extermination' and 'Jewish plague' mean for us today? They are no more than repugnant metaphors, grotesque and absurd. They are fragments of a shattered worldview, the bricks and debris of a house in ruins. For the Germans of the Nazi period, on the other hand, such metaphors entered into the administration of institutions and the management of companies. It is therefore no coincidence that the German company which delivered the mortal Zyklon B gas to the extermination camps was called 'International Company for the Fight Against Vermin' (*Internationale Gesellschaft für Schädlingsbekämpfung GmbH*).

Similarly, it is only through the metaphoric prism of purity-corruption that we can understand the logic of signs which began to appear on houses in German towns which announced that 'This house is free of Jews' (*judenrein*). The suffix *-rein* signifies 'made pure of'. Verbs too reflected and structured this tendency to think of the Jew as a disease menacing Germanic purity. It became fashionable 'to aryanise' (*arisieren*) businesses and institutions. A shopkeeper would declare his shop a *rein arisches Geschäft* ('a pure German store') as opposed to a Jewish store. Such signs soon disappeared from Nazi society, though, since Jewish stores soon ceased to exist and there was little left to 'aryanise'.

## BINARY DEFINITION

The fact that only 'the Jewish' could be 'aryanised' reflects the extent to which 'the Jew' acted as the necessary antithesis of the Nazi definition of 'the German'. Jew and German define one another in *Hitlerdeutsch*. The Jew is so indispensable for the German, that it is questionable whether the ideal of the German which was extolled by the Nazis could have survived the 'Final Solution'. Can you be a strong and noble Teutonic German, a spiritually inspired patriotic Fighter without the insipid and parasitic counterpoint to act as a contrast to your self-image and to give a meaning to your 'calling'? The complementary nature of the definitions of Jew and German in the language of the Third Reich is so evident that it seems difficult to imagine one without the other. The mutual dependence of the two terms entailed a complex set of antitheses, which is set out in Table 8.1.

These are adjectives, not metaphors, of course. They do not function like 'Black Plague' in transforming our representation of a thing by imposing another framework of understanding upon it; but these oppositions will engender metaphors, and they themselves will be consolidated by metaphors. Let us take the representation of the *judenrein* ('purified of Jewishness') aryanised shop whose shopkeeper considers himself as honestly respecting both his customers and the laws of his society. In contrast to him, Jewish shopkeepers are characterised as a 'race of parasites' profiting from impoverished Germans of the 1920s and 1930s. The victimised German is 'preyed upon' by the Jew, the incarnation

Table 8.1 Mutually defining concepts

| Jew | German |
| --- | --- |
| sly | earnest |
| artificial/superficial | authentic |
| deceitful | honest |
| decadent | cultivated |
| deprived of soul (*entseelt*) | inhabited by a sensibility for religion |
| intellectual | man of sentiment |
| homeless | patriotic and close to the earth (*erdnah*) |

of a carnivorous capitalism. This incarnation must be fought as much as the communism that (because of Marx's origins) is equally assimilated with the Jewish threat to the world-order which the Nazis take it upon themselves to save and safeguard by unleashing World War II. World War II was, however, represented as a just retaliation against a threat to the German nature, culture and civilisation. It was, besides, represented as a 'Jewish war' since the motivating forces behind the attack on German civilisation were believed to be the alliance between Jewish communism and Jewish capitalistic forces.

## ESSENTIALISATION AND EXCLUSION

It is difficult to understand the power of Nazi rhetoric and the force of its attraction for Germans of the inter-war period, unless we understand the way it uses the conceptual and rhetorical process of 'essentialisation'. All members of a category are reduced to one single essence which is supposed to define them. The essence is supposed to encapsulate their innermost, most fundamental nature. If that essence is good, as the German was idealised as the ultimate good, then all Germans partake in that essential and inalienable goodness. If the Jew is evil, then no Jew can escape from his nature, his essence, his essential evilness. This is a deterministic form of anti-Semitism which was to express itself in the mechanistic determinism which set up, organised and ran the concentration camps. It was, however, part of an ancient anti-Semitism implicit in Christian societies which, having adopted the Jewish tradition in accepting the *Old Testament*, wish to exclude the Jews from those Christian societies. The hostility and resentment Christians have often expressed throughout history towards Jews reached new heights in Hitler's regime in which Nazis used the conceptual world of the *Old Testament* to refashion their own New Order: 'anyone who doesn't know the Jew doesn't know the devil' ('*wer den Juden nicht kennt, kennt den Teufel nicht*') (Klemperer 2006: 163–5; 1975: 225) was to be read on *Stürmer* display cases. Klemperer rightly concluded that 'without the swarthy Jew there would never have been the radiant figure of the Nordic Teuton'

(2006: 164). Essentialisms often go in pairs. Glorifying and demonising are two sides of the same coin.

Essentialisms displace experience. We no longer view the world around us in an immediate, lucid and receptive manner. We take position in relation to a set of preconceived coordinates in which the object-reduced-to-essence is fixed, and in which my relationship to it is thereby fixed. I no longer respond to the world: I subject myself to the idea I have made of the world. At this stage, the individual's personal world becomes subservient to the reigning cultural mindset. Prejudice, at this stage is no longer simply a 'preconception' which 'predisposes' one to a certain attitude until experience shades and reshapes our ignorance. On the contrary, prejudice, once subjected to over-arching essentialisms, is perfectly capable of inducing us to select only what fits into its caricatures and encouraging us to reject what does not. Being reminded by friends or by reality itself of the limits of these caricatures will invariably provoke resentment or hostility, but that very resentment and that very hostility will only serve to entrench prejudice. The bigot, the racist and the rabid nationalist consequently believe they perceive the true underlying nature of society, while others simply bother them with insignificant details. Those details are the real living, breathing people of our social universe. For that very reason, we say that 'God is in the detail'. The detail, the individual, takes us back to reality, resituates us within diversity and multiplicity. Details displace precarious reductionisms.

Understanding the pull of prejudice and the power of essentialisation might help us make some way towards understanding the way thoughtful, considerate individuals, loving fathers and mothers, could have condoned the treatment of the Jews. If we accept that the Jew can be reduced to that – his very Jewishness, an inescapable nature, an incarnation of evil – then the Jew is no longer our neighbour. He is no longer our doctor or the man who serves us in the corner store. She is no longer the child playing with her friends beneath our window. With essentialisation, the Jews are already, conceptually speaking, annihilated. The Jew becomes a concept. Since these people are strictly speaking 'Jews', it is supposed that they must (contrary to appearances) participate in the essential evil of 'Jewishness', that corrupting influence which threatens Christianity, society, the Party, tradition and the world order.

This is sufficient to pose the problem: what shall we do with the Jew? But this problem is exasperated by the problem of homeland. The German is a Teuton and has his homeland in Germany. The race is secure in its home (*Heimat*) and strikes its roots deep into the *Vaterland*. The borders of this *Vaterland* are subject to controversy. They might encompass all German-speaking lands, all the lands of the Germanic peoples. They might extend towards the east, displacing the race of Slavs (believed to be inferior *Untermenschen*), as in the project of *Lebensraum*.

The question of homeland, however, logically entails a revaluation of the nationality of the Jew. If the real German, the 'authentic' German, belongs in Germany, where does the Jew belong? Where is his homeland? The Jew becomes a squatter in the home of the German, a foreigner, an enemy. Since we are dealing with essentialisms here, and since these essentialisms are not only mutually defining but mutually exclusive, we can begin to understand the German's indignation at the idea of a German-Jew or a Jewish German. In his binary worldview, such constructs are oxymoronic. The homeless Jew would seem to be the logical conclusion of the essentialist discourse which replaces people with categories. This logic brings its own problems, though: because the Jew cannot be strictly speaking considered to be a foreigner (which would imply he comes from another land) since he has no homeland. According to the tortuous logic of the Nazi mindset, the Jew is doubly excluded.

This exclusion explains the reactivation of the dead metaphor of the wandering Jew. In Nazi rhetoric, the Jew becomes a nomad. The very conception of the world of the Jews is a nomadic worldview ('*Nomadisches Weltbild*') (1975: 230), the Nazi concludes. The question then becomes: how are we to expel those who have no country? Very quickly, the 'Final Solution' proposes itself as the only logical means of resolving this conundrum. As the German people, uplifted by a neo-romantic conviction in its own sense of destiny, pursued its project of self-realisation, the realisation of its essence, the realisation of the future, the Jew was deprived of both country and project. In the mindset of the Nazis, the Jew had neither a place nor a destiny in the German homeland.

## ADOPTION AND INVERSION

The reduction of Jews to the essence of 'Jewishness' in the Nazi understanding of the term transforms humans with whom we speak and live, humans we can empathise and sympathise with, into a noxious element which must be eradicated in order to purify the German people. The perversity of this logic is matched by the perversity with which the Nazis adopted and recycled the conceptual frameworks of the Jewish tradition in order to denigrate the Jews and represent them as a frightening and repulsive menace to German lifestyle and culture. While excluding the Jews from the German culture, they constructed that German culture upon a borrowed basis. The assimilation of the Jew with the Devil is only one clear example of the dependence of Anti-Semitism upon Jewish concepts and analogies (Meschonnic 2001, 2007).

This adoption and adaptation of the conceptual resources of the Jewish religion is not confined to concepts; it also entails the recycling of religious narratives. The Jews wandered in the wilderness with Moses. The Germans are also told that they are a lost people, a people searching for their homeland and their destiny. 'Being lost' is clearly a metaphor in this case. The crisis of capitalism and the post-war trauma of the Germans was real enough, but it is transformed into a metaphor when the *Volk* are told they must find their way through this catastrophe. The German people usurp the role of the Jews of the Exodus, and are transformed into the chosen people with a world-transforming vocation. Curiously, the basis of this strange conception comes not from a German but a Frenchman, a disillusioned aristocrat who dreamed of the glorious past of the Francs, a Germanic tribe, which had degenerated in a world perverted by mercantilism and bourgeois pettiness. It was in 1853 that the celebrated man of letters, Arthur de Gobineau, wrote his *Essai sur l'inégalité des races humaines* (*Essay on the Inequality of Races*), glorifying the white peoples of Europe and attributing to them a privileged status in the world order. To the Francs, to whom Gobineau traced his own line, he attributed the role of the chosen people. The French are, unsurprisingly, less inclined to remind themselves that the main exponents of Nazi ideals were not German. The English have, unsurprisingly, also preferred to forget that Nazi doctrine relied heavily upon a certain English source of inspiration: Houston Stewart Chamberlain (1855–1927) (not to be confused with the statesman).

A Prussian whose mother was Jewish (Heine, for example), or a citizen of Vienna born in Moravia (Freud, for example) would no doubt have found the idea of a chosen German people unpalatable. Images of the noble Teutonic knight, the saviour of Christendom would no doubt have held little charm for them. But for many, the image reflected in the mirror that the Nazis held up for them was an enchanting and mesmerising reflection. The lost people were promised a great destiny. In Hitler they would find not only a leader but also a homeland. This is precisely what a colleague of Klemperer once tried to explain to him. Klemperer held the colleague in question in high esteem and was distressed and disturbed to hear her argument. She chastised him for objecting to her considering all virtues to be German virtues. Being 'German', she claimed, was the central principle of her newly adopted idealism. 'Everything is related to the issue of being German or non-German [*nichtdeutsch*], this is all that matters; you see that is what we have learned from the Führer or rediscovered having forgotten it. He has brought us home again!' ('*Er hat uns nach Hause zurückgeführt!*') (Klemperer 2006: 99; 1975: 137).

Hitler seemed to be bringing the people back home to the homeland. If we accept that the lost people is also a chosen people with a great destiny awaiting them, then all they have to do is to go back to the source of their being and replenish themselves from the fountain of their inner nature. Evidently, this journey to the origins of the essence of the people, this projection into eternity, requires a leader: therein lies the charm of the *Führer* ('leader'). By recuperating the conceptual metaphor of the lost-chosen people, the Nazis were able in one fell swoop to establish themselves as 'prophet-shepherds', while reducing the oh-so-glorified people to a herd of 'soldier-sheep'.

## INSTABILITY

As Lakoff and Johnson have often argued (1980, 1999), metaphors often contradict one another. At times the metaphoric representations of a single concept are mutually exclusive. This, Lakoff and Johnson rightly claim, is not necessarily a disadvantage. We can unveil different aspects of a concept by highlighting its various facets in ways which do not necessarily correspond to one unitary understanding, or to experience as a whole. Describing love as a journey allows us to speak of development in terms of motion, choices in terms of turnings, and hopes and desires in terms of destinations. Speaking of love in terms of a fixed point allows us to speak of the unchanging aspect of an enduring feeling or state. Both representations reveal real aspects of love without the two metaphoric constructs being compatible.

These metaphoric constructs of love, nonetheless, both show a desire to explain something. The question we are forced to ask when we enter the Nazi mindset is: do the Nazis wish to explain anything? The contradictions in their discourse and the complexity of their reasoning would appear to be the result of a refusal to think logically and coherently. Prejudices pile up upon one another. Instead of a conceptual construction, a building with several floors and diverse rooms, we find a derelict wasteland, a workplace in ruins. Upon such ground are the fluctuating metaphoric flourishes of Nazi rhetoric constructed.

The contradictions of Nazi metaphoric frameworks are not the fruit of an inspired vision which perceives the complex and diverse facets of one concept by approaching it from different angles. Those contradictions are the debris of a cluttered mind hostile to order and coherence. The Jew, to such a mind, appears one day as the nomad, the next day as the epitome of city decadence. Hitler, and above all Goebbels, abandoned themselves to a neo-romantic conception of the German people as a pastoral folk rooted in its own soil (*Boden*). Only by drawing its force from the soil, through its roots, could the People regenerate itself. This was the *Blut-und-Boden-Doktrin* – the 'blood and soil doctrine' (that Klemperer attributed to Spengler but which germinated in the thought of the Nazi, Walter Darré).

Because it had resisted supporting Hitler, Berlin had always inspired suspicion in Nazis. As all the true enemies of the Reich were essentially Jewish (inasmuch as all that was Jewish was evil, and all that was evil was Jewish), Berlin was often considered to have a Jewish heart. Berlin, in Nazi rhetoric was 'the asphalt monster' ('*das Asphaltungeheuer*') (Klemperer 2006: 225; 1975: 308). Asphalt was that manmade product which covered the soil into which the folk must strike its roots. The city was the antithesis of that regenerating force: the union between folk and nature. The city was decadent: asphalt had already been invoked in the German expression 'asphalt-flower' ('*Asphaltblume*') in 1890, meaning prostitute (2006: 225; 1975: 308). The Nazis were the auto-proclaimed saviours who would ram their NSDAP flag into the asphalt and fight valiantly against the path to ruin, the path down which the Germans were being led by those Marxist doctrines that would result in 'the loss of the Vaterland' ('*Vaterlandslosigkeit*'). This involved smashing the press unsympathetic to the Nazi party and in particular the Jewish newspapers (*Journaille*) which were 'asphalt organs' ('*Asphaltorgane*') (2006: 225; 1975: 308). For all these reasons, the Berlin workers (a great many of whom supported the communists) were a 'lump of homelessness' (my translation of the phrase: '*so ist der Berliner Proletarier "ein Stück Heimatlosigkeit"*') (1975: 309).

Confusion is the most complex of strategies, and this conceptual cluster requires some explanation. How are we to unravel the contradictions involved in this construct? At least four confusions are operating in this discourse:

1. The city citizen is confused with the Jew, and the two are said to be united in their decadence. The German is spiritual because he remains rooted in the soil, he is close to the earth (*erdnah*). The citizen-Jew confined to the asphalt world of the city, in contrast, is deprived of soul (*entseelt*).
2. The Jew is confused with the socialist. Because socialism was inspired by Marx (a Jew), all socialists were 'Jewish'. Because the Nazis saw themselves as liberating the world of (Jewish) communism and (Jewish) capitalism, they saw themselves as the heroes of the Second World War, the 'Jewish war'.

3. Socialism was confused with internationalism. Socialists, by supporting communism with its aspirations for world revolution, were attacking the nation. They were enemies of the people.
4. Internationalism was confused with the nomadic destiny of the Jews.

These are the equations upon which the logic of *Hitlerdeutsch* was based. This was their way of defining all that opposed them as 'Jewish'.

## CONTRADICTION

Once they had become the masters of Berlin, the Nazis found it incompatible with their interests to represent the city as 'a lump of homelessness'. During the war, Goebbels was to pay tribute to the citizens who bore up to bombardment with great courage. This might have encouraged Goebbels to change his mind, and to accept that his former condemnation of the city had been unfair or at least too sweeping. But such an admission belongs to the mind of a man who struggles to be honest with himself and with others, a man who finds himself embarrassed and ashamed when he finds himself in contradiction with his former opinions. A less brilliant orator than Goebbels would not have felt burdened by scruples of morality and intellectual honesty. He would have been satisfied simply to contradict himself and change his speech to suit the times and the interests of his party.

Goebbels was no ordinary orator, however. With as much panache as bad faith, Goebbels opted for denunciation: he denounced himself (without naming names, of course). He denounced those who had in days gone by maligned the citizens of Berlin. Nothing, he claimed, could break the citizens' will to live. '*Hier liegt die vitale Kraft unseres Volkes genauso fest verankert wie im deutschen Bauerntum*' (1975: 309.) This phrase gave the English translator, Martin Brady (2006: 225) some difficulty: he translated it as: 'The vital energy of people is as dependable here as it is amongst the German farmers'. This is a curiously 'de-Nazified' translation, though. It weakens the symbolic will to power of the Nazi expression *vitale Kraft* ('vital force') by rendering it as 'vital energy', and it evades the crucial (if clumsy) image which Goebbels wished to evoke. A better rendering would be: 'Here the vital force of our Folk is just as sternly anchored as in the German farming community'. The clumsiness which Brady no doubt wished to avoid was that of a city community enrooted in asphalt. This was precisely Goebbels's idea, however: the people which had been denounced as being rootless (*wurzellos*), were now being praised for the strength of their roots reaching down into the asphalt. The citizens of Germany's capital could not be 'uprooted' by the air attacks of the invaders.

The grotesque image of the plant living in asphalt is characteristic of Goebbels for two reasons. Firstly, it shows the opportunism of someone willing to contradict himself and denounce his former words as though they came from others. Secondly, it shows his reluctance to abandon his cherished metaphors, metaphors which he found it easy to refashion when the occasion required it. For us, such metaphors are simply repugnant. But if we are tempted to criticise the mixed metaphors of the Nazis, we are, nonetheless, forced to concede that neither Hitler nor Goebbels sought either beauty or clarity: they sought efficiency, and however much we might disparage it, history testifies to the force of Nazi rhetoric.


## ABSURDITY

The last form of metaphoric perversion which remains to be explained (if we can really begin to explain anything in this language which is deliberately obscure) is absurdity. A grotesque and menacing absurdity characterises much Nazi rhetoric. We have just considered the reapplication of the *Blubodoktrin* from the German peasantry to the Berliners, who become plants enrooted in the asphalt: but the greatest of metaphorical absurdities is found in the Nazi definition of 'man'.

It will be remembered that the Nazis celebrated the German as a man of sentiment and instinct. It was his animal nature that was fundamental to the German. This explains the perversion of two metaphorical spheres of reference. In the beginning, the Nazis sought inspiration in both sport and in the armed forces. But as the Nazis adopted sporting metaphors and as they militarised their movement, they ended up 'Nazifying' both sport and the armed forces. The soldier, the protector of the Fatherland became subsumed by and made subject to the State. Uniforms were worn by storm troopers who would beat up Jewish shopkeepers. Competitors in sports became an expression of the 'Will to Power', the will to destroy opposition. They asserted the Germanic ideal: sportsmen were hailed as *Übermenschen*. This perverted the noble aspects of both the sportsman and the soldier. The soldier was reduced to an animal that obeys his master (something approaching the German shepherd which Hitler cherished). The sportsman was reduced to a conqueror who imposed himself by crushing others. This was nowhere more evident than it was in the Nazi celebration of boxing. Boxers themselves were celebrated, and the German *Volk* itself was characterised in terms of a boxer who came back with his nose broken to slug it out and knock down his opponent (the allied forces). Given the extent of the destruction of Dresden and Berlin towards the end of the war, Klemperer could only marvel at the inappropriateness of the metaphors still being used. What it is important to stress here, though, is that the charm of the blond German beast for the Nazis was (and had always been) his capacity for bloody violence, his animal will to survive.

The body was, consequently, valued as much as, if not more than, the mind. The good soldier who craved only to follow the Führer was celebrated. The Nazi was encouraged to cultivate his body in order to transform it into a tool to be put at the service of the people. Goebbels' rhetoric fashioned the German as a gladiator, as though the slave-warrior who killed and died for the amusement of the Romans' entertainment were a worthy ideal (Klemperer 1975: 295–301).

This celebration of the animal nature of man is a far cry from Rousseau's noble savage. It hides within it that petty resentment and that mistrust of intellectuals which is common among soldiers and which is often found in uneducated spheres of society. The *Deutscher Geist* celebrated by the Nazis was not the Romantics' ideal: the spiritual man, the man inhabited by an *Einfühlung* ('empathy') for the universe which surpassed the faculty of Reason celebrated by the Enlightenment. It was the opposite of the Enlightenment ideal, the man deprived of spirit and mind, the man reduced to an unthinking body.

Dr Goebbels greatly contributed to this mistrust of intellectuals. He was a contradictory figure: he was clearly far more intellectual than the masses he inspired, but he shared their mistrust and contempt for intellectuals or, at least, he liked to play upon such sentiments when he addressed his rallies. For both Goebbels and Hitler, the intellectual was an insipid, soulless being.

Inevitably, this contempt for intellectuals was to be unloaded once more upon the Jews. The Jew became the epitome of the intellectual. Once more the Jew was confined to an essentialism. The Jew was no longer a labourer, no longer a shopkeeper, no longer a schoolchild. The Jew was an intellectual, the opposite of the man of sentiment.

This perversion was, however, at odds with the hierarchy which the Nazis were eager to impose, the hierarchy according to which the German was the man and the Jew was the beast (be it a worm, a rat or a pig). This contradiction engendered one of the ugliest forms of Nazi nonsense. This cult of obscurity realised its full potential in the invention of *Intelligenzbestien*. This obscure curiosity is a neologism which proves too much for the English translator, Brady, who renders it by 'eggheads' (2006: 185). This is a feeble translation, though, which does no justice to the bizarreness of the German construction. The French translator, Élisabeth Guillot, does more justice to the term in rendering it by *bêtes d'intelligence* (1996: 259), because this neologism means *Intelligence-Beasts* or *Intellectual-Animals*.

How are we to see clearly in this obscurity? The Teutonic German is a spiritual man, a blond brute, deprived of the capacity of reasoning, that very characteristic which allows us to define man as man. The Jew, on the other hand, is defined as the one who incarnates the analytical capacity for reasoning attributed to the intellectual (but characteristic of the human species as a whole). For this, he is relegated to the status of an animal, a being insufficiently soulful to be defined as a 'man'. The opposition is perversely balanced: the Nazis opposed a 'thinking animal' with an 'unreflecting man'.

## TWO GOEBBELS

*Intelligenzbestien*, beasts of intelligence, is the perverse conclusion of a logic which celebrates the primal elan and primitive drive of the Teutonic hero of Nazi philosophy. The beast of intelligence serves as the opposite pole in the caricature which opposes Jew and German. There is an implicit mistrust of thinking involved in this celebration of the animal nature of man. But men and women do, of course, think. However absurd and perverse it may be, *Intelligenzbestien*, as a concept, is a conclusion which is arrived at by following a sinuous logic which reflects, to some degree, the desire to order experience and bring organisation into thoughts and impressions about how the world works.

Thus far, we have traced different mechanisms and intellectual reflexes in the Nazi *Weltanschauung*. These reflexes, by compounding confusion and contradiction, demonstrate an antipathy for clarity and for reason. But how does this antipathy manifest itself in extended discourse, that is to say, in the thinking of individual men and women? If we follow the 'organisation' of texts or speeches, how will such reflexes function?

It is worth trying to enter into Goebbels's mind in order to see how Nazi conceptions and the logic of the Party shape the discourse of one of this worldview's main exponents. But where should we seek Goebbels? In his writings? In his speeches? Goebbels is a dark but fascinating character in that he represents something of a character-actor. There are various Goebbels. Certainly, there is the prolific propagandist, the 'eminent Dr Goebbels', the author of *The Fight for Berlin* (*Kampf um Berlin*) (1937), and *The Attack* (*Der Angriff*) (1935), to name but two of his 'historical' accounts of the rise to power of the National Socialist Movement. But in contrast to the rhetoric of such books (which is intended as a rousing and rejoicing celebration of power), there is also a much more pensive, personal Goebbels, the Goebbels of his diaries. It is worth contrasting the two discourses in order to follow the patterns of thought as they emerged in private and how they were paraded in public.

Goebbels makes no attempt to hide the violence of the Nazi movement. Indeed, the cartoon-like propaganda pictures that adorn his *Fight for Berlin* (*Kampf um Berlin*), from beginning to end, revel in violence. The book opens with a picture of the swastika, standing alongside two uplifted arms, one holding a sabre, the other a hammer, ready to sweep down. The significance is clear: the workers and the army will destroy all that opposes them. Likewise, the book ends (285) with a gigantic, square-shouldered Germanic hero in whose wake three symbolic figures (tiny in comparison) shrink and cringe. Each figure incarnates one of the enemies of the party. There is the communist, the policeman of the Weimar Republic and a bespectacled Jewish businessman. Business marks him as the ambassador of capitalism, the parasite which sucks the life out of German workers. And failing eyesight marks him as the insipid intellectual, of weak health, who represents a danger to the racial purity of the proud, strong German people. What makes the German hero of this picture different from those of preceding images – images of conquerors, soldiers marching, drawn sabres, clenched fists and towering giants planting swastika-bearing flags in despairing crowds of miniature enemies – is that this Teutonic hero bows his head under the weight of responsibility. This is no longer the rebel who struggles against adversity: he is the responsible hero of the regime, the one who takes upon his shoulders the arduous task of rebuilding Germany.

The cult of violence is clear, but Goebbels presents this as a necessary violence. For this reason, in his chapter entitled '*Terror und Widerstand*' ('Terror and resistance': 57–82), the terror is the terror inspired by the communists, the Red Terror:

| | |
|---|---|
| Meistens gab der 'Vorwärts' oder die 'Rote Fahne' den Ton an, und dann spielte das ganze jüdische Presseorchester die wüste und demagogische Hetzsinfonie zu Ende. | Most of the time 'Forward' or 'The Red Banner' [the communist press] set the tone, and then the whole Jewish Press-Orchestra played out the wild demagogical Slander-Symphony. |
| Hand in Hand damit ging auf der Straße der blutigste rote Terror. | Hand in hand, it followed the bloodiest red terror in the streets. (58, my translation) |

A cartoon-style illustration on the following page (59) depicts a brutal pack of communist activists who have stabbed a victim (presumably a member of the Nazi party) and left him bleeding to death in the gutter. The discourse of this book is difficult to follow, but the argument appears clearly enough. Violence is the violence of the revolutionary Communist Party and its activists. Their source of inspiration is a music and a culture which is intrinsically 'Jewish'. Demagogy is invoked, but Goebbels, one of the twentieth century's greatest exponents of demagogy, attributes it entirely to his enemies. The Nazis are the underdogs, the oppressed victims of unscrupulous demagogy.

Goebbels does not deny the violence of the Nazi movement, he justifies it. He represents it as the inevitable and only answer to Terror. The State is depicted as being entirely incompetent as far as containing communist violence and stamping out their Terror is concerned. The State attempts to crush violent Nazi activism. It must therefore be acting contrary to the interests of the German *Volk*, whose defenders and saviours the Nazis believe themselves to be. According to the binary logic of the Nazis' *Weltanschauung*, which sees the Jew as the root of all evil and corruption, the State must, consequently, be in the hands of the Jews. And, for that very reason, the State must be overthrown. This is a point which is obliquely approached. Cartoons on pages 157 and 235 represent the police as the naïve pawns, manipulated by the sly and malicious bespectacled Jew. And such arguments are sometimes put across not without a certain sense of humour (which no doubt makes them all the more efficient). On page 251, for example, a seriously injured Nazi activist, bloodied and unconscious, is carried into a police station. 'Did that man get run over by a car?,' asks one of the police officers. 'No, by the Berliner Polizei,' answer the shamefaced officers carrying the victim. The same sly, smiling Jew looks down approvingly from a portrait upon the wall.

The Nazis are disseminating a conceptual mindset according to which the Old Order has been perverted. It is manipulated by the Jews. And the State cannot preserve the Germans from the Red Terror. Two malevolent forces provide the Nazis with a situation which requires a solution. And it is in this light that their uprising is represented as a logical, necessary and, indeed, inevitable consequence. Thus begins Goebbels's grotesque fairy tale which announces the *Beginnende Ordnung* ('the Beginning of Order'), as he calls it in the title of chapter 3 of *Kampf um Berlin*. Goebbels does not hesitate to theorise this violent imposition of order. And he makes little attempt to hide the fact that the Nazis have learned this lesson from the Communists. As he puts it:

In der Politik entscheiden niemals allein die Ideen, die man verficht, sondern auch und in auschlagge-bendem Maße die Machtmittel, die man für die Durchfechtung von Ideen einzusetzen gewillt und fähig ist. Eine Idee ohne Macht wird immer, auch wenn sie richtig ist, Theorie bleiben. Ihre Träger müssen deshalb ihre ganze politische Schärfe darauf richten, die Macht zu erobern, um dann unter Einsatz von Macht die Idee zu realisieren.

In politics, the ideas you defend never decide things alone, but also, to a decisive extent, the means of power which you are willing and able to apply in order to realise your ideas. An idea without force will always remain merely theory even when it is right. Therefore, the supporters must concentrate their entire political energy in gaining this power, and then use it to realise their idea. (57, my translation)

The Red communist Terror was considered by the Nazis to be a chaos menacing civilisation. And the answer was the violent uprising of the German people, incarnated in the Nazi party, who accepted the challenge to save civilisation. This struggle was one of order against chaos, patriots against foreigners, health against illness, truth against lies, honesty against demagogy. This was the struggle which was supposed to smash those that taunted the Nazis with the slogan '*Berlin bleibt rot!*' ('Berlin remains red!') (58). *Kampf um Berlin* closes with the image of the towering Teuton who holds his head in a manner somewhat reminiscent of Rodin's *The Thinker*: pensively, he assumes his destiny to forge order and reassemble the German *Volk* after crushing the forces of destruction (the communists, the Jews and the police who do their bidding by upholding a system which humiliates and impoverishes the German people). Goebbels sounds the triumph in the closing four paragraphs of *Kampf um Berlin*:

Über Terror und Verfolgung, Bedrängnis und Gefängnis triumphierten Recht und Wahrheit und stieg schimmernd und leuchtend die Fahne unseres Glaubens wieder hoch. Man kann uns biegen, aber niemals brechen. Mann kann uns in die Knie zwingen, nie aber werden wir kapitulieren.

Wir jungen Nationalsozialisten wissen, worum es geht. Wir sind von der Überzeugung durchdrungen, daß, wenn wir verzweifeln, Deutschland in einem Chaos versinken wird. Darum stehen wir aufrecht und fest, verfechten unsere Sache, auch wenn es aussichtslos erscheint, und werden damit in Warheit der Forderung gerecht, die Richard Wagner einmal an das Deutschsein knüpft: Es heißt, eine Sache um ihrer selbst willen tun.

Over Terror and persecution, distress and imprisonment, right and truth triumphed, and the Flag of our Beliefs climbed, shimmering and luminous, higher and higher. People can bend us but never break us. People can force us to our knees, but never shall we capitulate.

We young National Socialists know what is at stake. We are penetrated by the conviction that if we doubted, Deutschland would sink into a chaos. Therefore, we stand upright and sturdy, defending our idea, even when it seemed hopeless: and we thereby fully realise the imperative of Richard Wagner when he defined fulfilling an idea for its own sake as an intrinsic part of German-Being.

Um 29 October 1927 mußte es auch dem Schwarzseher und Skeptiker klar werden, daß eine neue Phase in der Entwicklung der nationalsozialistischen Bewegung in Berlin eingesetzt hatte. Jener SA-Mann, der da mit umflorter Fahne stark und trotzig vor eine ergriffene Gemeinde hintrat und in hinreißenden und aufrüttelnden Versen seinem Zorn und Ingrimm Luft machte, hatte das ausgesprochen, was in dieser großen Stunde das heißschlagende Herz der alten Parteigarde bis zum Überlaufen ausfüllte:

By 29 October 1927, it must have become clear even to pessimists and sceptics that a new phase in the development had taken place in the National Socialist movement in Berlin. The SA-Man who stepped up, strong and unflinching, to a moved community, bearing a black-veiled flag, venting his anger and fury in inspiring and uplifting verse, was proclaiming, in that great hour, the very thing that sent the racing heart of each Old Party comrade overflowing with emotion:

'Zusammengehalten! Um das Banner geschart
Ein Wall von teutonischen Recken.
Den Kopf in den Nacken, den Trutz gewahrt!
Trompeter! Blase zum Wecken!
Hört die Signale, Ihr Deutschen im Reich!
Die Partei in Berlin verboten!
Sie wollen den Kampf, wir geben ihn Euch,
Und brechen den Terror, den roten.
Wir rütteln am Fundament der Gewalt,
Bis die jüdischen Throne wanken,
Und werden uns dann auf unsere Art
Bei Euch bedanken!'

'Stick together! Gather round the Banner
A rampart of valiant Teutonic giants .
Head held high, Remain firm!
Trumpeter! Sound the Awakening!
Hear the signals, you Germans of the Realm!
The Party is banned in Berlin!
They want the fight: we'll give it to them,
And break the Red Terror.
We'll shake the foundations of violence,
Until we shake the Jewish Throne,
And then we will pay you back
In our own way! (248–5, my translation)

The rhymed verses chant the Nazi worldview, and the assonance and alliteration of Goebbels's own words (*Bedrängnis und Gefängnis*, and *biegen, aber niemals brechen*) adorns and strengthens his rhetoric.

In private, as we might expect, we find an entirely different Goebbels. In the first volume of *Gathered Fragments from Joseph Goebbels' Diaries, 27.6.1924 – 31.12.1930* (*Die Tagenbücher von Joseph Goebbels: Sämtliche Fragmente, Band I*), we find a Goebbels less convinced by party doctrine, a dedicated but perplexed party activist often given to doubts about the party's success and unity. The diary is perplexing in itself in that it introduces us to the personal world of a man among other men, in contrast to the macabre figure that Goebbels has come to represent in the post-war imagination. This Goebbels is capable of estimating and analysing the success or failure of his own public appearances in meetings and rallies, and those of his leader, Hitler, who, according to him, is sometimes 'tired', and at other times, 'inspiring'.

This Goebbels shows a great sensitivity to the weather, which is recorded almost religiously in his diary. And changes in the weather affect his moods. The sunshine, at times, appears to come as the crowning success for some of his public appearances, and, at other moments, he waxes lyrical about the glory of summer weather. His diary is also the record of a young man who reminisces about estranged loves and who frequently falls in love with the wives of his political associates. But he returns to his vocation, and, curiously, though we tend to associate Germans with work, when Goebbels chides himself back into working, he turns to English: '*An die Arbeit, my Boy!*' he writes on 2 July 1924, as he prepares to return to reading Rosa Luxemburg's *Letters*.

It is worth trying to follow the logic of Goebbels's diary entries in order to gain some understanding of the way he tied ideas together and to fathom the reasons which pushed him to oppose reason in his obscure philosophising. In the diary we find a mixture of anti-Slavic, anti-Jewish sentiment. By a strange course of reasoning, his anti-Semitism induces Goebbels to identify as the arch-enemy of the National Socialist Movement, *Geist*, a concept which we usually translate as 'the mind' or 'the spirit'. At any rate, when it comes to countering the enemies of the Nazis, Goebbels is advocating that the Nazis counter 'intelligent reasoned discourse'. This fact appears clearly in his diatribe against Harden (a contemporary author):

Maximilian Harden, so ein verlogener polnischer Judenlümmel. Wie gemein manchmal. Diese unter scheinbarer patriotischer Tapferkeit versteckte Feigheit. Diese auf die Nerven fallende jüdische Rabulistik. Diese liebevolle semitische Selbstberäucherung. 'Ich handele nur aus reinsten patriotischen Gefühlen.' 'Sie können mich verurteilen, wenn nur die Nation gerettet wird.' Wie grausam dieser Judenbengel gegen die Männer <!> die in seiner Gewalt sind. An Harden kann man, wenn man die Augen aufmacht, die ganze Rassenfrage studieren. Dann das Gemeinste, damit die Gojims in der Provinz nichts merken. 'Ihr Name?' 'Ernst, Felix, Maximilian Harden, protestantischer Konfession.' Haha. Ein aufrechter Patriot! Ein Mann, der die Wahrheit liebt. Ich rühre nicht im Schlamm.

Maximilian Harden, what a lying, Polish, Jew-lout. How nasty sometimes. Under the pretence of patriotic bravery, hiding cowardice. This irritating Jewish sophistry. This loving Semitic self-adoration. 'I'm only acting out of the purest patriotic feeling.' 'You can judge me, if you will, as long as the nation is saved.' How cruel this Jew-rascal is with the men under his orders. If you open your eyes, you can study the whole Race Question by considering Harden. The meanest thing is trying to make sure the Goys of the Provinces notice nothing: 'Your name?' 'Ernst, Felix, Maximilian Harden, confession, protestant.' Ha ha. A real patriot! A man who loves the truth. I do not stir mud. (Goebbels 1987: 31–2, my translation)

The patriotic Jew is a contradiction in terms for the Nazis. For this reason, Klemperer, a decorated corporal in the First World War, is incomprehensible to Hitler, who served as a mere *Frontsoldat* (private infantryman). For Goebbels and Hitler, men like Klemperer and Harden were aberrations which should not exist, and which must be destroyed. The Jews had no home, the Nazis believed. The assimilated Poles had to be weeded out. Neither could be trusted to defend the homeland. And the very war that would come fifteen years after this diary entry was to be conceived of as a conspiracy of the Jews who had come to wreak chaos and destruction upon the German people, the pillars of civilisation, in the form of the Red Terror.

Goebbels's diatribe slips (without paragraph break) into a denunciation of the art of thought itself, because the Jews, Goebbels feels, are sly and dangerously subtle: they can twist things with their lies. They will mislead the German people. They will lead the nation into chaos, as they did (or so he believes) in the First World War. Therefore, Goebbels concludes that the mind itself cannot be trusted:

| | |
|---|---|
| Der Geist ist eine Gefahr für uns. Wir müssen den Geist überwinden. Der Geist quält uns und treibt uns von Katastrophe zu Katastrophe. Nur im reinen Herzen findet der gepeinigte Mensch Erlösung von dem Elend. Über den Geist hinaus zum reinen Menschen! | The Mind is a danger for us. We must overcome the Mind. The Mind torments us and drives us from catastrophe to catastrophe. Only in the pure heart does the tormented man find a release for his wretchedness. Move beyond the Mind towards the pure man. (32, my translation) |

In opposition to the *Ideenwelt*, the idea-world, proposed by Jewish idealists like Rosa Luxemburg, a world he condemns as phantasmagorical, unnatural and full of lies (32), Goebbels contends that only the intuition of the natural man can find a solution to the problems of the Fatherland. We do not need to learn how to love from 'Homeland-foreign elements' (*landfremden Elementen*) such as these Poles and Jews, he argues. And at this point Goebbels becomes deeply emotional and sentimental in reminiscing about his friends, Richard and Olgi, who have taught him to love with a love that death cannot kill. Sitting in the sunshine, admiring the beauty of nature, Goebbels feels sure that he is closer to nature, closer to the *Blut und Boden* ('the blood and the soil') of the Fatherland, than Jewish beasts of intelligence who (so he believes) can only pervert his perception of reality. The rejection of the intellectual and the lyrical celebration of the poetry of nature go hand in hand in this staunch affirmation of a basic and brutal German racism.

Ironically, though Goebbels proposes we can study the racial question in studying the assimilated Pole in his patriotic commitment to Germany, we, today, find ourselves studying his own words in order to open up the great seething confusion of love and hate, reasoning and delirium, which fuelled Goebbels's ranting and philosophising. These quotations will appear twisted and grotesque to most readers, but if they portray the way the perceptions of one sunny afternoon colour the personal world of a man who was steeped in the doctrine of the Party and who became one of its main exponents in disseminating its worldview, then we will have moved beyond the objective analysis of doctrine to grasp the way doctrine enroots itself in the mind and in the sentiment of men and women. This should go some way to elucidating the way the individual mind and memory, feeling and sentiment, fuel political movements.

## CONCLUSIONS

It should be clear by now that in investigating the relationship between metaphor and propaganda and between metaphor and ideology, we can no longer content ourselves with the traditional displacement model of metaphor. In speaking of propaganda and ideology, we might be inclined to conclude that words are 'misused' and that their meanings have been 'perverted', but we cannot explain this process of misuse by saying either that a word has 'lost its meaning' or that its meaning has been 'replaced' by a metaphorical stand-in. This would be Orwell's stance. But such claims take us back to a naïve view of meaning and language, a view in which words are attached to things. According to the fairy-tale approach to metaphor, a word is robbed of its rightful meaning;

and a great many scholars and political writers have pursued 'the robbers' in order to restore meanings to their 'rightful owners'.

This paradigm reveals itself to be dysfunctional as soon as we remember that words do not belong to things (and that most words, such as verbs, adjectives and prepositions, do not even signify 'things' but designate qualities or relationships between things). Meaning turns out to be shaped and structured through the dynamically flexible process of linking words together in order to allow us to model concepts out of them, and structure the relations between them. The lexical material of language can be seen as a pliable plastic material that offers itself up to be modelled by meaningful expression in discussion.

The question that arises when we deal with communist and Nazi rhetoric is whether these discourses strive to be meaningful. The first, Fidelius claimed, did make sense, though it was necessary to suspend disbelief in order to walk into the Czech communist mindset. The second appears to be wilfully obscure, incoherent and perverse. But this forces us to reconsider what we mean by the perverse strategies involved in rhetorical language.

If we look at the way the neo-conservatives represented the war in Iraq (see Underhill 2003), we can indeed observe a misuse of the word: a war was represented as something else, 'liberation', 'a solution', 'a logical destination' or an 'obligation to take up a challenge'. But this was only part of the process of perversion, a process which was coupled to a macabre subliminal manipulation of war metaphors used in representations of peaceful spheres of life. As the enthusiasm for the war overflowed into the discussion of the 'war' against poverty, the 'war' against disease, the 'war' against tax evasion, the press sympathetic to the invasion of Iraq helped prepare nations in the English-speaking countries psychologically for the war. It was by juxtaposing war and war metaphors that the imagination was influenced. That non-explicit juxtaposition acted not upon the rational but upon the impressionistic, emotional subconscious, and it was this process of merging between reality and figurative representations which contributed to giving a warm glow to the frightening term 'war'.

In our studies of communist rhetoric and Nazi discourse, we found ourselves caught up in forms of manipulation which were at least as complex as the one at play in the English representation of war. But neither what happened during the build-up to the second war in Iraq nor the studies of communist ideology or Nazi propaganda can be explained by the naïve critique offered by Orwell (among others) who denounce the use of metaphors for betraying the literal meaning of words. Besides, the philologist and the etymologist both know that the literal meaning of a term is often more elusive than its everyday usage.

My study of 'war' demonstrated how the shape and meaning given to the word in various situations involving a real war and various metaphorical wars was altered. Having established that most words are by nature flexible and polysemous, we cannot assert that propaganda kidnapped or effaced the meaning of the word, but we can suggest that a change in perspective destabilised the network of meanings the word had previously evoked in the English-speaker's imagination. Studying this process of destabilisation allowed me to establish four points of interest for our study of metaphor:

1.  The concept of 'war' is metaphorically constructed.
2.  Propaganda adapts and reshapes the metaphorical extensions which derive from and revolve around the concept of war.
3.  The remodelling of the concept of war and of metaphoric wars reshapes the relations between war and warriors, war and allies, war and enemies.
4.  Metaphor reshapes the relations between metaphorical wars and war itself, transforming warriors or warmongers into 'innocent victims' in 'political wars' in which pacifists wage 'war' against 'war'.

Though 'war' is part of the world in which we live, it would be an exaggeration to say that propaganda alters our 'worldview', if we take this term to mean *Weltanschauung*, in the usual sense of the word ('ideology'). Propaganda, in the case in question, altered what I would call our 'perspective' of war, our affective, intellectual and moral relationship to this phenomenon at a particular period in time. It remains to be seen whether this propaganda will have a lasting impact upon our mindsets and our imaginations. If this is

the case, then we might say that propaganda contributed to refash-
ioning our private and political worlds. If this tendency prevails,
our 'private world' and our 'cultural mindset' will then incline the
mind along the paths that propaganda has traced, and our mind
will only escape them by resisting the easy stroll along the grooves
that propaganda's language has impressed upon the imagination.

In the political study concerned with the language of
Czechoslovak communism, we can see a much more fundamental
transformation of language. Ideology exploits the spatial metaphors of grammar to set up its ideologically bound oppositions and
alliances between social factions. Everyday concepts such as the
'people', 'struggle', 'citizen', 'war', 'enemy' and 'traitor' are transformed: that is to say, they become 'authorised' to signify meanings
hitherto improbable or implausible. Ideology sets about 'making
sense' of the world by positioning these concepts, linking them
and weaving their meanings together. At this stage, it becomes
meaningful to say that a *Weltanschauung* or a cultural mindset
refashions the world by transforming language. Although the
influence of ideology upon speech is incontestable, and though the
Marxist–Leninist worldview in question has taken hold of many
different language systems, *Weltanschauung*, the emergent cultural
mindset, must always frame itself within the confines of the worldview engendered by the language system. In order to change the
way we speak, we must first enter into language-bound conceptual
thought that our worldview opens up for the mind. This binds us
to (and situates us within) the interactive frameworks of concepts
and thought patterns of speech. These are the unique patterns of
world-perceiving and world-conceiving which are specific to each
language system.

The Czechoslovak communist conception of *historie* may seem
to us absurd and nonsensical. An effort of the imagination and a
rigorous attempt at rational analysis, nonetheless, reveals a logic.
This logic, moreover, shares much in common with our own
concepts of historical progress, the dynamics of cause and effect,
the conception of objectives as destinations and the concept of an
ultimate destiny for Man.

Ideology restructures our world-perceiving and world-
conceiving. It rebuilds the dimensions within which we live. But

in this architectural transformation of our thought world, the materials used (its bricks and pillars, its beams, windows and its roof) are the familiar materials of our mother tongue. Rather than the rigid 'prison-house' concept of worldview, this leaves us with a form of cultural mindset and world-conceiving which must be considered 'flexible'. The ideology adapts to the language, and the language (whose words, concepts, and the relations between those words and concepts are by nature malleable) in turn adapts to the ideology.

While the perspective is simply destabilised by propaganda, the mindset is transformed by ideology far more deeply. This transformation expresses itself in at least four different manners:

1. The symbolic structures of concepts are transformed.
2. The relations between those concepts are transformed.
3. The associations evoked by concepts are radically altered to accommodate the mindset of the ideology within the socio-historical tradition of a culture, adapting the meanings attributed to and associated with words in order to ensure the ideology increasingly takes hold of consciousness.
4. By adapting past meanings to new modes of functioning, ideology thus transforms the way we feel about concepts, people, ideas, ideals, things, institutions, and even about the past and the future. This prepares the way for ideology to manipulate and direct our feelings along pre-established political paths. At this stage, the 'production' of loyal party-members becomes possible.

In this way, an ideology penetrates, invades and colonises a language. But 'penetrates', 'invades' and 'colonises' are all metaphors. So it would be naïve to suppose we can escape symbolic forms of expression to find refuge in an apolitical hinterland, a land beyond metaphor. In politics, there are only positions, and the 'no-man's-land' is unlikely to prove a haven of peace. It would seem that in language there are no 'free-thinkers'. Thought is language-bound. For this reason, it is appropriate that we do not forget in our discussion of politics and metaphor the manipulation of our own modes of thought in English. Focusing on neo-conservative propaganda and the hold it gained over the imagination of American and British citizens should at least prevent us from sneering at the duplicity of Czechoslovak communists and the gullible nature of those seduced by their ideology. And if we condemn the Nazis, then we will do so knowing they were succumbing to forms of conceptual laxity, bad faith and intellectual laziness to which we are all at times prone.

Nevertheless, though all languages at all times are open to political manipulation and though we admit the symbolic origins of all thought and speech, our discussion of political metaphors should not lead us towards relativism, if we mean by this reductionism, the cynical belief that no system of thought is better or worse than another. A study of metaphors should allow us on the contrary to formulate three essential questions that will help us evaluate the validity and reasonableness of different mindsets:

1. Are the premises of an ideology well founded?
2. Are the concepts clearly defined?
3. Are the arguments rationally explained and do they lead us to logical conclusions?

A study of metaphor can hardly establish whether our idea of history is apt, but it can help us analyse in greater detail the limits of its construction as a concept, and this in turn may help us evaluate how well founded it is. A study of metaphors can establish the clarity with which concepts are defined and linked to one another. A study of metaphors can, finally, assess the logic and reason which structures and directs the arguments of a discourse.

In the language of Czechoslovak communism, the premises often appeared to be based on shaky foundations. Its concepts were often ill-defined: a word like 'people' begins to exclude many of the 'people' within a nation. Dissenters are transformed into class enemies and class enemies are transformed into homeland-less non-citizens. A small group of people represents the will of the Party, which in turn sees itself as the directing force of the State, which in turn justifies itself in oppressing the people because it *is* 'the People' (or its essential nucleus). However, throughout our discussion of this ideology, Fidelius demonstrated that the Party wished to explain itself, promote itself and justify itself in clear, rational terms. The Czechoslovak communists lived in their own world, 'another world', but they sadly looked out at those who refused their own vision of the world, and they hoped with both conviction and sincerity that those 'dissenters', 'cynics' and 'reactionaries' would take the step to join them in their world. They invited others into their world; and reason and logic were the tools and materials with which they hoped to build a bridge between the two worlds.

What happens, though, when a political regime seeks not to include but to exclude? What happens when an ideology rejects reason and logic and appeals not to the mind but the heart? What happens when a discourse no longer tries to convince those it addresses, but strives to persuade them by acting upon their emotions, their fears and desires? It was in order to consider more fully these questions and the role that metaphor plays in such regimes that we took it upon ourselves to plunge into the perverted rhetoric of *Hitlerdeutsch*.

On entering that world, with Klemperer as our guide, we strove to understand obscure strategies and the perverted logic which sought to diabolise the Jews and turn all enemies into one great menace to the noble German culture. The black confusion of the world which the Nazis offered the Germans, and the nightmare they lived through with the destruction of their Reich and the defeat of the Germans in World War II, were the results of a propaganda which was based upon misconceived hypotheses concerning the nature of the Jews, the Germans, their neighbours and their enemies. Arguments reposed upon ill-defined definitions, and relied upon a wilfully perverted logic paraded by those unashamed by confusion, contradiction and such ignominious oxymorons as 'Intelligence-Beasts'.

Though Lakoff and Johnson are no doubt justified in arguing that metaphors can allow us to think, the metaphors of Nazis do not allow us to think, or at least, not to think clearly. They do not draw us closer to the world: they lead us into illusion. That is why it is necessary (as Lakoff himself often argues) to consider the aptness and the consequences of the metaphors we use. Those listening to Goebbels did not have the lucidity or the cultural background to resist the metaphors that he used to seduced them. Perhaps Goebbels himself was seduced by his own metaphoric musings, carried away and lost to himself, in the way that, as Plato suggests, all demagogues lose themselves in leaving reason behind.

# CHAPTER 9

# Language in Metaphors

## THE FRENCH LANGUAGE IS SO BEAUTIFUL, WE HARDLY DARE TOUCH HER

In his sardonic book-length account of the various representations attributed to the French language throughout history, *De la langue française* (1997), Henri Meschonnic quoted Rivarol, one of the 'great priests' who knelt down before the majesty of the French language, celebrating its purity, its clarity, its logic, its perfection and its universality. French at the time of Rivarol (the end of the eighteenth century) was the preferred language of European elites from Madrid to Moscow and was widely used as the language of diplomacy; and this was enough to convince Rivarol that the French language was 'universal'. It was, he felt, the natural tongue of humanity, who logically inclined towards it as the most eloquent and appropriate means for expressing ideas. Rivarol even went as far as chastising himself for violating the perfection of the French language in his work as a lexicographer. Cutting up this work of perfection into words seemed to him almost indecent: '*Ma besogne du* Dictionnaire de la langue française, *me fait penser à celle d'un amant médecin obligé de disséquer sa maîtresse*' ('My task of writing the *Dictionary of the French Language*, makes me think of a lover-doctor who is called upon to dissect his mistress') (Meschonnic 1997: 114). It is a curious state of affairs when a lexicographer chastises himself for explaining terms, as though extracting words from texts and contexts somehow maims the language. It will no doubt appear even more disconcerting to the English-speaker that a language should be represented as a loved one, and no ordinary loved one, but rather as a mistress, imperious in her capacity to command her disciple-lover. French, nonetheless, for many men of letters throughout history, has often been considered as an object of veneration and desire. Rivarol's remark is hardly out of place in a tradition which, from the seventeenth century onwards, has tended to extol the French language and advocate its celebration and adoration.

The representation of the French language as an object of adoration harnessed the grammatical fact that *la langue* is feminine. Metaphoric representations are not imprisoned by gender, and speakers experience no difficulty in comparing an object of a feminine gender to another of a masculine gender in French. It is perfectly possible in French to compare a language to a fruit (*fruit* which is masculine), just as speakers can, if they choose, compare it to a flower (*fleur* which is feminine). Likewise, although 'truth' is feminine in French (*vérité*), in German (*Wahrheit*) and in Czech (*pravda*), all three languages allow speakers to compare 'truth' to masculine nouns.

Nevertheless, despite the seemingly arbitrary repartition of nouns into genders, gender often reveals a deeper unconscious relationship to a concept. As Simone de Beauvoir pointed out, 'Man feminizes the ideal he sets up before him as the essential Other, because woman is the material representation of alterity' (de Beauvoir 1988: 211). Language is only one of those ideals enshrined in alterity and elevated to a feminised ideal:

> Woman is Soul and Idea, but she also is a mediatrix between them: she is the divine Grace, leading the Christian towards God, she is Beatrice guiding Dante in the beyond, Laura summoning Petrarch to the lofty summits of poetry. In all the doctrines that unify Nature and Spirit she appears as Harmony, Reason, Truth. The gnostic sects made Wisdom a woman, Sophia, crediting her with the redemption of the world and even its creation. (211)

But what exactly does it mean to say that language is 'feminine' in French, and that it is 'feminised' by French culture? This will force us to reflect upon the word 'language' itself; because our word 'language' covers two concepts which are each attributed different terms in French. While the 'language' of a culture or nation (*langue*) is feminine, the 'language' we speak of when we mean the vocabulary or style of speech characteristic of a person or a group (*langage*) is masculine. Interestingly, the latter has not been elevated to the status of a venerated mistress to whose commands a writer is enslaved.

Language, in the sense of the language of the nation, the language uniting the French-speaking countries throughout what has increasingly been called *la francophonie*, has been elevated into a cult in a way that the English language has never been, however much our language is loved by its speakers. Language is the object of fascination but not of adoration in the English culture. The majority of references to 'language' in *The Oxford Book of Quotations*, for example, refer to language in terms of vocabulary and style of speech rather than to the idiom of our linguistic community. We might speak of Yeats's or Blake's language for example, or 'the language of the gutter press', but devotion to our language *per se* remains rare and contrary to the spirit of Anglophone culture.

Rivarol's reflection on his mistress-language is in no way remarkable in the tradition in which he takes his place, but it is revealing for our study of metaphor in two important ways. Firstly, it reminds us that while we have been studying metaphors in language, language itself is invariably represented in metaphors. The medium which allows us to construct metaphors is itself a metaphor-bound construct. What we say about language and what it does for us, involves the activation of complex metaphoric frames. If a language is said to be 'rich', that implies that it is a 'possession' (part of our 'inheritance'). This representation also has the inconvenience of implying that other languages are 'poor' or 'not so well off'. Following the same logic, this metaphoric frame allows us to speak of a period of decline in the 'life' of a language as an 'impoverished' state. If, on the other hand, language is said to be a means of communication or a 'tool', then we remain within a mechanistic, utilitarian framework of thought, a conception which emerged during the industrial revolution when such mechanistic conceptions began to hold currency. The idea of 'language use', one of the most fundamental conceptual frameworks used to conceive of language as an object of scientific study, presupposes this historically situated, mechanistic, utilitarian conception of language. And it is only by reaching beyond that conception that we will come to see the limits of our metaphor-bound definition which frames our debates on language in contemporary linguistics. Reaching beyond this metaphoric paradigm might enable us to extend the horizons of our perception of language and offer us greater insight into what we are involved in doing when we speak and write.

The second thing which strikes us when we consider Rivarol's conception of French as a mistress is that different linguistic communities conceive of 'language' differently, and those differences are, of course, metaphorically bound. In this chapter, we will only be able to skip nimbly through a few different conceptions of language which have emerged in English and French. A fuller study of the parallel developments of the concept of 'language' in English and French would be of interest, but since our aim here is simply to demonstrate that all representations of language are both linguistically and culturally situated, juxtaposing a variety of conceptions should suffice to prove the point.

For the English-speaker, the cult of the French language might appear either quaint or pretentious, but the development of this celebration of *la langue française* and its modern counterpart, *la défense de la langue française*, cannot be understood without grasping that this celebration is born of struggle. As Trabant pointed out, the Romance languages were engaged in bolstering their own prestige in order to convince speakers of the sixteenth and seventeenth centuries that each of the national languages, Spanish, French and Italian, could replace Latin as the language of culture (Trabant 1992: 92–102; 2007: 69–72). This involved three distinct stages. For French, the first stage was that of the defence of French as a means of expressing ideas and as a vector of culture, a task which was taken upon himself by Joachim du Bellay who in 1549 published *La Deffence et Illustration de la langue françoise*. Initially, du Bellay did not dare to claim French could equal Latin, the treasure-house of culture for the French-speaking nation. But in the second stage, one hundred years later, Vaugelas, in his *Remarques sur la langue françoise* (1647), was already claiming rival status for French by extolling the authors of its language who, in his opinion, had proved that 'the French language has all of the majesty of Latin and all of the sweetness of Greek' ('*la langue Françoise a tout ensemble la majesté de la langue Latine, & la douceur de la langue Grecque*') (qtd in Meschonnic 1997: 96). It will be noticed that both 'sweetness' and 'majesty' are feminine in French, and thereby contribute to the feminised idealisation of the French language.

In a public speech given at the *Académie de Soissons* in 1710, just over sixty years later, the concept of the French language had already entered its third stage. At that point in time, French was said to have reached its perfection. That perception was held to be made manifest by both the classic literature of the time and by the *Dictionnaire* of the *Académie*. And yet, French at that very moment found itself in a precarious position at the giddy height of perfection. A danger that was courting the French language was soon to make itself felt. Up to that point, it had been possible to speak of 'progress' and 'improvement' (*perfectionnement*) when speaking of linguistic change, but as soon as the language was held to have reached the height of its perfection, it had no further objective to reach; it could only decline, if it was not maintained, preserved, in that state of perfection.

This is the danger that was to besiege French linguists and men of letters for the following four hundred years and which torments linguists up to this day. Since the French language was held to be perfect, then its perfection had to be protected from change, since change itself became associated with harm and perversion. The case for purism and the preservation of the language intact should not be overstated. To be fair, French writers often stressed that French would profit from adopting words from other languages and by translating foreign literary works into French. Rivarol himself was a translator (and called himself Rivaroli when he ventured to the other side of the Alps). In a very different vein, he argued that 'The French language will not receive its full perfection without visiting her neighbours' (qtd in Meschonnic 1997:

113). This was Rivarol's way of promoting his prose translation of Dante's *Inferno*. Nevertheless, the burden of the French language's perfection outweighed such invitations to cultural openness. The French language, it was argued, had been 'held' or 'fixed' (*fixée*) in its perfection by Malherbe, a poet and man of letters (1555–1628). And the first edition of the *Dictionnaire de l'Académie françoise*, in 1694 paid tribute (or rather homage) to the tradition of Malherbe and those that followed him. This inaugurated a tradition which saw men of letters entrenching themselves in what could only become a reactionary stance with relation to language change.

A marriage between writers and grammarians and accepting the task of maintaining language in its most perfect form seems a strange idea from the perspective of the twenty-first century. After over one hundred years of aesthetics and poetics which have invariably associated literary movements with reaction and rebellion, rule-breaking and innovation, it appears almost perverse to ascribe to writers the role of preserving the purity of the language intact. French writers have never contented themselves with simply recycling a given form of linguistic perfection. The reactionary linguistic aesthetics espoused by men of letters has never hindered writers from expressing themselves in their language or from furthering the expressive potential of French. Hugo and Baudelaire explored reality. Their innovative language and the expression they gave to lived experience and to the potential of the imagination continue to inspire readers today (even in translation), and that certainly seems to prove that French of the nineteenth century was changing and adapting, growing and remoulding itself as the reality of French culture changed and as individual impressions of that culture emerged. And yet, parallel to this ongoing development of language, the will to assign the task of 'preservation' and 'maintenance' to writers is evident in the works of grammarians and men of letters.

The logic of celebration was often incoherent. Celebration of the French language-in-a-permanent-state-of-perfection could only be maintained if it was contended that change had not in fact 'changed' the language. For this reason, in the preface of the 1835 edition of the dictionary of the *Académie*, it was argued that the French language retained the same 'identity'. This curious balancing act was formulated in somewhat incoherent terms: *'Depuis deux siècles, en effet, la langue française est la même, c'est-à-dire également intelligible, quoiqu'elle ait beaucoup changé pour l'imagination et le goût. C'est ainsi seulement qu'une langue est fixée'* ('Indeed, for two centuries the French language has remained the same, that is to say it has remained equally intelligible, though it has changed greatly in terms of imagination and taste. This is, besides, the only way a language is maintained') (Meschonnic 1997: 189). Elsewhere, the lexicographers of the *Dictionnaire* were to admit that the 'idea of maintaining a language' (*'la notion de fixité'*) was false (191). However, since the *Académie* had over-invested in striving to maintain the language in its present state for over two centuries, it could only reserve for itself the role of slowing down the process of change. Change was pernicious, the *Académie* believed: change could only be conceived of in terms of decline.

By the 1930s, four forms of perversion were said to endanger the French language: foreign words, technical terms, slang and grotesque expressions (191). Any etymologist writing in English, German or Czech will welcome the introduction of new concepts from foreign languages. The introduction of new words enriches the language and allows us to adapt to our changing everyday reality. It would be wrong to dismiss French linguists and etymologists as being reactionary and culturally inward-looking. Such an attitude is alien to the work of Alain Rey and his wife, Josette Rey-Debove, who have directed the compilation of the most widely consulted French dictionaries in recent decades, and linguistic protectionism is entirely absent in Rey-Debove and Gagnon's *Dictionnaire des anglicismes* (1980). Contemporary linguists in France often disparage or despise the *Académie*'s moribund nostalgia. But it would seem that linguists, etymologists and lexicographers often exert less influence over politics and the Zeitgeist when it comes to the conception of the language shared by a culture at any given period than men of letters and the well-meaning politicians who pick up their ideas and rehash clichés.

Of course, the *Académie* of 1932 did little to prevent the introduction of specialised scientific terms or foreign words (notably anglicisms). Culture continues; speakers do not ask permission to tell jokes, play with language and introduce expressions which jar the ear of those who prefer conversation to follow the tried and tested patterns of expression our fathers and mothers hand down to us. Yet, in contrast to this living and developing culture, for more than four hundred years now, there has existed a force which celebrates constancy over innovation and which perceives innovation as an inevitable but invariably detrimental force. Throughout this period, that reactionary force has remained just as constant as the French language itself has proved impervious to its will and inconstant to the timeless perfection that the *Académie* has sought to preserve from 1694 onwards. It is thus in the spirit of this resilient nostalgia for lost perfection that Marcel Arland expressed himself when in 1955 he lamented that 'all originality is illness' ('*toute originalité est une maladie*') (Meschonnic 1997: 108). For Arland, the French language was a perfect body, and all outside influence was conceived of in terms of a corrupting illness. Such metaphors do not bear up to analysis. After all, bodies constantly take in and expulse elements from outside: bodies breathe, bodies feed, bodies sweat and defecate. The inaptness of Arland's analogy can no doubt be attributed to the fact that he is simply adopting a traditional or hackneyed form of expression without investigating the heuristic potential of the corporeal metaphor to express a real trait of language.

Such conceptual laziness is not rare. Linguistic reactionaries are faithful to their dogma of the preservation of perfection. Their devotion is that of adoration, an almost religious adherence which all but excludes thought. However, in fairness to the *Académie*, we are forced to concede that it has survived. And if it has survived and has been able to perpetuate its linguistic conformism and its conceptualisation of the French language, it is because it has been able to adapt to the changing historical, political, cultural and literary situation in which French people find themselves. This involves both the preservation of a creed and the reinvention of arguments in different contexts. Meschonnic lists the delicious absurdities which have been put forward at different epochs, but even as he demonstrates the vacuity of such arguments with his inimitable *Schadenfreude*, Meschonnic is forced to express almost admiration at the ingenuity of these defenders of the French language: 'What is surprising, with these defenders of the French language is the diversity of their bad arguments,' he exclaims (1997: 293).

The three forms of representation which come up again and again in the celebration of French, and which have resisted the course time and the attacks of linguists, are the representations of French as being chaste, ordered and clear. We have already seen one expression of French as the feminised ideal, the mistress, in our quotation from Rivarol. This is a particularly resistant form of representation. Dominique Bouhours in 1721 expressed himself in the following terms:

Quoique nos moeurs ne soient peut-être pas plus pures que celles de nos voisins, notre langue est beaucoup plus chaste que les leurs, à prendre ce mot dans sa propre significa-tion. Elle rejette non seulement toutes les expressions qui blessent la pudeur & qui salissent tant soit peu l'imagination mais encore celles qui peuvent être mal interprétées; sa pureté va jusques au scrupule, comme celle des personnes qui ont la conscience tendre, & ausquelles l'ombre même du mal fait horreur; de sorte qu'un mot cesse d'être du bel usage & devient barbare parmi nous, dès qu'on peut lui donner un mauvais sens.

Although our usages are perhaps no more pure than those of our neigh-bours, our language is far more chaste than theirs, if the word is taken in its proper meaning. *She* [our language] rejects not only all of those expressions which hurt her sense of discretion and which soil even slightly the imagination, even to the extent of rejecting those which risk being misinterpreted. *Her* purity is scrupulous, just as for those of a tender conscience, even the shadow becomes a source of horror. Thus, a word ceases to be considered acceptable to our tastes and barbaric as soon as one can attribute to it a bad meaning. (Bouhours, qtd in Meschonnic 1997: 193, my translation)

For Bouhours, language is not a means of expression, a tool we use, but an active personified force which dictates the way we should treat her. And the French language is most definitely a 'she'. French rejects vulgarity. French and vulgarity are incompatible: this is the implicit argument. Yet, what Bouhours is advocating here is, of course, a policy rather than an observation. Bouhours is speaking of his ideal of French rather than of the reality of linguis-tic usage. The French of Bouhours is not the French to be heard in the streets of France. French is a dialect (belonging to Paris and Versailles) and it is a sociolect (restricted to polite society). *Le français* of Bouhours is the French of aristocrats, not the speech of French seamstresses and cobblers. For Bouhours, it would, of course, be beneath his dignity to stoop to contemplate such language, and to call it 'French' would no doubt be regarded by him as an insult to his idealism. Even to this day, when people correct non-standard expressions or turns of phrase and grammatical forms accepted in certain social circles and in certain dialects, it is customary to stress, '*Ce n'est pas français!*' ('That's not French!'). An idealistic aesthetics circumscribes the limits of French culture and determines who is accepted within its exclusive linguistic community.

French has, of course, an unbroken and vital tradition of slang and vulgarity, and the great writers whom the *Académie* were gradually to integrate into its canon – from Villon in the sixteenth century and Molière in the seventeenth down to Baudelaire in the nineteenth century – have contributed to that vital tradition. But that vulgarity has no place in the conception of the French language which Bouhours is trying to promote. This will towards exclusion involves a constant struggle. Not only must the *Académie* guard against change, it must also deny much of what is happening in speech in France in order 'to protect' French. There is an amusing parallel here in this contorted rhetoric concerning the 'chastity' of the language. According to the logic of this metaphoric frame, just as French should not be vulgar, women should not be promiscuous: they should be chaste. The reality at every period in time contradicts the ideal, but this does not debunk the ideal. Idealism is ever impervious to reality. The celebration of the mistress-language persists, and the defenders continue deluding themselves as to the nature of women, language and language change.

At the beginning of the twentieth century, the ideal of the chaste language was still intact. The celebrated writer, Anatole France, extolled 'her' in terms similar to those used by Bouhours:

| | |
|---|---|
| La langue française est une femme. | The French language is a woman. |
| Et cette femme est si belle, si fière, | And this woman is so beautiful, |
| si modeste, si hardie, si toucha- | so proud, so modest, so bold, so |
| nte, si voluptueuse, si chaste, si | touching, so voluptuous, so chaste, |
| noble, si familière, si folle, si sage, | so noble, so familiar, so mad, so |

| qu'on l'aime de toute son âme et qu'on n'est jamais tenté de lui être infidèle. | wise, that we love her with all of our soul and we are never tempted to be unfaithful to her. (France, qtd in Ripert 1993: 236, my translation) |

If metaphors are to enlighten us, then they must light our way by revealing the unfamiliar in familiar terms. This implies, of course, that the term of comparison is familiar to us. This would seem to be the underlying logic at work behind comparing language to a woman. We all know what women are, after all, do we not? This is far from certain, however. The 'nature' of woman changes from period to period. The concept of femininity quoted here appears out-dated, almost absurd at time in which women's liberation and sexual freedom have been promoted almost as moral obligations by the media and our institutions for at least two generations. Besides, Anatole France's conception of woman piles contradiction upon contradiction, revealing he adheres to all of the traditional clichés foisted upon women by men who fantasise about the diverse roles they feel women should play in order to satisfy their manifold and often contradictory desires. A woman must be chaste but voluptuous, proud and distinguished but also familiar (the term *familière* in French means 'intimate', just as *hardie* means not only 'bold' but also 'brazen'). No doubt the author would argue that French is also full of contradictions. But if this is so, then it is because 'she' is a woman. The logic is circular. Woman is contradictory by nature (so runs the traditional cliché). And that is why men love her.

At this point, we might be justified in feeling the metaphor of the *langue-femme* has lost any heuristic value. What it does indicate, for our study of metaphor, however, is that metaphoric representations of language are themselves often couched in culturally bound concepts. Not only does 'feminising' language impose upon language a gendered representation, that gendered representation partakes in and consolidates (in its own modest way) the gender roles imposed upon women. The metaphoric paradigms which asserted themselves in the written language up until at least halfway through the twentieth century were, of course, predominantly paradigms forged by and maintained by the masculine imagination, though it is undoubtedly true that women maintained the tradition of a 'feminised' French.

The incoherence of such arguments never prevented them from gaining wide currency, from persisting in the imagination over time or from resisting change. Such celebrations of the chastity of the French language will, perhaps, have difficulty in facing up to feminism, however. Since our concept of woman has undergone a radical change, celebrations such as those of Bouhours and Anatole France might soon be rejected. On the other hand, given the resistance of certain of our clichés concerning women and given the capacity of the defenders of the French language to adapt to changing circumstances, we might also anticipate a reformulation of the 'mistress-language' metaphor in the coming decades.

## THE AESTHETICS OF ORDER

The concept of order takes on a whole new significance when it is harnessed in the representation of the French language. Of course, we can speak of 'disordered speech', 'unordered paragraphs' or a 'disorganised argument' in various languages, but such expressions refer to discourse and not to the language system itself. The representation of language-as-order is a much more far-reaching concept in French. According to a certain well-established tradition, French as a language system is said to reflect the very principle of order in and of itself. Advocates of this dubious hypothesis are, of course, forced to have recourse to literature and speech (*discours* and *parole*) to consolidate their arguments with illustrations, but the examples found in literature and speech will be used to make a general affirmation about the language system itself: French is inherently ordered. Examples such as the prose of Voltaire or the poetry of Malherbe are held to be mere expressions of that innate and transcendent principle of order which is intrinsic to the language of those writers. This concept of French first appears in the sixteenth century and triumphs in the seventeenth century, and it is far from extinct today (Meschonnic 1997: 161). Upon what basis is this idea founded?

The argument advanced is that the organising principle of

words within the sentence follows the order, subject–verb–object. This order is said to characterise the French language in contrast to others. (In fact, it is common to many: we might say *Jean remarque le chat* in French but we also say 'John notices the cat' in English, for example.) This order is, nevertheless, celebrated by French linguists at various periods in history and held up to be the only logical order of organisation. Here, we are not simply talking of syntactic logic and grammar; we are speaking about the logical organisation of ideas. Because the French sentence follows the order of subject–verb–object, it is held to reflect and engender Natural Reason. This makes French the language of Reason itself. The Enlightenment is brought to bear upon the discussion of grammar, and French grammarians and *hommes de lettres* elect themselves as the heralds of the Enlightenment. If the French can enlighten the world with their culture, it is argued, it is because the French are inhabited by the light, that clarity (*clarté*) of vision and understanding which is denied to other cultures whose speakers are not so fortunate as to be belong to the French culture. Bouhours argues that 'the French language is perhaps the only one to follow exactly the natural order of ideas and to express them in the same manner in which they are born in the mind' (qtd in Meschonnic 1997: 161). Order structures and organises the French language, while clarity adorns French with a coat of varnish for its perfection. Louis Le Laboureur had already developed this idea in 1669:

> If it is true that our speech expresses our ideas, it is certain that the construction of speech which imitates most fully the order of our thoughts is the most reasonable, the most natural and consequently the most perfect. We for our part, follow that order without violating it in any way in both prose and verse, in our writing and in our speech. (Le Laboureur, qtd in Meschonnic 1997: 161–2, my translation)

Nature is order, and order is reason. French combines order and reason and remains true to the nature of both order and reason, true to nature itself. French is untainted by perversion. Other languages invent contortions which twist the organisation of ideas as they are born in the mind. French, on the other hand, holds true to the logical representation of thought in language. Here we encounter the commonly held concept of language as the 'servant' of Reason. Inner thought, according to the logic of this argument, uses language for its outer expression. Ideas, for Enlightenment philosophers, were born outside of language. The Enlightenment philosophers did not have Humboldt's understanding of the inextricable relationship between language and thought. For them, language should serve thought, and French served it admirably, the French felt. For Duclos, the order and simplicity of French made it appropriate for philosophical discourse (Meschonnic 1997: 162). For Rivarol, 'good sense would choose French' (163). Greek, Latin, English and Italian were perfectly adequate when it came to persuading people, moving them or tricking them, but when it came to instructing, enlightening and convincing people, French was a peerless language. French was the language of truth (163).

Light for Enlightenment philosophers (who were either Christians, like Lessing, or Theists, like Voltaire) is the 'Light' of the Lord, the 'Light' of Revelation. That light illuminated creation and engendered the reason within us, the reason by virtue of which we can be considered to resemble our Maker. French, it was argued, was illuminated by that self-same Light. This engendered a circular, self-affirming logic: French was true to nature, and by virtue of its nature, it was true. What was held to be unclear was not accepted as 'French' by thinkers who celebrated the clarity of the French language. Clarity could be considered a form of inner illumination, a spiritual as much as a grammatical or logical quality.

For the conception of clarity to survive, it had to adapt, of course. Bernard Grelon, writing in 1995, claimed '*la clarté était un élément de la démocratie*' ('clarity was an element of democracy') (Meschonnic 1997: 185). Grelon could have been writing in 1790, because the French revolutionaries were eager to embrace the idea that the French language was the model of clarity and reason, the means by which the French would enlighten all men. The clarity of the French language became part and parcel of the universalism of French revolutionary republicanism. French was the language of reason and of humanity. For this reason, those who did not speak it were not (and could not be) fully enlightened. As a consequence, the state policy following the revolution was to investigate ways in which languages spoken by minorities (Breton, Alsatian, Basque) and dialects such as those found in Flanders and in Provence might be 'annihilated' (see de Certeau et al. 1975). Only by the annihilation of such languages and dialects could men be instructed and enlightened as to the ideals of the French revolution, the inspired project of Reason to transform the world.

Those asked to report back to Paris on the project for wiping out dialects and regional languages invariably proved 'enlightened' by the same ideals as those who were militating for the expansionism of the Paris-Versailles sociolect, *le français*, which the Revolution had elected for its vision of the world. Pierre Bernadau, for example, reported that Gascon dialect spoken by the 'lower people' ('*le bas peuple*') of the South-West of France lacked the precision and the energy of French. It had, moreover, inherited English terms and expressions from the period between the twelfth and fourteenth centuries, during which time the Realm of England had possessed parts of the region. Bernadau saw no inconvenience in destroying the dialect, though he expressed doubts as to the possibility of preserving the purity of language since 'the low people' of towns always 'corrupt' language, he claimed (de Certeau et al.: 197–202). The parish priest of the Upper Alps region complained that the people of his region spoke a dialect which had evolved through the superimposition of several layers of the Celtic language of the Gauls, and which had been subject to Greek, Latin and Germanic influence before taking on many words from Spanish and Italian. The people understood French but were incapable of speaking it, he reported (279–81). The first task of the revolution which claimed to represent all men was to make sure that all men spoke the language of the revolution, the language of clarity and reason, French. At this stage, the aesthetics of the representation of language were brought to bear on the political organisation of the Republic. Words like 'order' were harnessed in an altogether more pragmatic sense. Order could only be imposed on the provinces if the people of those provinces agreed to enter into the language of the New Order.

This celebration of order did, of course, force the defenders of clarity to reject a great deal of what might legitimately be considered as 'French'. This exclusion went beyond a predictable contempt for sociolects and dialects: defenders of *le français* took arms against individual styles of writing and spoken expression. Beauzée, for example, writing in the *Encylcopédie*, was forced to admit the existence of inversions, but he concluded that such inversions went against nature of the French language (Meschonnic 1997: 167). Bally quoted sentences which showed a suppleness which bordered upon the capricious (*capricieuse*) and which rebelled against the inflexible rules of French. Bally argued that such rebellions were not 'proper to French' but rather belonged to a Classicism which was not in keeping with Latin and the mother tongue (169). The inherent contradictions in such arguments are absurd. At times, defenders of French will use literature to demonstrate the nature of the language and at other times, they will exclude literature from the language, as though literary works break with the fundamental nature of the mother tongue.

Following such reasoning and trying to grasp the basic premises upon which it was based takes a considerable amount of energy for the English-speaker unacquainted with such an aesthetic idealisation of language. Criticism comes easy; and yet we should ask ourselves whether we ourselves are any better placed to understand the relationship between language and literature, between stylistic expression and the maintenance of norms within the linguistic system. Because we do not have the necessary terms to allow us to distinguish between the language system and the language used by individual speakers or authors: both are referred to as 'language', in English. This becomes painfully obvious if we argue, for example, that Shakespeare's language transformed his language. If the *Académie* has one virtue, then that virtue lies in the fact that it forces us to engage in the debate as to what role literature has to play in improving and maintaining the language of a linguistic community.

At the end of his survey of the tortuous arguments invoked in celebration of the glory of the French language, Meschonnic concluded that most of the authors quoted failed to perceive that what is at stake is not the way language-use risks perverting and destabilising the language system, it is the capacity of language as a system to be perpetuated by the expressive and meaningful use of it in everyday discourse and in literature. While the *Académie* shudders every time the rules of syntax are stretched, each expressive adaptation of language helps maintain it as a flexible mode of expression which not only serves our need to express our ideas, but which allows us to take our place within social relationships by defining ourselves as we speak. Meschonnic concluded: '*C'est le langage qui est en jeu dans la langue, pas la langue dans le langage*' ('It is language [our use of it] which is at stake in our language [French], not French [which is at stake] when we use language') (306).

In contrast to the resilient and vibrant nature of spoken French and in contrast to the success of French literature and cinema, Meschonnic finds the veneration of the French language, as it is celebrated by the *Académie* and its sympathisers, a rather sad party game: '*Le moralisme démoralise*' ('moralising demoralises'), he claims (192). Happily, these killjoys have never had very much influence on French literary production (however much their influence has been felt upon politics and in the State's bodies). '*Les passéistes n'ont jamais empêché l'avenir d'arriver. La fin du monde était prorogée*' ('The reactionaries were never able to prevent the future from coming on. The end of the world was adjourned') (Meschonnic 1997: 289). French culture resists the reactionary forces at work within it. Each generation sees defenders who rise up to condemn the corruption of the language, but the language lives on, despite (and often thanks to) the influence of new transgressions.

For this reason, Meschonnic sees his own attempt to reappraise the celebration of the French language not as an attack upon French, but as an attack upon the ancient and persistent conservatism of certain 'cultured spheres of society' (284). If the French language is in danger, if it is ill, then its illness is that celebration of a pure, fixed and inflexible model which has never and will never correspond to any living language. The pessimism and defeatism of the *Académie* is a symptom of that illness. Attacking the myth of the French language does nothing to undermine the heritage of French, it is simply a question of defending the French language against its defenders, Meschonnic claims (284). The *Académie* has always been willing to exclude most French people and the way they express themselves from the French language. But the French language has perpetuated itself as a language system thanks to that community and thanks to those writers whom the defenders of French have often viewed with such suspicion.


## NEW DEFENCES

It is now more than a decade since Meschonnic wrote his satirical account of the wide variety of arguments used to defend the French language, those dark and obscure celebrations of clarity. The French language has had to contend with a major upheaval in the organisation of world politics and global capitalism, and with the transformation of our way of handling information from the level of the individual company to the international organisation. Globalisation itself has tended to consolidate the position of English in international negotiations, be they at G8 meetings or encounters and projects involving the workers of global groups. French-owned multinationals such as the hotel giant, Accord, now use English as the working language for meetings and seminars. Europe itself has widened her frontiers with the entry of new members; and though France welcomed the entrance of those members, it should, however, be pointed out that the proliferation of national identities has tended to consolidate the position of English, while undermining the role of French as the *lingua franca* of European administration. Slovaks and Poles often speak English and German, and they learned Russian up until the 1990s as part of their school curriculum, but they rarely speak French. There is a cruel irony in this. For, in contrast to the representatives of the new Member States, English representatives in Brussels and Strasbourg have always been expected to master French (with German as an option). Increasingly, it is non-native speakers who insist on speaking English at European meetings, and this fact is largely responsible for the dramatic change in the prestige of French in Brussels.

The impact of information technology and the World Wide Web on language is somewhat more complicated. The Web was initially perceived as a menace by many who felt it would consolidate the position of English. And it has incontestably done so. But the vast amount of online material in other (often very rare) languages has enabled linguistic communities other than English-speaking ones to bind together in virtual communities. Finnish and Czech websites offer untold possibilities for cultural projects. Email and webcams allow members of fragmented diasporas to link up with fellow native speakers in ongoing everyday exchanges.

The associations and institutions which have taken on the role of promoting and defending the French language make ample use of the Internet. The *Ministère de la culture*, for example, has a site called the *Délégation générale à la langue française et aux langues de France* (General Delegation for the French language and for the languages of France). This oxymoronic title spells out the contradictory task which the French government has taken on: that is, to conjointly promote French as the language of the nation while supporting other languages spoken on French territory. This policy involves the launching of various projects which are advertised in the press and new media. The French Week (*Semaine de la langue française*), for example, now an annual event, is promoted using the wide-ranging means provided by the Internet.

How has this transformation in communication affected the representation of the French language? What metaphors are at work in framing the discourse of such sites? The language of sites promoting the French language is characterised by worn-out clichés, hand-me-down thoughts and prejudices. Their authors are characterised by the kind of intellectual laziness which Orwell condemned when he argued we should never make use of images where concrete language would do. On such sites, the French language is a 'treasure' (*trésor*), part of the French people's 'heritage' (*patrimoine*). Since language forms part of our identity, *Le Figaro* (2005) argued that 'Classical French was a common house in which everyone felt at home' ('*Le français classique était une maison commune dans laquelle tout le monde se sentait chez soi*'). Benoît Duteurtre, in the same article, complained that 'American English jargon contaminates the French language' ('*le jargon américano-anglais contamine la langue française*'). The 'house' becomes an 'organism'; and the organism is 'ill'. Contact with other languages perverts its purity and the great disease that menaces the French language is English. The parallel with racist rhetoric is striking; and at times, articles on both integration and the purity of the French language are found in the right-wing press next to one another. What the language of the French written and online press make clear is that metaphor is enrolled in the representation of language at three levels. French itself is metaphorically represented. Other languages entering into contact with French (for example, English) are represented in terms of metaphor, and the relationship between the two languages is metaphorical in nature. Advocates of exchange will extol linguistic borrowings as a form of 'cross-fertilisation', while protectionists like those quoted above revel in metaphors of perversion, contamination and decadence.

Elsewhere English is frequently perceived and presented in terms of an invading army. Interestingly, this rhetoric has had some success in spreading from France. In his successful popular account of the Spanish language, *Defensa apasionada del idioma español* (*A Passionate Defence of the Spanish Language*), Álex Grijelmo devotes no fewer than fifty-eight pages to his chapter entitled '*La invasión del inglés*' (153–211). Grijelmo also shows a predilection for organic and biological metaphors which not infrequently generate metaphors of contamination. Interestingly, the loaded rhetoric of the 'invasion of English' is occasionally adopted in English and ironically paraded, as in an article in *The Economist* (21 December 2002), 'The English invasion'. Such articles lack, however, the triumphant tone of celebration which characterise the defence of the French and Spanish languages. In the more sober English accounts, mutant forms of English expressions in Hindi and Italian are invariably regarded with an amused curiosity.

The degree of hostility shown towards the invader, English, in French articles, essays and books varies from author to author, but the rhetoric follows the set pattern laid out for those who adopt the metaphor of invasion with its metaphorical extensions: defence-attack, victory-defeat, penetration-violation, submission-revolt. At the time of the French revolution, the Gascon parish priest, Bernadau, quoted above, evoked the ancient hostility of the French to their English enemy when he spoke of the traces of English upon Gascon. Yet this hostility is deeply enrooted in the French language and culture as a whole. Consequently, in March 2008, in what was otherwise a balanced review of the languages which are studied in France, published in *Le Monde de l'Éducation*, the writers returned to the loaded metaphoric paradigms which held currency at the time of the revolution. English was considered '*indétrônable*' ('impossible to usurp from its throne'). English is a king, but interestingly it does not resemble those glorious kings of France's past. English represents the old order, the King against whom the French revolution struggles in order to liberate the world and guide it towards the future and towards progress.

These one-sided accounts of English and French should not be allowed to eclipse other more ambivalent feelings towards English, however. Feelings and ideas about language reflect the complexity of society, and it would be a gross misrepresentation to claim that the French people as a whole have a simple and antagonistic relationship with the English language. Even claiming that the right-wing press is anti-English (as the article from *Le Figaro* might lead us to conclude) would be misinformed. On the contrary, magazines like *Capital* and *L'Entreprise* revel in anglicisms derived from the spheres of management and commerce, and, on the whole, they promote the neo-liberal vision of the global economy that the American right has embraced. Among the most pro-American French-speakers are those executives who have spent several years either in the USA or in international companies and who return to France as converts to the global economy. Such converts seek to impose upon their French colleagues a whole range of American expressions and badly translated concepts which they have assimilated while abroad. Ironically, these converts probably contribute to anti-American feeling as much as Americans themselves, if not more. A parallel in British culture would be those hosts of cheese and wine parties who affect a love of French culture and slip French expressions into their conversations. Since this parading of French culture is often carried out in a condescending and pretentious manner, it often does little to endear the French to most English-speakers.

In contrast to the defenders of the French language, the global executives who convert to the American worldview form only one group of people in France whose linguistic attitudes are not reflected in the discourse and the metaphors of defence. But there are many others: teenagers and young people for at least two generations have borrowed and adapted words and expressions from English, though after a generation it often becomes hard to tell which expressions should now be considered as 'French' and which have been borrowed (see Rey-Debove and Gagnon's *Dictionnaire des anglicismes*, 1980). Contemporary French-speakers are also constantly innovating upon and experimenting with the English expressions they borrow: *Je speed* ('I'm stressed out' or 'I can't calm down') is derived from English but has no direct equivalent in English. Other words such as *black*, are used in French to avoid connotations associated with *noir*, when speaking about people of colour. French pop groups also show little resistance to English and often adopt the language for their songs for reasons of rhythm and melody as much as fashion.

Of course, the *Académie* and *Le Figaro* would have us believe that 'uncultured' businessmen and teenagers can be expected to know no better. In general, such groups are portrayed as the barbarians from whom French-lovers are trying to save their culture. The guardians of culture look for 'remedies' (*Le Figaro* 2005) while these groups encourage corruption and contamination of the pure language. The defenders are, however, labouring under a sad misconception. While young people show an expressive vitality in their slang and in their songs, in the way they adopt and adapt linguistic resources which come from English and other languages, and while businessmen and IT engineers use newly adopted commercial, financial and technical terms with an expert precision of which the layman is incapable, the style of language used by defenders of French is, on the whole, remarkable for its lack of originality, precision or accuracy. This is the language of prejudice: and prejudice prefers those comfortable armchairs, received ideas, to the uncomfortable truth of complex reality. *Le Figaro* waxes nostalgic about the lost unity of past centuries, the 'house' in which each inhabitant found his or her home and knew his or her place, but in doing so it brushes to one side the multilingual past of France and refuses to acknowledge the harsh policies of linguistic repression used to crush minority languages and dialects at school, in the French administration and, most of all, in the French army.

This language of prejudice is on the whole rather rare in linguistic literature in France. Defence is a policy, and policies are political. The defenders have therefore sought to impose their ideas upon politicians and to propagate their ideas (or rather keep them alive) in articles published in the media and on the Internet, or in books intended for a wide audience comprising mainly teachers or other educated readers. The ignorance paraded in such literature is often its most remarkable quality. The essay by Dominque Noguez, '*C comme une crise du français?*' ('C as in the crisis of French?') (2000), for example, is a case in point: Noguez is armed with a bibliography of two authors who published their works in 1928 and 1973. The latter, Étiemble, wrote a witty, tongue-in-cheek account of the death of French. Sadly, as is the case with many humourists, Étiemble's fans have none of his sense of humour. Noguez takes the death of French very seriously. She seems to see her lack of research as no obstacle to giving her diagnosis as to the demise of French: she contents herself with remarks concerning advertising billboards and ruminations on the development of the language and culture of France. The metaphors she recycles, though predictably hackneyed, are alarmist. Noguez appears to believe that over-statement can compensate for 'underthinking'. 'The French language is the victim of treachery. And all of us [French-speakers] are more or less to blame for it,' she announces (Noguez 2000: 39). French is a cherished possession and French people are being robbed of it. French is a dear one who commits suicide (42). Noguez transforms the defence of French into a 'cultural war' ('*guerre culturelle*') (47) and, taking up a favourite metaphoric narrative of contemporary defenders of French, she warns the English and the Americans that 'every Goliath one day meets his David' (47). Noguez seems exhausted by the effort of contemplating the cultural war and the demise of her language-culture, however, and she resigns herself to the cruel fate awaiting French and French-speakers: '*il n'y a rien à faire qu'à accepter cette dépossession et cette suicide*' ('there is nothing left to do but to accept this theft and this suicide') (47).

Other defenders are less apathetic, and eagerly seek allies. Defenders have a special weakness for foreigners when it comes to celebrating French. Bernard Pivot's book programme *Bouillon de Culture*, a successful late-evening show which was broadcast till the end of the 1990s, was remarkable for inviting Francophile English authors. The authors invited spent little time speaking

of their books but were politely prodded into expressing their
adoration of French wine, the French countryside and, of course,
French literature. In the same vein, Julia Kristeva, the prestigious Bulgarian psychoanalyst and literary theorist, was invited to
express her feelings about French in the same Flammarion edition
which published Noguez's impressions on the so-called 'crisis'
of the French language. Kristeva does, it must be admitted, have
a certain stylistic flair, and makes some attempt to reformulate
the metaphorical paradigms on which her account of the French
language is based. Language, she posits, is like 'skin': a second language becomes a 'skin-graft'. The question then becomes, will the
graft take? (Kristeva 2000: 66). The mother tongue later becomes
water for Kristeva (66). This is somewhat more predictable for
the psychoanalyst, equipped with images of the liquid womb of
our first personality-forming experiences. The mother tongue is
simultaneously a body, but Kristeva 'murders' her metaphor: the
French education she received in Bulgaria followed by her exile
from her homeland, she tells us, 'ended up transforming that old
body into a dead one' ('*a fini par cadavériser ce vieux corps*') (67).
Links to language are links to land and to blood, Kristeva goes on
to tell us (68). This is conventional enough, but borders upon the
mixed metaphor. Can we be 'enrooted' in blood? Kristeva seems to
suggest that exiles are 'uprooted from language and blood' ('*enrac-
inés dans aucun langage ni aucun sang*') (68). With a feminist twist
to Freud's claim that all men crave to kill their fathers, Kristeva
claims that 'there is a kind of matricide in abandoning your native
tongue' ('*il y a du matricide dans l'abandon d'une langue natale*') (69).
Kristeva is not writing an academic article, of course, it must be
admitted: she is offering us a very personal essay. That essay does,
however, tend to indulge in a dubious literary style: '*la souffrance
me revient, Bulgarie, ma souffrance*'(69) reads like a tacky rewrite
of Françoise Sagan's *Bonjour Tristesse*, which was no doubt the
reading of Kristeva's adolescence in her French school in Bulgaria.

On the whole, when Kristeva moves beyond the personal experience of emotional trauma linked to moving from one language to
another and considers the French language in itself, she returns
to the traditional clichés which have remained in currency over
the past four hundred years. French represents clarity. Bulgarian

represents the 'Black Sea of passions': '*La clarté logique du français, l'impeccable précision du vocabulaire, la netteté de la grammaire séduisent mon esprit de rigueur et impriment – non sans mal – une droiture à ma complicité avec la mer noire des passions*' ('The logical clarity of French, the impeccable precision of its vocabulary and the clear-cut nature of its grammar attract my rigorous mind and impress – not without difficulty – a form of rectitude upon my complicity with the Black Sea of passions') (69). France is the enlightenment. But what, then, is Kristeva's Bulgaria? The antithesis of the enlightenment? If it exists, her Bulgarian will certainly have difficulty in finding its place in the European Union. If we to are believe her account of her mother tongue, Bulgarian, it is so incapable of semantic distinctions, lexical precision and grammatical correctness that misunderstandings must be the rule and not the exception in that language. Of the Bulgarians I have been able to consult on these questions, not a single one concurred with Kristeva's representation of her mother tongue. Is it possible, then, that Kristeva has allowed her mother tongue to die within her, and has entirely lost touch with it? It would certainly seem that, in abandoning it, her consciousness has taken root in another tradition. From this short account, it would appear that Kristeva thinks and feels about her adopted language and mother tongue with the conceptual frameworks of clarity, order and reason, the fundamental paradigms used to defend *la langue française*.

A far more interesting view of French is to be found in the work of the French-speaking Algerian academic, Mohamed Benrabah. This writer turns on its head the party game played by foreigners like Kristeva who render homage to French by endorsing the clichés of that language's supposed clarity. Benrabah is certainly not interested in attacking French, however: he is interested in tracing the representation of French in Algeria. Benrabah argues that since the 1960s, the Algerian government (which was elected after the declaration of independence on 1 July 1962) has been promoting an anti-French campaign. This forms part of the post-colonial trauma which Algerians have undergone, Benrabah explains in his book, *Language and Power in Algeria: the History of a Linguistic Trauma (Langue et pouvoir en Algérie: histoire d'un traumatisme linguistique)* (1999).

The French revolution endorsed universal ideals and proposed a universal project which was supposed to provide for or promote the respect of each and every man, each and every citizen. Evidently, colonisation would set up a form of government and social order which was antithetic to this fundamental egalitarianism. Benrabah explains that British colonisers were content to pillage, exploit, and set up commercial structures and industries designed to profit themselves. Nevertheless, they did, on the whole, show either tolerance or indifference to the culture and religious practices of the indigenous population. The French revolution, on the other hand, made such an option inconceivable. The idealism which inspired French republicanism and structured its institutions and its bureaucracy made it necessary to convert those the French colonisers reigned over. Those who were oppressed had to be 'liberated': which meant turning them into French citizens (albeit second-class citizens). The government in Paris was a centralised project, a centre which enlarged its sphere (or circumference) of influence throughout France and throughout its colonies. The conversion of the indigenous population often involved destroying schools and cultural and religious establishments, and the attempt to eradicate local customs. Most of all, it involved converting those classes of the indigenous population which were amenable to the French colonial powers, those classes whose members who could take on a role in the administration of the colony. The cultural oppressors of the Algerians became the Algerians themselves: those, at least, who had adopted the French culture.

The revolt against that culture inevitably led to a strong anti-French feeling, and identity movements focused upon eradicating the influence of that French culture which had helped destroy the indigenous culture and had deprived the Algerian people of their identity. But what was that identity? Benrabah explains that the post-colonial government launched itself into a radical promotion of the Arabic culture which was to replace the French colonial influence. There were three fundamental objections to this policy. Firstly, France had undeniably made an enormous impact upon the Algerian culture, and had helped structure and maintain the modern institutions of its society. Secondly, many

Algerians are Berbers who speak Kabyle not Arabic. And thirdly, those who do speak Arabic, speak their own very particular version of Algerian Arabic which is related to, but very distinct from, the so-called 'pure Arabic' which is spoken in Saudi Arabia, Lebanon and Syria. In an article entitled '*The Multilingual School in Algeria: An example of a negative educational policy*' ('*Éducation et plurilinguisme en Algérie: un example de politique linguistique educative "negative"*') (2002), Benrabah explains the catastrophe of linguistic planning and the horrific effects it has had in disrupting the socialisation of Algerian children. Those children found themselves deprived of their language in education, deprived of a linguistic context in which they could learn to study successfully, deprived of the means of constructing together their identity, an identity which would enable them to take their place in society and to find a job.

Benrabah's study is interesting from our point of view of metaphor for four reasons. Firstly, it helps explain the rhetoric of the Algerian government which has promoted the purity of the Arabic language by appropriating the metaphoric resources used by elites to defend the superiority and purity of French. Secondly, analysing the metaphoric representation of the rhetoric of 'Arabisation' allows us to understand how French has been denigrated and attributed the role that certain French people have attributed to English: that of a 'corrupting influence', the language of power and oppression, the language which 'wipes out' culture and refuses to tolerate otherness. Thirdly, Benrabah's study shows how the elite of the post-colonial administration, from its very beginnings, acted duplicitously in disseminating this anti-French propaganda in order to secure its own power by representing itself as the force of liberation, while that elite continues to send its children to French bilingual schools. Finally, Benrabah's study shows that the elite governing Algeria today knows just as well as Kristeva how to adopt the clichés which certain French people entertain in flattering themselves as to the uniqueness of their culture and the treasure of their language. With a shameless display of double-speak (which was no doubt given little publicity at home), the Algerian President Bouteflika pandered to the ministers of the *Assemblée nationale* in the following terms:

| | |
|---|---|
| La langue française et la haute culture qu'elle véhicule restent pour l'Algérie, des acquis importants et précieux que la réhabilitation de l'arabe, notre langue nationale, ne saurait frapper d'ostracisme. C'est là une richesse à même de féconder notre propre culture. | The French language and the high culture it brings with it, remain for Algeria important and precious possessions which the restoration of our national language, Arabic, will not ostracise from us. It is one of the riches that is able to fertilise our own culture. (*Le Monde*, 17 July 2000, qtd in Benrabah 2002: 79, my translation) |

While a generation of young Algerians try to navigate their way through a barrage of racist rhetoric which demonises the contamination of Arabic's purity by foreign languages and denounces the influence of European countries on North African society, and while their ignorance of the language of their former colonisers, French, denies them access to employment at a professional level, the Algerian elite stigmatises French at home while continuing to sing the praises of French abroad, using the usual metaphors and singing the same tune they learned from their colonisers. In this way, for more than forty years, the powers governing the country have been building a linguistic wall between its people and the colonial power which shaped its past and which plays an essential role in its post-colonial economy. French ministers were no doubt delighted to hear of the multilingual school which the Algerian President Bouteflika boasted would soon be opened in Algeria, but, as Benrabah explained, this school merely represented an advertising campaign for those abroad while it will function as a mechanism for consolidating social segregation at home.

## HAGÈGE'S GARDEN

One of the most respected and most erudite contemporary defenders of the French language, Claude Hagège, became a member of the *Académie française* in 2007. Taking his place in the *Académie* was a logical step for Hagège: he had already been awarded the *Prix de l'Académie* for his book *Man of Speech* (*L'homme de paroles*) published in 1985, and in 1995 he had won the prize of the *Chevalier de l'Ordre des Arts et des Lettres*, awarded by the research institute of the French government, the CNRS. His work shows a vast erudition and his style is remarkable for its prolific (but disconcertingly naïve) use of metaphor when it comes to describing language. Metaphors, for Hagège, are not simply a means of comparison, they are the tools for dissecting the 'body' of language. This introduces one of the central metaphors at work in Hagège's work: a language is a living thing: '*Les langues humaines naissent, se développent et meurent. À cet égard, elles possèdent des caractéristiques qui les apparentent aux espèces vivantes*' ('Human languages are born, they develop and they die. In this respect, they possess the [same] characteristics as other living species') (Hagège 2006: 235, my translation). The living organism is more than a simple analogy. This rhetoric frames Hagège's thought on language and furnishes him with the titles for his books, *The Breath of Language* (*Le souffle de la langue*, 1992) and *Stop Language Death* (*Halte à la mort des langues*, 2000). For Hungarians, their mother tongue is 'a breath that defies death', Hagège claims (2000: 21). Language is a 'vital principle', a 'principle of life' ('*principe vital*') (21). We invest our cultural inheritance in language. If that language is a 'treasure' – as Hagège claims – (19), then this is because language can act as a 'storage place' for depositing our culture and our identity. The celebration of language's cycle of life continues in Hagège's dithyrambic exposition of grammar and word-formation: newly coined words form part of 'the rich crops of neologisms' ('*les riches moissons de la néologie*') (56).

Hagège's celebration of the French language forms part of his celebration of language as a human faculty. It is not simply the pretext used to justify ranting against English. Hagège, unlike the journalists quoted in the previous section, does not revel in resentment, and he is anything but prejudiced. Hagège is resolutely broad-minded, and his enthusiasm for other languages is clearly sincere. His enthusiasm does tend to attach itself to rather arbitrary paramours, however: at times, dead and dying languages are almost Christ-like for Hagège. If they die, we need not despair, he claims, for like Hebrew, those languages can be 'resurrected'. The metaphorical lyricism of Hagège goes far beyond the images of flowering and cross-fertilisation found commonly in the rhetoric of specialists of translation theory and linguistics. Hagège embraces the rhetoric of ecology and calls himself an *ecolinguiste*.

'Ecolinguistics' is more than a mere fashionable posture. Hagège is taking a position when he claims linguistic diversity is necessary for life. His position rests upon a reasoned argument, and it is at this juncture that the danger of English is introduced into Hagège's model. Uniformity (that is, the domination of the world by English, one single worldview) will lead to barrenness and sterility, he argues. The diversity of insects and the diversity of languages fill Hagège full of wonder (2000: 33). And it is Creation, the intelligent, self-orchestrating plan of Nature, that must be preserved in linguistic diversity.

Hagège is no botanist. On the contrary, he takes pains to disassociate his arguments from those of Schleicher, the German nineteenth-century botanist-linguist who adapted Darwin's ideas on language to invent his philosophy of linguistic determinism and the natural selection of those languages which were 'fittest for survival' (Hagège 2000: 28–34). The 'combat' metaphor does, nonetheless, figure in Hagège's reflection on the interaction between languages. The metaphor was used as the basis to his book, *Le français: histoire d'un combat* (1996) and was taken up ten years later by him in another book, *Combat pour le français: au nom de la diversité des langues et des cultures* (2006). But increasingly, Hagège sees this combat as a combat against the domination of English, while we can only suppose that the logic of the German linguist, Schleicher, would have forced him to concede that the success of English was the outcome of an inherently healthy process of natural selection.

Hagège's combat, on the other hand, is twofold. He takes up the defence of the underdog. Interestingly, he presents French as the defender of diversity and the defender of all other minority languages. French, in Hagège's combat, becomes a rallying point. Clearly, what makes French worthy of its prestige throughout the world is that it can incarnate the combat of other less fortunate, less successful languages. French becomes, in Hagège's paradigm, the 'top dog' among underdogs.

The role of French is historically determined. French, he argues in the conclusion to his 1996 work, 'has known a dazzling past' ('*un passé éclatant*') (1996: 167). And this means it 'is invested with a vocation: to testify in favour of all other languages' (167). This will, Hagège claims, enable French 'to keep its rank (*'conserver son rang'*) in the contemporary world' (167).

In other words, it is because it represents an alternative to English, that the speakers of less privileged and less prestigious languages can identify with the privilege and prestige of French. This in itself, for Hagège, justifies the status of French as an important world language. At the same time, though French has been displaced from the central role which Rivarol claimed for it as the universal language by the arrival of Global English, that very displacement has taught French-speakers a certain humility which allows them to identify with the speakers of endangered languages and allows them to represent them in their struggle against the dominance of one single global language. Why French-speakers should be more apt for this linguistic empathy than Hungarians or Navajo Indians is left unexplained.

This flimsy argument runs throughout Hagège's work, and the metaphors he employs are the cogs and spokes used to maintain a dynamic opposition, a combat between the mechanical forces of machinery imposing uniformity, and the dynamic organic principle of Life itself, which French and linguistic diversity are supposed to represent. These are the implicit suppositions upon which Hagège's metaphoric rhetoric reposes; and to what extent he is aware of the implications of his arguments is unclear. The charm of his arguments works at a subliminal, non-rational level, and he himself is perhaps carried away with and duped by his own lyricism. English, in his paradigm, represents a force for uniformity which constitutes a threat to that creativity which is essential to life, and Hagège relies on his readers having a gut reaction to the reduction of choice which comes with uniformity. The languages of the world, in contrast, are laid out in all their diversity for the reader to admire.

There is a certain degree of bad faith at work here. There is no indication that the reader is supposed to become interested in these languages themselves, or that he or she should make any attempt to learn them. These languages are showcase specimens. Hagège is not a philologist who loves the literature of the language he studies. He is a modern linguist who limits himself to making fairly superficial comparisons of languages at a structural level, and he compares languages which for the most part he does not speak. In this, his project is radically different from the one Humboldt set out for himself (though Hagège does quote Humboldt in passing – 2000: 35). Humboldt, contrary to Hagège, was fascinated by the meaning of languages, by the worlds that each language system opened up to its linguistic community. What fuelled the energy of Humboldt's own philology was a striving to enter into foreign worldviews. Humboldt's struggle to come to terms with foreign languages was a twofold struggle, one which involved him in grappling with the language as an organ of understanding, and one which meant striving to perceive the way in which individuals take their place within their language by striking their roots into it, and formulating their own personal worldview. To distinguish between these different concepts of worldview, I have preferred to refer to the *personal world* of the individual who inhabits an ever-changing *world-perceiving* and *world-conceiving* which his mother tongue opens up for him. The interaction between world-perceiving and individual personal worlds does not find any place in Hagège's project, however.

Hagège's love of languages (albeit unquestionably sincere) pales by comparison with Humboldt's project of investigating worldviews. Hagège is a defender of languages and linguistic diversity. The emphasis on defence in his work begins in 1992, with his description of the French language's fight to assert itself in the face of Latin and other contestants in the nation-project which will engender *le français* as *langue nationale*. His rhetoric mutates, however, into an increasingly 'defensive combat' in 2006, when he makes France the hero of the underdogs in the face of the 'violence of neo-liberal mercantilism' represented by global commerce and Global English (2006: 239).

Metaphors once more shape and structure his argument. The influence of English is represented as 'oppression' and 'invasion'. French liberates, English enslaves. We have already noted this loaded metaphorical paradigm which sets English upon a throne only to imply that progress should bring about liberation from monarchy. Once more a Frenchman invites the world (and all people who are born equal) to rebel against domination and realise themselves. The sole prerequisite is that French be allowed to lead. French was of course the language of a colonial power and of slave traders, something Hagège would certainly not deny, but his rhetoric plays down the darker side to the influence of French throughout the world. French influence does not 'invade', as English does in Hagège's oeuvre. If, for example, French is represented as a king then it is the 'Sun-King', a *Roi–Soleil*, whose rays beam down upon the earth and stimulate growth. French is 'fertile'. French is on the side of Life. For Hagège, the rays of French continue to stimulate the cultural soil of Africa. The 'flourishing [*floraison*] of French on foreign territories' proves, Hagège argues, that there is no contradiction between the influence of French and the development of independent identities (1992: 118). He quotes Switzerland, Belgium and Canada as examples. Curiously, this involves Hagège in complex rhetorical gymnastics. On the one hand, he wishes to present himself as a champion of cultural difference, on the other, he is clearly nostalgic for the era of Rivarol, and refuses to abandon the project of 'universality'. This leads him to conclusions of a very precarious nature: cultivating other identities, he claims, 'has defined its universality [*universalité*]' for French (118). The new universal message which France has to offer the world is that of the example of 'an alternative model [to the] single instrument of communication which wipes out [*lamine*] their individualities' (by which he means Global English) (118).

Three elements must be disentangled in this rhetoric. French is invested with a vocation to save mankind. French can cultivate a New Order of bio-linguistic diversity. By accepting to endow French with this role, other languages can hope to keep themselves safe and preserve their identities.

What this strange argument comes down to in practice will be seen if we turn to Hagège's proposition for linguistic policy in Europe. Europe's role is twofold, Hagège argues in *The Breath of Language* (1992). Because it is multilingual, Europe can show the world that linguistic diversity is a viable model. Most of the countries of the world are multilingual, of course, but the dominant model in the world today is the English-speaking American model. Europe, as a strong geopolitical force, can, Hagège argues, act as a counterpoint. But it can only demonstrate the viability of linguistic diversity if all of the languages of Europe are protected. Hagège suggests therefore that all Europeans should master at least two languages. This is in fact a policy that the European Union has adopted. The two languages should not necessarily be English plus the mother tongue, however; Europeans should be encouraged to learn other languages also. Very rapidly, however, Hagège's ambitions for French transpire. He takes pains to avoid a head-on collision with English because that would be a fight French cannot possibly hope to win. He prefers to posit that there are three European languages which have a 'vocation' to fulfil in Europe, namely, English, German and French: English because of its global prestige, German because of its prestige in central Europe and French because of its importance in North Africa, Canada, Switzerland and Belgium. The celebration of diversity and the love of dying linguistic communities, expressed so eloquently in *Stop Language Death*, here takes on a rather limited and selective approach to preserving diversity. Europe is to become a trilingual model in which Spaniards, Czechs and Greeks are supposed to see their identity reflected in one of the three languages which call upon them to assemble themselves in their ranks. Portuguese or Polish businesspeople might find the idea of protecting and promoting the languages of all European nations a reasonable policy, but if that means they have to learn French while the French clearly have no intention of learning Polish or Portuguese, then they will understandably become impatient with French people who refuse to speak English at international meetings.

This brings us to the end of our short tour of policies regarding the defence of French. We have encountered representations of languages as the victims or oppressors, as rich treasure-houses of culture, as invaders and as Sun-Kings, fertilising foreign soil with their rays, as people committing suicide, as defiled feminine objects of veneration and as contaminated organisms. These are the analogies that are at work in the arguments used to direct the debate on the future of languages at the level of the classroom and at the level of international business and diplomatic negotiation. Metaphor shapes the thought that forms the basis of language policy in private enterprise and world governance. The incoherence of certain metaphors reveals an incapacity or a refusal to think clearly. In the case of French, there is probably a certain strategy at work which linguists are loathe to avow when they seek to promote their own language while playing the defender of the underdogs. The underdogs, if by that we mean the Portuguese and the Poles, will be unlikely to heed their call in the Europe that is emerging.

Despite this seemingly obvious state of affairs, debate in France and at the European Union, over the past decade, has been framed in terms of two incompatible ideals, promoting a workable multilingual model based on a limited number of languages while promoting each and every minority language. Pierre Encrevé (2007) points out the absurdity of a policy which leads to France being forced to advocate the respect for and promotion of seventy-five different languages on its territory throughout the world. Abram de Swaan (2007), a Dutchman, regards the European cultural contradiction with irony. He argues that the policy of protectionism is fuelled by a sentimental bad faith:

> The European Commission is not in a position to launch a debate on the question of languages in the European Union. If it did so, France would insist upon its privileged position being maintained, Germany would demand equal rights, Spain would refuse to be pushed aside, as would Italy. Holland would thereby be forced to defend its own linguistic interests. Thus, though the Commission is supposed to be promoting a policy of linguistic equality, it has had no influence because the impact of the policy has been (as expected) nil. And by its lack of action, the Commission has contributed to the consolidation of the situation of English as the sole outlet for linguistic confusion. (de Swaan 2007: 94, my translation)

If English is indeed left to be 'the sole outlet for linguistic confusion,' then it is unlikely that Hagège's metaphors will be those imposed upon the developing consciousness of the European imagination. So what metaphors will shape that imagination?

## GLOBAL ENGLISH

If Rivarol's celebration of the universality of the French language continues to inspire a certain nostalgic tradition in French thought today, it is partly because of the charmingly effervescent style of the lyricism he used to celebrate his mother tongue. Rivarol was convinced his language could and would enlighten the world, and that conviction gave wings to his imagination. He may have been concocting a cocktail of clichés and received ideas, but he did it with a certain panache and elegance which made him a success in the salons of Paris and which won him fame in foreign parts, as in the intellectual circles of Prussia. Consequently, in gloomier times, those people depressed by the present state of the French language (or rather, by their own pessimistic estimate of it) tend to hark back to Rivarol and yearn for the times which fired his imagination.

Given the seemingly unstoppable spread of English throughout the world, we might have expected from English-speakers a triumphant celebration of the uniqueness and the superiority of the English language. Such a style of rhetoric can be found, but it does, however, appear to be rather rare. Why is that? The less flattering answer to that question is that for most English-speakers, other languages hardly seem to exist at all. The complacency with which most English and American people avoid or reject language-learning is legendary. Our laziness leads to an inevitable naïveté: or, to put it more bluntly, a gross ignorance. Most English-speakers find it hard to grasp that speakers of other language conceive of things differently from them. In this, they are not alone. Indeed, many thinkers have shared their indifference, and even Aristotle seems to have believed that different languages were simply different lists of words used to designate the same things. The idea of language playing a role in concept-formulation was foreign to Aristotle (Trabant 1992). It is no doubt because this very attitude is so widespread that English thinkers who are interested in the worldview question are so few.

If the strategy of championing English is rare, it is partly because championing one language implicitly recognises competition, and alternatives. For many English-speakers, the idea of other languages representing an alternative and even a superior mode of communication is all but inconceivable, precisely because we take so little notice of other languages. Consequently, even in the more 'enlightened' discourse of specialists, it is rare to hear English-speaking linguists trumpeting the genius of English as a superior framework for understanding the world. So what discourse will such linguists use in order to discuss the spread of English? What metaphors will frame and structure their thinking and the expression of that thought in English?

David Crystal, the famous linguist and editor of the remarkably user-friendly *Cambridge Encyclopaedia of Language* (1997), takes up the task of describing the 'success' of English as a world language. His is only one of many accounts, but it is an interesting example for our study of metaphor. The importance of Crystal's influence both as a linguist and as the author of his encyclopaedia means that the language he uses is likely to influence students and scholars for at least the next generation. Crystal has the same breadth of knowledge as Hagège and shares his curiosity for languages in all their diversity. Indeed, as we shall see in the following part of this chapter, Crystal takes up the ecolinguistics quest of saving endangered languages from 'language death'. This campaign will tug his language and his metaphors in opposite directions. On the one hand, he is tempted to celebrate the success of English, and on the other, he militates to alert the world as to the danger of world languages like English which are encroaching upon other cultures and inadvertently menacing them.

Crystal's sensitivity for other languages was cultivated by his bilingual childhood. Crystal, it must be remembered, is not English. Though born in Northern Ireland, he grew up in Holyhead in Wales before moving to Liverpool. And he was engaged in promoting the Welsh language during the 1960s and 1970s. Recently, he has channelled the same enthusiasm he showed for protecting and promoting Welsh into his crusade to save disappearing languages. This makes him far less inclined to indulge in self-affirming clichés which have seduced the speakers of other dominant languages. 'Why does a language become global?' Crystal asks (2003: 7–10). His answer to this is down-to-earth and pragmatic: power:

A language has traditionally become an international language for one chief reason: the power of its people – especially their political and military power. The explanation is the same throughout history. Why did Greek become a language of international communication in the Middle East over 2,000 years ago? Not because of the intellects of Plato and Aristotle: the answer lies in the swords and spears wielded by the armies of Alexander the Great. Why did Latin become so well known throughout Europe? Ask the legions of the Roman Empire. Why did Arabic come to be spoken so widely across northern Africa and the Middle East? Follow the spread of Islam, carried along by the force of the Moorish armies from the eighth century. Why did Spanish, Portuguese, and French find their way into the Americas, Africa and the Far East? Study the colonial policies of the Renaissance kings and queens, and the way these policies were ruthlessly implemented by armies and navies all over the world. (Crystal 2000: 9)

The tone of such language has the taste of most post-colonial discourse: it is relentless in rejecting idealistic and romantic accounts of the spread of language and culture. The self-congratulating praise of the culture of the victors or the celebration of the language of the ruling elite have no place in Crystal's account of the spread of languages. Alexander remains 'Great' in title only, in Crystal's account, and Crystal clearly attributes little 'greatness' to Alexander. Invaders are believed to be tyrants, and all power is 'ruthless' in post-colonial accounts such as Crystal's. In the same way, Crystal asks us to concede that if English has become an international language, it is principally because of its empire. Its power and prestige also came about through the 'growth of competitive industry and [he adds] business brought an explosion of international marketing and advertising [. . .] Technology, chiefly in the form of movies and records, fuelled new mass entertainment industries which had a worldwide impact' (Crystal 2000: 10). All of this has tended to consolidate the power of English throughout the world.

This is Crystal's staunch reply to those tempted to formulate arguments similar to those adopted by the promoters of the French language:

It is quite common to hear people claim that a language is a paragon, on account of its perceived aesthetic qualities, clarity of expression, literary power, or religious standing. Hebrew, Greek, Latin, Arabic and French are among those which at various times have been lauded in such terms, and English is no exception. (7)

The most common advantage claimed for English is its supposed simplicity, since it has no genders and has retained only some rudimentary remnants of the declination system it inherited from Old English, preserving the accusative and the dative. Crystal hastens to reveal such arguments for the misconceptions they unquestionably are: languages such as French, Latin, Russian, Spanish, Greek and Arabic found their genders no obstacles to their dissemination, and the consolidation of their power at different times throughout history (10).

There is an implicit pragmatism in Crystal's thought, though. If English has become a global language, it is also because it serves a useful purpose. This begins as a question. English-speakers are invited to consider on page 12 of his *English as a Global Language* (2003): 'The prospect that a lingua franca might be needed for the **whole** world is something which has emerged strongly only in the twentieth century.' But a page later, it is already an affirmation: 'The need of a global language is particularly appreciated by the international academic and business communities, and it is here that the adoption of a single lingua franca is most in evidence.' The reality of Internet exchanges between physicists which are conducted in English is, to Crystal's mind, a celebration of the encounter of humans from around the globe. But the necessity of speaking English is the very fact that French linguists such as Hagège resent, the necessity feared by many academics who not only feel uncertain as to their ability to express themselves in English, but who also believe the specific language-bound nature of their thought will be deformed by translation into what is often called 'Globish' (*globalais* in the French term advanced by Trabant 2007: 67).

Crystal is resolutely more optimistic: English serves a need. Globalisation engenders exchange and people will naturally gravitate to one mode of communication. Crystal sees this as a natural step. Here he is clearly 'selling' English to his audience. The consumers of English 'appreciate' the product, Crystal likes to claim. Others, like Hagège, see this 'consumption' of English as a constraint. These differing perceptions of the influence of English reflect the respective conceptual frameworks which exist in different cultures and their languages. While France sees itself, its culture and its language in terms of the centralist policy upon which its government administration is based, English culture was already fragmented throughout the world with bases in America and elsewhere when the English came to gain great status as imperialists. Consequently, in our culture we say that English 'spreads', and globalisation is understood as an extension of this process of cultural spreading. This process seems perfectly natural and legitimate to the English-speaker. French-speakers, however, perceive this 'spreading' in terms of 'penetration'. English 'invades' French: globalisation 'invades' France. Our culture sees itself as part of one great wave, and in translating English, many cultures (the Czechs, for example) often adopt the metaphor of 'spreading'. French people, on the other hand, tend to see France's relationship with the English language and with the world of global commerce in terms of rivalry. This posits a relationship between France and the world which 'excludes' France from the world. The 'world', which is expulsed from the imaginary domain of the French, returns to encroach upon the citadel. France is 'menaced' (*menacée*) by globalisation. A similar paradigm is at work in much of the demagogic anti-European popular press in Britain which conceives of Britain as being 'a part of' Europe while positing it as somehow standing 'apart from' Europe. This fundamental contradiction is pervasive in media discourse in which Britain (and most of all England) is portrayed as wishing to take its place in Europe though it perceives Europe ambivalently as a force seeking to enslave it.

Those who worry about the influence of English are not without their arguments. Undeniably, English has been encroaching on different spheres of life and work in other countries in recent decades. Crystal, for his part, is highly critical of the complacency of English-speakers when it comes to language-learning (2003: 17–19), and he underlines that this tendency is growing. In one European Business Survey carried out in 1996, 38 per

cent of British businesses had an executive who could negotiate
in at least one other language. By 2002, this figure had fallen to
29 per cent (19). In other words, the more effort speakers of other
languages make, the less effort English-speakers make. Many
English-speakers, Crystal affirms, feel that one language is sufficient. He also affirms that there 'is no shortage of mother tongue
English-speakers who believe in an evolutionary view of language'
(15). As he puts it, many English-speakers espouse the philosophy,
'let the fittest survive, and if the fittest happens to be English, then
so be it' (15). Such people would seem to be reviving the linguistic
determinism espoused by the German nineteenth-century linguist,
Schleicher.

Is there a parallel here with the championing of French? There
is one obvious difference between the fate of English in the twentieth and twenty-first centuries, and French in the eighteenth and
nineteenth centuries: the prejudice of the supposed superiority of
English has never been enshrined in state policy. Neither has it
come to be a cherished cliché of the intellectual elite. English has
no Academy or state-guided culture (though the BBC has always
aspired to play that role). On the whole, English and American
culture develops as a social force largely free of state-direction,
if by culture we mean music, literature, and the arts in general.
Culture is therefore left to the forces of popular taste and the
forces driving the market which are allowed to impose themselves.
Those forces, however, as far as the spread of English is concerned,
appear to be proving far more resilient and aggressive than the
French *Académie*: and those forces are often animated by a new
primitive version of 'linguistic Darwinism'.

Crystal is acutely aware of the potential danger English poses
for the maintenance of other languages, but, despite certain fundamental similarities, his analysis of the situation turns out to be
very different from that of Hagège. Crystal worries about the economic necessity of learning English, about its prestige which tends
to encourage communities to denigrate their own language and
culture, but ultimately, he concludes:

> it is the linguistic imperialism position which is naïve, disre-
> garding the complex realities of a world in which a historical

conception of power relations has to be seen alongside an emerging set of empowering relationships in which English has a new functional role, no longer associated with the political authority it once held. (25)

In other words, to Crystal's mind, English can no longer be considered the tool of a colonial power. Gandhi's words might have been meaningful in 1908 when he affirmed: 'To give millions a knowledge of English is to enslave them' (qtd in Crystal: 124). But to hold such an attitude today, Crystal obviously believes, would be absurdly anachronistic. Blaming English as the sole culprit for the 'disastrous effects of globalization on global diversity' (25) is, Crystal argues (taking the term from Lysandrou and Lysandrou) tantamount to 'linguistic luddism'.

This is a curious metaphor to adopt. Ned Ludd was an artisan who saw clearly that industrial progress and machines would render the skills of his profession obsolete. By standing in the way of industrialisation and smashing the machines that were brought in, Ludd became a symbol for all those who stand in the way of progress. The Lysandrous (and Crystal, who adopts their term) are clearly implying that English lies on the road to progress. Or does English pave the way to progress? Crystal's discourse suggests that English is to be both the destination and the shaping force that leads us to that destination. He in no way approves of a 'laissez-faire attitude' when it comes to linguistic planning and language protection, but he believes that English has 'a new functional role', and working towards that goal involves a certain idealism. He congratulates himself on being 'happy to be an idealist' (25), and looks forward to a world in which English will empower minorities. In a few simple steps, Crystal has turned Gandhi on his head and made English a liberating force for those enslaved by the global economy.

There is, however, nothing inevitable in the fate which is to befall English or the role it is capable of playing. Crystal's idealism is not blind, and he contradicts Sridath Ramphal, who ascribes the dominance of English to a fate that must be faced up to, when Ramphal laments: 'there is no retreat from English, no retreat from the English-speaking world' (qtd in Crystal: 27). Geopolitical forces could set events moving along a different course. The dominance of English 'will be an interesting battle 100 years from now', Crystal predicts (27). Yet in that battle, he invites linguists and all those who feel concerned by the crushing effects of globalisation upon cultural and linguistic diversity to see in English a force of empowerment. Their diversity might be saved by or through English.

Though Crystal contradicts the argument adopted by linguists such as Hagège who warn against the enslavement to a single global language, it turns out that this is less because of any fundamental difference in the logic of his argument, than because of an implicit rivalry. Crystal is usurping the role that Hagège wishes to reserve for French. In the new global world, Hagège is arguing for 'oligarchy' and invites the 'lesser nobles' to entrust their 'protection' to a 'ruling elite' made up of a 'few select representatives'. Crystal clearly has a 'one-man-state' in mind, 'kingship'. English, as a language, has moved beyond the national level and has become international; and in the international context, Crystal seems eager to crown English with the role of mediator. The arguments of 'disinterested neutrality' (often adopted by monarchs) are soon to follow in Crystal's account.

One obvious strength of English over French is the fact that its spread throughout the world has not been hindered by a centralist policy which protects the interests of one clearly defined group of people, and no single group has attempted to impose one single form of English upon other countries which adopt the language. This means that creoles and mutant forms of English, such as the Singlish of Singapore, have grown up naturally and have come to be used as a mode of communication which expresses the identity of those who use them.

This contrasts with the traditional French position which sees the influence of French culture as the imposition of one essential culture upon other civilisations, which are asked to recognise in the French model a transcendental, universal nature which has been identified in humanity by the French and perfected within their nation. Such a model depends upon the image of the circle. This cultural model assumes French is like a pebble tossed into a lake: its influence will ripple out in ever-expanding circular waves.

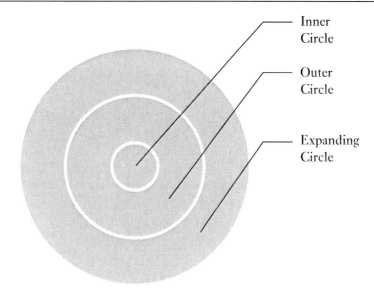

Figure 9.1 Kachru's three concentric circles of English-speakers

This conception is probably common to most imperial nations, but it has outlived France's colonial age. In contrast to this, the model advanced by many English linguists since it was introduced by Braj Kachru in 1988, is the model of English based upon three interacting circles (see Figure 9.1).

In Kachru's model, the 'inner circle' refers to the traditional bases of English (USA, UK, Ireland, Canada, Australia and New Zealand). In the 'outer circle', Kachru places those nations which ascribe to English an essential role as a 'second language' and have adopted it in the functioning of their chief institutions. In the 'expanding circle', Kachru places those nations which have no historical relationship with English as a colonial language, who do not need English to mediate between rival national languages (as in India), but which recognise the importance of English as an international language: obvious examples would be Russia and China. The essential difference between this model of language and the traditional colonial conception is that in Kachru's model, the ripples roll both ways. As the expanding circle expands, the influence of the English adopted in that circle will ultimately make its influence felt upon English as a whole and, consequently, upon the nucleus, the inner circle. In generations to come, the speech of Glaswegian teenagers and Tennessee factory workers is likely to be influenced by the English generated on the Internet by non-native speakers, just as American English has been encroaching upon the BBC's sphere of influence for the past two generations.

CNN International already employs non-native speakers as newscasters in anticipation of this trend. The world is invited to identify with English. English is global. English institutions are parading a rejection of the single nation-based conception of culture and language in favour of a celebration of a new synthesis of global diversity. And linguists are recognising this as the accurate reflection of a reality in an ongoing state of change. David Graddol, comparing the proportion of the world's population to have English as its first language in 1950 with expectations of the proportion in 2050, points out that it will probably fall from 8 per cent to 5 per cent (qtd in Crystal 2003: 69–70). In other words, though English is spreading, English-speakers as a group are dwindling, proportionally speaking.

Crystal affirms that English offers access to knowledge (80–3). Crystal is clearly arguing that English will become the vector of cultures, helping them to assume their identities in the world. There is an implicit inversion here: colonial powers appropriate the riches of a country. Yet the very nations who adopt English are portrayed as 'appropriating' the language. They are not being deprived of their language, they are receiving a rich, useful and politically empowering possession. Crystal is bordering upon the very thing he set out to avoid, celebrating English. In a telling slip, he adopts the rhetoric that trumpeted the glory of Victorian imperialism when he adapts for the English language the celebration of empire: 'English has become the language 'on which the sun never sets' (75). Crystal's stance turns out to be reactionary rather than radical: English is clearly being assimilated by him with the civilising process of enlightenment. Because of the diversity of English bases, and because English has been refashioned by so many cultures around the world, it has come to be perceived as a 'neutral language', he affirms (85). The desire of the Anglophone to flatter himself and his culture proves, in the end, irrepressible. Despite his efforts to resist championing English, Crystal cannot resist the short step, the change of a single syllable which turns which 'neutral' into 'natural':

> So many developments were taking place at the same time that we can only point to the emergence, by the end of the nineteenth century, of a climate of largely unspoken opinion which had made English the *natural* choice for progress. (Crystal 2003: 83, my emphasis)

'Natural' is one of the most obscure and complicated words in the English language. The 'nature' of nature is refashioned by each generation, and each group adopts 'natural' to justify the order which it imposes upon reality and upon the world. 'Nature' is always a cultural concept, whether it be the industrial capitalist conception of nature which encourages Darwin to describe bees as 'good workers' or a Social Darwinist conception which encourages Schleicher to see disappearing languages as being unfit for reproduction in the 'survival of the fittest'. Elites and racists will always see the dominance of their own interests as 'natural'. Linking 'nature' and 'progress' in this portrayal of the role of English is, therefore, far from innocent in the mouth of an English-speaking linguist.

The complexity and contradictory nature of ideas found in the work of thinkers who gain great recognition in their day is often inevitable. People such as Rivarol embody a certain kind of confusion which is constituted from the crystallisation of received opinion and contemporary currents in the thought of their day. Like Hagège, Crystal loves language and loves languages. He loves language change. Inevitably, therefore, his love of language extends to a celebration of the fragmentation of English into what Tom McArthur, the Scottish linguist, has called 'the English languages' (in his book by that name, 1998). Crystal sees a great charm in the creativity of these new forms of English with their hybrid forms of neologisms and constructions which could potentially enrich English for the inner circle of native speakers. Take, for example, 'car lifter' and 'luggage lifter' which are used in Pakistani English, and derived from 'shoplifter'. Crystal celebrates code-switching,

218 CASE STUDIES IN METAPHOR

the subtle process by which minorities shift cultural emphasis by moving from one language system to another in order to change the mood of the conversation or highlight some emotion or evoke certain connotations. He quotes the following exchange between two Kuala Lumpur women lawyers who speak 'Malenglish', the creolised form of English often spoken in Malaysia:

> CHANDRA: Lee Lian, you were saying you wanted to go shopping, *nak pergi tak*?
> LEE LIAN: Okay, okay, at about twelve, *can or not*?
> CHANDRA: *Can lah*, no problem *one*! My case is going to be adjourned anyway.
> (Crystal 2003: 166, my emphasis)

For Crystal, languages impose themselves upon the world because of the power their cultures gain as a result of historical, social, military and political conditions. Crystal obviously sees English as a power play with diverse players, however. He sees English as a 'battle' or a 'battleground' upon which actors who shape English will assert themselves in a world in which English will not enslave those people but 'empower' them. Ultimately, this battleground will be portrayed by Crystal with an aesthetic touch. English will be a 'lexical mosaic' (177), a concept which Crystal points out is not new. Crystal does not see English in terms of the American cultural model, that of the 'melting pot', but in terms of the Canadian model, the 'mosaic'. In adopting the rhetoric of the Canadians, though, he adopts that self-congratulating smugness with which the Canadians champion their own model. That very opposition serves to promote one system and stigmatise the other. While the Sun-King claimed, '*L'État, c'est moi*,' the slogan of the global era is 'We are Diversity!' English may be winning in the battle, but the democratic inclusion of diversity is not dissimilar to the French celebration of universalism more than a century ago. English-speakers certainly do not question their right to reign over that new global diversity, and it would be naïve to take the arguments used to promote English as a natural and practical solution at face value.

## ECOLINGUISTICS

Jugglers perfect the art of keeping five or six burning sticks up in the air at once, but Crystal already has his work cut out in juggling his two projects. Crystal wants to save endangered languages which are being crushed by institutions which have imposed and promoted the use of dominant languages, and which are subsequently being abandoned by their linguistic communities. At the same time, he wishes to celebrate English as the language of empowerment. The contradiction in these mutually exclusive desires creates a tension in Crystal's thought, but that very tension inspires a lyrical vein in his prose when he sets about defending diversity, a vein which had remained untapped in his celebration of English up until then. He claims:

> It is time to promote the new ecolinguistics – to echo an ancient saying, one which is full of colourful and wide-awake green ideas [. . .] It needs to be promoted urgently, furiously, because languages are dying as I write. Everyone should be concerned, because it is everyone's loss. (Crystal 2000: ix)

Languages are endangered in two different ways. A language can become extinct, but a language can also become impoverished. Indeed, we often find that one language (English, for example) has supplanted another language and excluded it from one particular sphere of life. Crystal quotes a Dutch senior project manager who claims that a language can be gradually displaced in the workplace and finally become excluded from that field of existence. Over time, it can become restricted to the language of intimacy, the language of the family. This process (in my own experience) follows a series of stages. In Switzerland or the Czech Republic, for example, the 'shrinking' of a language will begin with the adoption of English at work or as the language of teaching a specific subject (economics, for example). For a short time, the terms and concepts offered by the native language and the adopted language will exist side by side: that is, they will compete, and the contrast between two lexicons will inspire lively discussion and reflection. After less than a generation, however, the terms and concepts of the adopted language tend to displace the terms and concepts of the mother tongue, and those terms themselves become tainted: they come to seem outdated. Soon, young people who assimilate the foreign terms and concepts as the frameworks with which they think as they are educated will find the terms and concepts of their own language strange, foreign and somehow inappropriate. Soon those terms will fall into disuse and cease to resonate with the meanings they once designated. At this stage, a language-community is well on the way to believing one sphere of existence cannot be adequately expressed by their own language. Hagège (2000) and Trabant (2007) offer similar accounts of the way in which different facets of existence can be eclipsed and the way a language shrinks as a result.

For his part, Crystal (who three years previously had been extolling code-switching, in the first edition of *English as a Global Language* in 1997), argued in 2000 that speakers' switching from one language to another is the symptom of the fact that speakers clearly feel some languages are clearly better adapted for expressing certain aspects of life. Consequently, a dramatic increase in code-switching can reveal a potential danger for a language's future (2000: 22). Crystal's style is crystal clear in his presentation of the threat of language death. His entire book reads like a moving speech on the subject, a position structured by a series of rhetorical questions. Why should we care about language death? Because language expresses identity. Because languages contribute to the sum of human knowledge. But also because we need diversity.

These three arguments are designed to convince different groups. If a language is inextricable from a culture's identity, then that culture should, Crystal believes, protect its identity and preserve its language. In the context of post-colonial academia, such an argument clearly hopes to convince those with a conscience, those who believe that each cultural identity should be preserved. Though many people may prove indifferent to such a claim, Crystal is unlikely to find any real opposition to such a claim in the university today. There is an implicit problem here, though, which neither post-colonial critics nor Crystal are willing to face up to. Both the discourse of post-colonialism and Crystal's defence of other cultures are based, on the one hand, upon an idealisation of culture as the riches of a nation, the accumulation of knowledge, wisdom and art. Yet, at the same time, Crystal (like many writers of the post-colonial era) obviously espouses a cultural relativism which maintains that each culture is equally rich. This metaphorical framework has the inconvenience of implying that each culture is equally 'poor'. More importantly, the argument in no way offers an explanation as to why a people would be losing out if it dropped one culture and replaced it with another (equally rich) culture. Why should changing languages imply impoverishment if we accept the tenet of relativism?

Crystal is stating a truism when he argues that diversity increases the knowledge of humanity. Such a claim would appear to be unassailable. But Crystal embraces a certain idealism which gives a rosy tint to his account of the way in which humanity synthesises the knowledge of different cultures. The famous French anthropologist, Lévi-Strauss (1961), had a far more sceptical vision of the question. For Lévi-Strauss, cultures are able to adopt only what they can understand. For example, if a culture is mercantile, then it will adopt means of counting, storing and making money through trade if it encounters better modes and practices in this sphere of existence in another culture. In the same way, the relatively primitive techniques of our European farmers were transfigured by the knowledge gathered from the Aztec gardens when Cortez invaded Mexico. Yet, if Lévi-Strauss is right, we are only capable of appreciating, adopting and preserving what we understand. This means our own value judgements limit our ability to grasp what we encounter in other cultures. Ultimately, we are wholly incapable of grasping the true significance and value another culture invests in many things, practices, ideas and ideals. The value of such things is always structured in terms of the patterned relationships of meaning which bind the fabric of a culture together. As we adopt the peanut and the potato, we cast aside the 'pearls' that we (the invading swine) are incapable of appreciating and recognising for what they represent to the indigenous population. Inevitably, from the point of view of the vanquished, all invaders are barbarians.

Crystal shows a great sensitivity to language and a desire to acknowledge the otherness of foreign culture. Crystal is a linguist of great erudition and wide learning, a man of energy and conviction who is capable of transforming that energy and conviction into acts. At another level, though, he remains a pragmatic materialist, a product of our post-industrial capitalist culture. Language is a 'possession' for Crystal, a 'treasure'. In saving languages, Crystal seems to be drawing up a balance sheet. The world 'possesses' thousands of languages: should we stand aside, he seems to ask, and watch while the world is robbed of its rich store of resources? And yet, the very concept of 'possession' proves to be a dubious one when it comes to linguistic diversity. The earth can hardly be considered a person, and no one single person knows more than a handful of languages. So who knows these languages and cultures? Do we even know how many languages the world 'possesses'? Or how many languages are in peril? Nettle and Romaine, in their moving account of language death, are forced to admit they have no answer to this question: 'How much of the world's linguistic diversity is endangered? The honest answer at this stage is that we don't know precisely' (Nettle and Romaine 2000: 39). So what can be meant by the claim that humanity (or the world) is 'losing' languages? Ultimately, neither Crystal nor anyone else can be said to enjoy the great banquet of diversity that the hundreds of thousands of languages are supposed to represent.

Crystal extols the diversity of worldviews which linguistic diversity implies. But who is capable of entering fully into the profound variety of those alternative worldviews? Like Hagège, Crystal makes abundant use of the term 'world-view', a term he attributes to Humboldt in his encyclopaedia; but it is significant that he does not quote Humboldt in that encyclopaedia or in his book on Global English or in *Language Death*. In fact, Crystal's concept of 'world-view' is very much the vague concept found in everyday usage, one that can be attributed to neither Whorf nor Sapir but rather to that vulgarised catch-all concept, the 'Sapir–Whorf hypothesis'. Humboldt, on the other hand, was far closer to Lévi-Strauss, who claimed that we approach other cultures like trains that pass by us (1961: 44–5). Speeding along, in the opposite direction, we catch a glimpse of them, no more. Humboldt, for his part, claimed that even a detailed knowledge of a foreign language never allows us full entry into its worldview (*Weltansicht*). We cannot fully disengage ourselves from our own worldview and the prisms of its conceptual frameworks through which we understand the world. Our own 'world-perceiving' and 'world-conceiving' always shape our understanding of those modes of perception and conception we strive to enter into when we learn a foreign language.

Exponents of dominant languages, Hagège and Crystal are altogether more confident. They do not appear to doubt their capacity to enter into foreign worldviews and to save them from annihilation. The humility of Lévi-Strauss and Humboldt are absent in the arguments of Hagège and Crystal on language death. Though both are modern men, products of the post-colonial age, animated by a love of languages and a very solid erudition, ultimately, they both believe unconditionally in the march of progress. Mankind is moving towards one synthetic ideal in which knowledge from all cultures will be assimilated in a new order. Crystal sees no obstacle to our assimilating another culture and ultimately to our assimilating much of it into English, if that culture is given a chance to survive. This bears a close resemblance to the false representation of 'world culture' which Lévi-Strauss critiqued. The civilisation of the world (*civilisation mondiale*), Lévi-Strauss claimed, is not composed like the patchwork costume of the Harlequin (1961: 50). When we extract one aspect of a culture, as, for example, we adopt paper from the Chinese, we fail to grasp that these elements in and of themselves are less important than the ways in which each culture orders and groups them within its society. In the multiculture of globalisation, we take what we can use, and are indifferent to losing the significance which those newly acquired elements formerly held in the societies which invented them.

Crystal appears to believe in harmony and synthesis in social groups. The idea of different linguistic communities living side by side in ignorance of each other's ideas, ideals and concepts is wholly absent from Crystal's approach, though it is, in fact, the reality of most modern cities today. To adapt Lévi-Strauss's train metaphor, we might compare the interaction of the languages in the modern city to a city's bus network. Buses cross each other's paths, and at times follow one another for a block or two, but they soon lose sight of one another as they trundle off on their own routes. Speakers of different linguistic communities coexist with a large degree of indifference. Neither is the juxtaposition of languages that can be heard on the undergrounds of London, Paris or Prague anything new. The juxtaposition of linguistic communities has been the lot of humanity throughout the greater part of its existence: in fact, there are only a few periods and places in which monolingual cultures emerge. Consequently, we might conclude that cultures do not 'clash' but rather fit together and juxtapose themselves as necessity requires. To argue that this process creates one unified collective work of art, however, a 'mosaic', is merely wishful thinking. Foreigners and minorities can be added or withdrawn from the whole of society without a society falling to pieces or losing its overall sense of composition, if society can be said to have such a sense of itself. Mosaics and Harlequins' outfits are an entirely different matter.

There is an inherent positivism in Crystal's idealism. But what begins as a call to protect the worldviews of other languages is a project which soon transpires to be a call to assimilate other perspectives into English. For what other language system can Crystal have in mind for the debate on the future of the worldviews of other languages when he says: 'The context of this book demands a special focus on those languages which are most endangered, but the rhetoric of the present section requires that we adopt an appropriately universal viewpoint' (2000: 52)? This would seem to imply that all worldviews can be refashioned within the worldview of English, an idea which would have been inconceivable for Humboldt (and probably also for Lévi-Strauss). While French was already 'universal' for Rivarol, English, if its speakers prove broadminded enough, is capable of embracing the universe and all its points of view; so Crystal would seem to have us believe.

Sceptics among philologists and anthropologists will not hesitate to contest this argument. It is Crystal's third argument, however, which is the most questionable: we must protect dying languages because we need diversity (32). This is actually the first and foremost argument Crystal advances, and it underpins the whole rhetoric of his ecolinguistics. Like Hagège, Crystal becomes if not dogmatic, at least resolutely naïve, when he adopts the ecological metaphor with its framework of thought and the logic of its arguments: 'the arguments which support the need for biological diversity also apply to language', he tells us (32), and:

Increasing uniformity holds dangers for the long-term survival of the species [. . .] The need to maintain linguistic
diversity stands squarely on the shoulders of such arguments.
If diversity is a prerequisite for successful humanity, then the
preservation of linguistic diversity is essential, for language
lies at the heart of what it means to be human. (33–4)

What do such arguments mean? What are their consequences
for us, if we take Crystal at his word? Let us leave to one side the
curious phrase 'successful humanity'. What success and failure as a
species means is far from clear, and it is doubtful whether Crystal
as a cultural relativist would be able to point to any group which
incarnates the 'failure' of humanity. But is he really arguing that
our 'long-term survival' depends upon linguistic diversity? Let
us consider the heuristic potential of this analogy. If the hedges
of Britain are destroyed, the predators which live there will find it
difficult to find a habitat. Mice and rats upon which they prey will
multiply; this might in turn contribute to wiping out other species
which find themselves in competition with mice and rats. The
introduction of the rabbit and the cat to Australia with catastrophic
consequences for marsupials is widely documented. Because of the
nature of the food chain, species and plants interact and depend
upon one another. To touch one link in the chain will, therefore,
set off a 'chain reaction'. But is this so of languages? Will the
demise of Czech, for example, make a difference to Turkish? Hindi
now has the potential to become a major world language, but if it
was stopped in its tracks and the Hindi-speakers of the world were
subtracted from what Crystal likes to consider as the world's stock
of languages, would that endanger the future of German? Quoting
Russel H. Bernard, Crystal argues that 'Any reduction of language
diversity diminishes the adaptational strength of our species'
(34). Crystal bolsters this argument by quoting Geoff Pogson:
'Language diversity, like a gene pool, is essential for our species
to thrive . . . If we are to prosper, we need the cross-fertilisation
of thought that multilingualism gives us' (34). But is multilingualism likely to find itself in danger at any time in the near or distant
future? Cross-fertilisation has been celebrated by translators for
centuries, but translators had in mind the exchange of thoughts

and works between only a few different languages. The 600,000 languages said to be in existence today did not come into the equation. Besides, in contrast to the concept of cross-fertilisation by translation, the idea of exchange Crystal and Hagège have in mind seems obscure, if not superficial. Whether more than a few dozen languages do actually influence a single linguistic community to any considerable degree is highly questionable.

Crystal's urgency is engaging, but his diagnosis seems spurious. It is his prognosis, however, which must above all else be questioned. In order to save languages and to maintain the rich exchange between them, he argues it is sufficient to maintain the diversity of our pools of native speakers. Crystal has no intention of going out to learn the languages he intends to save; he believes they can be saved for humanity simply by maintaining native speakers alive in a community. Diversity would seem to require merely that a wide variety of languages simply exists. How exactly the worldview of the Bushmen is supposed to be introduced and assimilated into Crystal's Enlightenment project, to educate Mankind and lead it onwards in its quest for progress towards a 'successful humanity' is far from clear, on the other hand. At this stage, it would seem that Crystal's tendency to think in metaphors such as gene pools has obscured his capacity to appreciate and analyse exchange between languages.

On 26 February 2008, the Norwegian government founded the Svalbard Global Seed Vault on the island of Spitsbergen, located 700 miles from the North Pole. In a sandstone mountain, 394 feet above sea level, out of the reach of water even if the caps melt, seeds were placed in order to preserve for future generations the plants which might, in the event of a nuclear war or natural disaster, be eradicated from existence. A similar motivation underpins Crystal's arguments for saving languages. He claims that 'with the death of each language, another source of potentially invaluable information disappears' (55). The key word here is 'potentially'. If the world 'possesses' a stock of languages, it can dip into its cold storage and withdraw the information when required. Whether culture works like this at the level of individual linguistic communities or at the level of global politics is highly debatable. At any rate, Crystal's sense of urgency is animated by the motto 'just in case'. His argument that language is the 'most valuable single possession of the human race' (an argument he shares with Hockett, qtd in Crystal 2000: 66), and his argument that 'what it means to be human is enhanced by a knowledge about those who think and act in a different way' (66), are arguments which put Crystal on the side of the Enlightenment philosophers, with their fascination for alternative cultures which was to lead to the founding of the discipline of anthropology. Such arguments make him the friend of the French authors of the *Encyclopédie*. They bring both Crystal and Hagège closer to Humboldt, who set out to open up his own mind to other dimensions of the human spirit's potential by attempting to enter into the unique forms of world-perceiving and world-conceiving that shaped and structured languages other than his mother tongue, German. But while the vibrant curiosity of Humboldt's desire to broaden the horizons of his own potential for conception, perception and feeling caused him to pore over texts in French, English, Latin, Greek, Sanskrit, Kawi and a number of Amerindian languages, the broad ambitions of Hagège and Crystal to embrace and cherish all languages (indiscriminatingly) makes their love of languages of a rather lukewarm (if not insipid) affair. In contrast to philologists like Benveniste, who incarnated the traditional language-lover, the 'philologist', and Meschonnic, who is concerned with the specific mode by which an individual takes his or her place within his language, Hagège and Crystal appear somewhat like museum curators.

This has not stopped their work from gaining wide praise and support, however. Crystal in particular is not concerned with simply convincing people of the necessity to struggle against the tide of language death, though. Crystal wants to act himself. And he realises all too well that languages cannot be artificially maintained. This leads him to examine the reasons which encourage the members of a linguistic community to abandon their language. This involves rooting out the 'misconceived elitism' of the dominant language which has been assimilated by a marginalised group. By 'Fostering positive community attitudes' (102), Crystal hopes we can help combat those 'Negative attitudes towards one's own language [which] are surprisingly common' (102). Far from leaving dying languages alone, as some linguists have suggested doing,

Crystal claims, 'a policy of total non-intervention in indigenous affairs, however well-intentioned, would be a blatant disregard of the realities of history' (107). We must and can save dying languages, Crystal argues. He consequently disparages those who find it 'far too easy to evade responsibility' (107).

At this point, Crystal will turn Humboldt's approach on its head. While Humboldt was sceptical about our ability to reach within another culture and experience its language fully as our own worldview, Crystal claims that 'Living "inside" a language, it is not possible to see its distinctiveness' (109). It is, therefore, up to specialists of another language to instruct or at least 'help a community discover what is unique about its heritage' (109). This was exactly what Lévi-Strauss was suggesting was impossible when he spoke of the train which passed us in a flash, giving us only a glimpse of the people who belong to the passing culture and only a vague idea of where they were going.

Certainly, 'linguistic apathy or despair' (Crystal 2000: 112) are unlikely to save languages from extinction, but whether the meaning and significance of a culture and its language can be saved by instruction dispensed by outsiders seems highly unlikely. The project Crystal is advocating and the metaphors which frame and structure his thought (metaphors of language as a possession, a treasure, a resource, a species of plant or animal) make it obvious that his project bears little in common with Humboldt's linguistic anthropology. Crystal is very different from Sapir, who was interested in the way personality forges itself in language and maintains language alive by virtue of the creativity of individuals and the interaction of speakers. Crystal is much more akin to Whorf, who envisaged language-learning as the expedition of an explorer who sets out to seek out the final frontier. The more exotic the language, the better; the more languages, the better. But Crystal and Whorf both remain at the level of lexicology and grammar without tackling texts or actual living, breathing individuals producing real speech.

Crystal attributes to himself, as an outsider, a bird's-eye view of languages, and prescribes a broad political programme. In response to language death, Crystal advocates a process of 'revitalization' (125). Revitalisation Teams should be set up to convince communities of the necessity of the task at hand, helping them to find a new dignity in their lost or dying traditions and in their language. Crystal extols the 'visionary language rescuer who managed to motivate the local [Rama] community' (129). The post-colonial era has seen indigenous majorities and minorities reclaim land, by invoking arguments formulated by the societies that invaded them and claiming the land 'belongs' to them. Such claims are often disingenuously juxtaposed with claims that the materialistic worldviews of the languages of Western cultures make 'us' think of the land as 'ours', whereas the Mother-Earth in fact belongs to no one. The history of nations and frontiers has, however, proved indifferent to such claims. The countries of the East and the West were carved out of invasions and occupations and were only ever defended by defence and alliances. All ownership is theft, when it comes to nations and territories.

Crystal's idealism belongs to the post-war era which dreams of a more 'humane' future for humanity, a future which turns its back upon the bloody history of competing cultures. It is in this vein that Crystal speaks of the 'violation' of 'language rights', as though the legal rights of communities thus far marginalised and oppressed were somehow already established as a binding contract. Contracts, and legal rights, can, however, only be established between mutually agreeing, mutually self-interested parties, forced by necessity to respect the desires of one another. To attribute such bargaining power to disappearing cultures would seem optimistic, to say the least.

Whatever the motivations of the individual members of these Revitalisation Teams might be, if they are established, they will most probably be animated by that curiously cold and indiscriminating form of well-intentioned fraternal love that animates such institutions as the European Community and the United Nations. They will be fuelled by post-colonial guilt. But they will also no doubt be partially blinded by that intellectual smugness which makes would-be altruists impervious to criticism and unable to accept that they are incapable of knowing or understanding what should be done. In championing English as a new means of empowerment, what Crystal is calling for is a new form of 'stewardship'. Whether he knows it or not, the idea of stewardship is derived from a conception of 'vocation' proper to Protestantism. Man was put on the world to watch over nature and to cultivate the garden given to him by God. When Coca-Cola claims on its website to respect the planet by protecting the environment, it invokes the rhetoric of 'stewardship'. In a similar style, Crystal makes his Revitalisation Teams the new 'stewards' of ecolinguistics. They will save languages and thereby save humanity (because language is the most 'human' possession and because diversity makes humanity more human).

Such idealism may find advocates, but such dreams do not taste sweet: they have the acrid aftertaste of colonial rhetoric. For there is something deeply condescending in imagining that our Western culture will watch over the worldviews of ailing communities; and among the Western cultures, there seems little doubt which language these Revitalisation Teams will be speaking.

## SPRACHSINN

In their own different ways, both Hagège and Crystal represent two of the most erudite and respectable proponents of two fundamentally contradictory desires: the desire to champion one's own language, and the desire to play the defender of less prolific languages. The underlying chivalry in their discourse is the chivalry of the nobles of the Middle Ages, those nobles who were convinced of the importance of their own values, but considered it their duty (in theory at least) to benevolently watch over those less elevated and rush to the rescue of those in distress. This is a distinctly Christian vision of social and political relations, and it remains uncertain whether parallels of this form of protectionism exist in other cultures. Certainly, the ancient Greeks, for example, would have had little patience for such a policy concerning foreign cultures.

Humboldt, sadly, has no place in the debate on the disappearance of languages. He has been given no place, since his thought on language has had almost no impact upon English-speaking scholarship. Those who (like Hagège and Crystal) quote the 'Humboldtian tradition', such as Penny Lee in her insightful book on Whorf's unpublished writings (Lee 1996: 84), show no knowledge of Humboldt's philosophy on worldview. Humboldt does not exist for English linguistics, and those who pursue the path of discussions on worldview do so from the perspective of modern linguistics, contenting themselves with the cataloguing of grammars and the consideration of etymological roots. Philology became increasingly marginalised in language study in the twentieth century as linguistics asserted itself as a discipline. With philology, the concern for literature and the focus upon the individual use of language became overshadowed by the 'scientific ideal' and the objective consideration of isolated elements of the linguistic system.

Crystal, for his part, does, of course, show a concern and a sensitivity for individual speech (and he reserves a place for literature in his encyclopaedia). Nonetheless, when it comes to language death or the spread of English, Crystal considers the relationship between language and identity from the point of view of the culture as a whole, and for the most part he considers the culture from afar, invariably relying upon secondary sources. As a result, the speaking man or woman, the individual engaged in communicating to other people, is pushed out of sight. Comparative linguistics has, on the whole, become blind to individuals and deaf to their speech. This, in itself, is a minor disaster for linguistics because as Humboldt, Benveniste and Meschonnic knew, the only real source of our knowledge of what language is and does is speech. Meschonnic may pour irony on the French defenders, but he would be forced to admit that, on this point at least, those defenders were two steps ahead of Crystal. Firstly, they had an intimate knowledge of the language they were defending, and knew its potential for generating a vigorous sense of identity. Secondly, they were animated by a stimulating literary tradition, which had established models and norms against which to match the individual identities of French-speakers as a whole.

Those French defenders were no doubt at times prejudiced to the point of wilfully perpetuating their own ignorance and insensitivity to other cultures (a fault Hagège and Crystal can hardly be charged with), but they were closer to Humboldt in their understanding of the relationship between language and identity. They understood the intrinsic role that speech must inculcate in the individual, the role of cultivating individuals' understanding and allowing them to take their place within his society. As Trabant puts it:

> Humboldt 'posited a *sensus linguisticus*, 'sense of language' (*Sprachsinn*) which as the supreme form of imagination, as the intermediary between sensibility and understanding, generates language as both image and sign. (1992: 8)

*Sprachsinn*, the sense of language, represents the means by which men and women cultivate their imagination, their sensibility and their capacity to conceptualise the world with finesse. Perhaps because linguistics has scientific ambitions, and because the sciences have tended to cut themselves off from that cultivation of perception which is privileged in the study of the arts, modern linguistics has focused upon conception at the expense of perception; and when it considers perception, it often does so at the expense of feeling. In contrast to this tendency, imagination and feeling were inextricably bound up together for Humboldt. Language directs our thought to physical reality, alerting us to subtle distinctions of smell, touch and taste by the catalogues of categories it sets up. Synaesthesia, the use of the terms of one sense to describe the experience of another sense in metaphoric form, cultivates our perception and enriches our expression. For this reason, we constantly speak of 'the poetry of ballet', of 'symphonies of colours' or 'odious behaviour'. Not only do such expressions define obliquely (but poignantly) what we mean, they often serve to awaken us to reality.

This was the value of language for Humboldt: *Sprachsinn*. It was because French writers were so inspired by their own linguistic system and its potential for expression, so proud of the riches that writers had stored up for the expression of generations to come, that they wished to preserve it and offer it to others (even if that meant imposing it upon them). This sense of language, this *Sprachsinn*, is absent from the debate on language death in both English and French today, however. The authors who defend other languages do so because they take it as an article of faith that each language must constitute a worldview, and, consequently, must hold within it the riches which both Hagège and Crystal find in their own mother tongues, riches which they no doubt cherish as much as the defenders of the French language of the seventeenth century cherished theirs.

This leads both Hagège and Crystal to formulate movingly lyrical accounts of language death and to invent a chivalrous role for their own language to play in coming to the rescue. This chivalry in itself entails a narrative, a scenario Hagège and Crystal wish to play out. It is one which is fuelled by a rich stock of standard metaphors combined with innovative adaptations and original metaphors invented by the authors themselves. In their accounts, we are asked to attribute to languages the roles of victim, oppressor, treasure, endangered plant or animal, neutral means of negotiation, natural choice, mosaic and means of empowerment.

The logic of many of these analogies proves to be untenable. Languages are not living things, as Hagège and Crystal claim. They do not have a limited lifespan. They have no biological parents. They do not interact as species or individual links in a food chain. Even the very 'nature' of 'nature' posited by these two ecolinguists does not bear up to scrutiny. After all, what is so tragic about death? Death is part of nature. The dead bark protects the living cells in the trunk of a tree. Cancer, disease and contamination are all part of nature. Darwin would not have excluded bacteria from nature. Neither was Darwin convinced that mankind was progressing towards a higher form. He pointed to simple life forms which were perfect in and of themselves though they had not changed for hundreds of millions of years, simply because they had proved to be perfectly suited to their environment. And recent research seems to prove that these (rather than the mammals) are likely to survive if climate change or other catastrophes drastically alter the ecological equilibrium.

Darwin did not celebrate the predator as the Social Darwinists did in their attempt to enlist Darwin in the ranks of mercantile industrial capitalism. Yet neither did he exclude the predator, and he would have found the idea that one language should not 'devour', prey upon or 'stamp out' another language, a bizarre notion. Hagège and Crystal are both men of our times in that they entertain that romantic view of nature which invites us to see in the environment the harmonious orchestration of mutually beneficial partners. Predators such as tigers, parasites which suck the life out of what they feed upon (as bats or ivy do), death, disease and decomposition have no place in their fairy tale.

Crystal is motivated by the desire to be fair and just to other less fortunate languages than English. Hagège seems more directly concerned, as though he is worried that the fate which awaits dying languages may one day menace his own mother tongue. For this reason, he adopts and reframes arguments from the *Académie* with a certain urgency. Idealism, touched by pessimism, borders upon alarmism at times in Hagège's prose.

Ultimately, however, the nostalgia and pessimism of French defenders is misplaced. French goes on creating itself in the mouths of French-speakers who adopt and adapt it to their needs as they position themselves in dialogue with one another. The imagination of French people resonates with echoes of a vibrant literary and cinematic culture. Rhymes from songs reverberate to give a special meaning to a word or phrase for a certain generation. This coupling of words traces out patterns which the imagination can follow, or leads the imagination to destinations from which it can start out afresh to seek out other forms of expression. For families, everyday words and expressions continue, in France as elsewhere, to take on a special shared meaning derived from each family's shared memory of the times and places connected with those words and expressions. 'Paris' and 'Parisian' means one thing to a family living in Toulouse and something else to a family living in the northern suburbs of Paris itself.

Though contemporary defenders of French display a certain dissatisfaction, there is another form of dissatisfaction which is proper to language itself and which stimulates innovation. At crucial moments in their lives, people feel dissatisfied by speech and seek new forms of expression adequate to their experience of reality. Lovers are exemplary of this creative dissatisfaction. Language is born anew in the words that punctuate lovers' sighs. The most ludicrous cliché is capable of taking on a weight and significance which is almost overpowering, and even tongue-tied and unimaginative people find themselves reaching out for metaphors in their attempt to conceive of and express what is happening when they fall in love.

The imaginative person, the person with a reputation for wit, the joker and the writer all perpetuate this essential quality, the sense of language, *Sprachsinn*. *Sprachsinn* is what makes language meaningful for us. *Sprachsinn* stimulates a language's capacity to welcome us into its world, enabling us to express that world and thereby act within and upon it. This is what needs to be protected in language. To my knowledge, *Sprachsinn* is fit and well in English, French, Czech and German. *Sprachsinn* is not ill or in danger. Since the human species is innately creative, it seems unlikely that imagination is in danger of drying up, or that the languages of the world will one day fail to allow humanity to live 'successfully' (to return to Crystal's curious expression). Whether the *Sprachsinn* of the other languages in the world is equally alive, is a question which no one individual can be expected to answer. Neither are Hagège nor Crystal better qualified to answer this question than other linguists. Their distress can, consequently, be credited with no profound insight into what is actually happening when a language begins to disappear.

Only the speakers of a language can perpetuate it as a means of expression. The means of expression of the Bushmen remains a mystery to most of us. Their worldview is beyond our ken, and I for my part am unable to imagine the 'worth' of that language, just as I would be wholly incompetent when it comes to estimating the 'loss' to humanity which the demise of that language would represent. It may be true to say that when a man dies, a library is burned down. If that is so, it may well be logical then to believe that when a culture dies, the loss to the world is infinitely greater. But to speak of such things is to speak of that of which we are ignorant. To claim that we evade our duty when we neglect the fate of other languages, as Crystal suggests, is absurd. It is the absurdity of idealism, but that very idealism is fuelled by a certain vanity, the vanity of one who belongs to the master class and who believes he can and should save his inferiors. It remains to be seen if English-speakers will in future be able to afford such condescension. This role of English may well be altered over the next two generations. And if English dies one day, shall we blame the Chinese? We shall see.

# A Final Word

At the end of this tour of worldviews, what are we to conclude? Ultimately, this will depend, to a large extent, upon our own worldview. The pessimist and the fatalist will conclude that ideology and cultural mindsets are inescapable. From such a perspective, a worldview appears as a confining space, a prison. And, indeed, it seems true that in thinking and in expression, metaphor (one constitutive element of all worldviews) is ubiquitous and inescapable. The social sciences, with their objectifying rhetoric and, not least of all, their conception of the relationship between society and individuals (the 'products of social processes'), tend to push us towards a fatalism in which we conceive ourselves as the passive (and innocent) 'victims' of 'inhuman' ideology. This seems to be reductive. And it also invites us to side-step the moral question of human responsibility in society, culture and, by extension, language. That Klemperer and Fidelius refused to accept such linguistic complacency should suffice to contradict such an interpretation of the way language affects us.

Fatalism is entirely foreign to Humboldt's project, the attempt to understand and compare the characters of languages and the worldviews that each one opens up to its speakers. Fatalism fails to understand the efforts of the engaged writer who seeks to resist the reigning ideology. Klemperer, Orwell and Kundera become incomprehensible from such a perspective. But so too do Shakespeare and Emily Dickinson, who seek to explore the possibilities of language and to push back the limits of understanding which everyday speech promotes.

All of the three case studies confirm that metaphor is fundamental to conceptual thought. The conceptual patterning of our languages depends to a significant degree upon metaphoric paths which we follow (and therefore confirm), resist (and modify) or refuse, as we strive to break out into alternative, original modes of thinking. What the two ideological case studies serve to prove is that concepts tend to cluster together: concepts such as the State and the people (*Volk* and *lidé* in our studies) become harnessed together. The underlying intention of those promoting the reigning ideology is evidently to direct thought along predefined lines of reflection. In such a system of thought, in such a cultural mindset, the State can set itself up as the organ which both enfolds and protects the people, while preserving it from its 'enemies'. At such a point 'the people' becomes an 'essentialisation' which envelops the majority (without seeking its consent), and which ostracises and stigmatises a minority of individuals, who will in turn be set up as 'the enemy within' which must be 'purged' for the good of society as a whole. Such a process can only be understood in metaphoric terms: society is an organism (suffering from a non-terminal sickness), and the cure lies in the long-discredited medical process of 'purging' (letting blood).

As our study of language showed, not only is language itself inescapable, all of our attempts to define language and to compare languages or to explain their relations to other linguistic communities must necessarily be formulated in metaphoric terms. A language is seen either as an invading force, a colonising power, or as a source of animation and inspiration in the 'cross-fertilisation' of cultural exchange. Linguistic philosophies cannot evade this inevitable propensity towards metaphoric representation, no matter what model is adopted or adapted. Translators are fond of the 'cross-fertilisation' metaphor. Staunch defenders of linguistic purity prefer metaphors of 'invasion' and 'colonisation', and frequently indulge in metaphors of 'purity' and 'pollution', 'decay' and 'decadence'. Most of these latter metaphors repose upon a conceptual given: languages are assumed to be living organisms, fragile and susceptible to disease.

At times, cultures will harness opposing rhetorical strategies. It has become commonplace in intellectual circles in contemporary France to lament the invasion of French by English (usually implicitly identified as a corrupting 'barbaric' influence). At the same time, the influence of French upon other European languages in the eighteenth and nineteenth centuries and upon North Africa in the nineteenth and twentieth centuries is invariably characterised by those same critics as a civilising influence, as the 'radiating' influence of culture (*rayonnement*).

Language and metaphor may be inescapable, but what all writers and politically engaged individuals believe is a simple premise, namely that we can make a difference. Though worldviews are inescapable, worldviews are not imposed upon us by inhuman forces. A dominant discourse reigns though the complex hierarchy which defines the organs and institutions which disseminate it, the educators and informers (journalists and writers) who agree to confirm it, and the people, the individuals, who choose to endorse it and conform to its dictates. Only by their identifying with the dominant discourse can that discourse survive. Cultural mindsets, ideological worldviews, are maintained by people, and by people alone.

For this reason, metaphor critics such as Lakoff, Goatly and Eubanks suggest we 'wash the brain' (to adopt Goatly's expression) of pernicious thought patterns, in order to seek a more relevant, more truthful expression of those issues which are essential for us in the social sphere and in our own private lives. This turn in cognitive linguistics is a healthy one, but we should be wary of attempts to characterise it as a 'new beginning'. In many ways this critical turn is one that simply extends the vast project of 'critique' (in the sense that Marx would have understood the term), at tradition which includes writers such as Theodor Adorno, Raymond Williams and Michel Foucault, a tradition which finds its expression in contemporary literature in critical discourse analysis.

At a more fundamentally linguistic level, Meschonnic and Wierzbicka prove closer to Humboldt in seeking to uncover both the strategies of discourse and, most of all, the interactive conceptual constructs and the conceptual patterning which shape a discourse and which take root in the language system. The crucial point about such work is to understand that no one level of worldview imposes itself unilaterally upon another. This is the belief which both inspired my book on Humboldt and which gave the impetus to write this book. The perspective of the individual confirms the contours of his or her personal world. And cultural mindset depends upon the ability of ideology to penetrate and shape the personal worlds of individuals. Ideology, like bacteria, cannot live outside of organisms. Individuals must accommodate and associate themselves with the cultural mindset if it is to be preserved. This involves an inevitable process of ageing and mutation. Worldviews must resonate within consciousness. They must enable individuals and peoples to give expression to their thoughts and feelings. They must enable us to live together as communities. Ideology is thus constantly modified by individual expression, and therefore subject to innovation.

Paradoxically, even the most conformist thinker transforms his or her language by dimming its possibility for immediate, spontaneous expression. As that capacity for meaningful personalised speech wanes, the way is prepared for a rejection of overused, hackneyed, hollow forms of expression. And even when a radically new worldview begins to gain power and influence, individuals such as Klemperer emerge to critique the pervasive means by which the ideology is beginning to modify the fundamental thought patterns which take hold within our consciousness, and beginning to legitimate actions which would have previously seemed grotesque, absurd or unthinkable.

Literature, because it creates worlds, can be considered the sovereign domain of critique. And because metaphor, imagery and symbolism are paramount to literary expression, they have always been analysed with great care and sensitivity by literary crtiticism. For reasons of space and coherence, no full-length literary study could be included in the present work. But this should not obscure the fact that literature reveals something fundamental about language as a whole. Language constantly produces forms of representation. But, as the fictional writer and the political critic amply demonstrate, it also provides us with the means to critique our forms of representation.

Meschonnic believed that critique culminates in literature. He believed in a poetry which transforms life, and in a life which seeks to transform language. This is the celebration of the free-thinking individual, but it is also the celebration of the linguistic subject who can realise himself only in language. We have side-stepped literature in the present book, but we cannot side-step language.

Neither can we side-step Humboldt if we wish to face up to worldviews, those that seek to englobe us, and those which we ourselves adhere to and accept. This book is intended neither as a celebration of metaphor nor as a celebration of worldviews, but rather as a celebration of language. It is not the dominant discourse which must be unmasked and denounced. The sensitive readings of Adorno, Williams, Foucault and Goatly might lead the hurried reader to conclude that this is the principle vocation of language study. But our concern is more fundamental. What is at stake is 'the sense of language', the capacity for thought which language enables. This is what Humboldt called *Sprachsinn* ('the sense of language'). And that concept involves our capacity to extend our thought and feeling, our individual sensitivity and our shared understanding as a linguistic community. The sense of language involves our capacity to transform the 'worlds' which present themselves in the discourse around us. And, at a time when cognitive scholars are tempted by biological explanations provided for thought by neuroscience, at a time when generativists harken after a universal grammar which eclipses the consideration of the intrinsically specific nature of culture and language, this sense of language is the essential capacity which must be celebrated and defended in the discussion of the relationship between language and the mind.

# Glossary

---

**Allegory** Term derived from Greek (*allēgoria* 'speaking other-wise', which in turn derives from *allos* 'other', and *agoreuein* 'to speak'). An allegory is a story of varied length in either verse or prose which can be read at two levels. The surface level often involves talking animals (donkeys, scorpions, frogs, and so on) and the far-fetched plots characteristic of fables and fairy tales. But allegories have a deeper meaning which becomes apparent in the moral of the story, and which is invariably intended as a statement about human nature and the workings of society or of the world as a whole.

**Analogy** Term used in common speech to denote any form of similarity or parallelism. By extension, analogy came to mean a parallelism used to explain the way something works. Plato uses analogy abundantly to explain, for example, the nature of the forces governing the soul (two horses, one wild and passionate, one calm and aware of its ultimate goal), or the art of good states-manship (governing as the captain governs his crew). The adjectives 'analogical' and 'analogous' are rarely used today. The verb denoting to explain or consider by analogy, 'analogise', has also fallen into disuse. Though analogy is used in linguistics to denote any form of similarity or parallelism found in different languages, literary scholars tend to avoid the term. Neither Cuddon (1991) nor Brogan offer definitions of analogy in their encyclopaedias.

The pedagogical virtue of analogy is, nonetheless, evident in the examples offered by Plato. And cognitive linguists have argued that analogy is fundamental to the way we organise and package meaning. Fauconnier and Turner (2003: 11–14) hold analogy to be central to understanding, but they argue that the apparent simplicity of analogy is deceiving. Though any child soon learns to master analogical thought, the organisation of meaning in what appears to be a fairly straightforward statement often proves complex under examination. They cite the example 'Chaucer's London bore no resemblance to the London of today' to make their point (13). This short phrase allows us to divide one single object into two distinct categories in order to contrast differences of period and social and economic activity. Division becomes opposition, which in turn fuses once more into the complex dynamic whole, 'London'.

**Ascription** Term used by Eubanks to denote the discursive strategy of attributing (ascribing) a conceptual metaphor to another party. Often metaphors are invoked only to be denounced. Eubanks quotes examples of speakers criticising those who act as if trade is war, though they themselves claim to find such a concept grotesque or absurd. Ascription does not preclude bad faith: we often condemn in others what we ourselves practice. Just as the pot (in proverbial wisdom) calls the kettle black, many politicians and CEOs justify aggressive economic policies by claiming they are merely retaliating to a trade war started by another country or company.

**Attributed world conception** The idea that each language must engender its own specific world conception (usually referred to as 'worldview'). This is commonly expressed in the equation, 'a language is a world'. While there is much evidence to support such a claim, and knowledge of a variety of foreign languages makes such an idea seem plausible, there is, in fact, no evidence to prove that it is justified, nor can any such evidence be reasonably expected from further research. Empirically proving this hypothesis would require us to know all languages, or rather 'to master' them, in order to be able to compare and contrast the different worldviews to which each language gives us entry. Since such a sovereign mastery of all languages remains inconceivable, it would therefore seem wise to avoid stating as a truth what in fact is no more than an opinion or an article of faith. The equation according to which a language constitutes a worldview is best considered as a 'working hypothesis' which evidence gathered from the fields of comparative philology and translation studies tends to support.

**Blend** A third concept which emerges from the fusion of two concepts. For example, the fusion of the word 'tunnel' with 'channel' provides us with 'chunnel'. The concept of blending was considerably developed by Turner and Fauconnier, who stressed that an interactive model of metaphor and analogy is insufficient. The comparison between the two primary terms as fixed concepts (as they are usually conceived) cannot account for the ways in which the comparison itself changes the way we perceive the two terms within the framework of the new emerging concept. If, for example, we compare a man to a dog, this provides us with a 'dog-man' which can then be endowed with a series of complex characteristics which no longer bear any strict reference to our real experience of dogs. The world in which men and dogs are known and described has been left behind, and we find ourselves in the realm of the imagination, faced with a new construct in its own right.

Turner and Fauconnier have pioneered the integration of blending into cognitive linguistics and cognitive poetics. For these two scholars, conceptual blending constitutes a fundamental mode of complex thought which involves extended metaphors and hypothetical scenarios. As an example, they quote the desire expressed by the Right in the USA in the 1990s to see 'a Margaret Thatcher', an 'Iron Lady', come to the rescue of the US economy (2003: 18–21). This hypothesis involved combining Thatcher's qualities and characteristics with those of a potential US president, and playing out the scenario in which the new invented 'Thatcher', an 'American Iron Lady', would face the problems, obstacles and oppositions US society would place in her path. A common response to this hypothesis was that 'Margaret Thatcher would never get elected here because the labor unions can't stand her'

(18). This scenario involves a complex comparison of the UK and US societies, their needs and the forces at work within them.

In his study of the language of the Third Reich, Victor Klemperer shows the way the Nazi system of beliefs was partly conditioned by metaphors of a military nature. He then goes on to show the way in which the military was influenced (or perverted) by this system of beliefs. Lakovian metaphor theory would account for this mutual influence as the interaction of two frames of reference. Turner and Fauconnier would presumably consider that the two initial domains had given rise to a third emerging concept, the 'Nazified' conception of the military.

Similarly, Klemperer shows the way in which both Hitler and Goebbels conceived the Nazi German to be a sportsman, often a boxer, a fighter (*Kämpfer*). This entailed conceiving of social interaction in terms of struggle, sport and competition, and this, in turn, transformed attitudes to sport. Sport was increasingly conceived of as a preparation for war. One disadvantage of the Turner–Fauconnier model is that it tends to imply that two domains will give rise to a third, while in both of the above examples, the new emerging blends (military–politics and sport–as–war) actually transformed both the two initial terms of each of the equations. If this is often the case, then blending should be seen as a 'usurping force' which, once engendered, will consume its parents. This state of affairs is not excluded by the dynamic interactive model proposed by Lakoff and Johnson.

**Catachresis** Term which derives from a Greek term meaning 'misuse': often used to denote the misapplication of a word. Cuddon (1991: 122) quotes Milton's 'Blind mouths' as a specific form of catachresis, mixed metaphor. Preminger and Brogan (1993: 172) quote a much celebrated example, Hamlet's 'To take arms against a sea of troubles'. But as Preminger and Brogan point out (following, among others, Quintilian), catachresis involves 'a deliberate wresting of a word from its proper signification' (172). Catachresis, they argue, can procure humorous effects, semantic compression, expressive intensity and tension. The equivalent French term, *catachrèse*, is used primarily to denote a new concept for which language offers no available term. Originally the 'leg of the table' and the 'foot of the hill' were English examples of catachresis, metaphoric innovations, which will always be implicitly condemned by the naïve conception of language according to which it is assumed that words belong to things (that is, words are terms, limited to a single possible denotation). Viewed from such a perspective, all metaphor is 'misapplication'. The vast extension of our lexical resources that metaphor has allowed should be sufficient to make us wary of the definition of catachresis as misapplication. All innovative and creative thought which responds to new situations by inventing neologisms to define new experiences and objects of understanding inevitably reaches out to analogy and metaphor to form those neologisms. Since such forms of thinking involve considering something new and unknown in terms of something familiar, they have a heuristic and pedagogical value. Expressions like 'spaghetti junction' and 'concrete jungle' retain a striking and expressive meaning for us. The extension of the lexicon provides us with a rich variety of examples of catachresis, though specialists of poetics, stylistics and cognitive poetics tend to prefer to use the terms 'dead metaphor' or 'lexical metaphor'.

**Cliché** Common or hackneyed expression, for example, 'You are as sweet as a rose'. We should distinguish between the 'cliché', the 'dead metaphor' and the 'idiom' or 'idiomatic expression': we do not notice dead metaphors such as 'rosy cheeks', 'foot of the hill' or 'table leg', since they have undergone a process of 'literalisation' (see below), that is, they have been assimilated into common speech and now carry a primarily literal meaning. In the example above, 'sweet' is a dead metaphor since it has taken on the literal meaning (endearing and charming). Clearly, nobody really thinks of sucking the girl's arm to see if she tastes like sugar! Idioms, on the other hand, are colourful expressions which draw attention to themselves in discourse, for example, 'He keeps his cards close to his chest' or 'It's an open and shut case'. They are 'foregrounded' and often used intentionally for the sake of effect. All speakers use idioms and a language's stock of idioms is usually felt to be a part of its linguistic wealth. Older generations often carry on the tradition by continuing to use idioms which are gradually being lost or replaced by new forms of expression by younger generations.

While we often speak of the 'poetry of a language' when we speak of idioms, their use is never inspired or original. Neither do they pose as original expressions. 'Clichés', on the other hand, have literary pretensions. They pose as poetical niceties supposed to embellish one's discourse. Poets generally abhor clichés (though many of them are not above using them). In aesthetic terms, the use of clichés reveals a penchant for pseudo-sophistication: a failure to understand the nature of linguistic innovation. While an original metaphor like Macbeth's 'So full of scorpions is my mind' might stun us with its originality and force, a cliché like 'You are graceful as a swan' leaves most people unimpressed. The problem with the cliché is that it tries and fails to impress. It draws attention to itself, but does not seem to deserve the attention it demands.

**Cognitive poetics**  In the work of Mark Turner, cognitive poetics is a branch of scholarship which attempts to explore the workings of our mental operations as they play out in artistic or aesthetic behaviour. Cognitive poetics constitutes a certain form of literary criticism which originated from the merger of concerns of scholars engaged in metaphor theory using the Lakoff–Johnson paradigm and scholars influenced by cognitive science. Cognitive poetics focuses upon the interpretation of the literary text and analyses what are traditionally considered to be style and literary tropes. Much recent scholarship in this field has been devoted to reader-response criticism. In other branches, literature such as Turner's *The Literary Mind* (1996) attempts to show how literature high-lights the way in which all brains process and organise information. Cognitive poetics has been criticised for failing to take on aesthetic questions. It has been argued that attempts to demonstrate that all minds are 'literary' implies that cognitive poetics has yet to establish a criterion upon which the worth of literary works can be judged.

**Cognitive unconscious**  Term used by cognitive linguists to describe the relatively small number of conceptual metaphors and metonymies that define our various 'folk theories' (see below) about the nature and functioning of the world (Lakoff and Johnson 1999: 541). Lakoff and Johnson (like Whorf before them) argued that philosophical thought could not gain access to any form of transcendental reason, being itself language-bound. They argued: 'The existence of the cognitive unconscious at the heart of our thinking and reasoning undermines any view of reason as transparent and directly self-reflective, as well as any aprioristic view of philosophy' (540). Lakoff and Johnson conceive of cognitive linguistics not as an attack on philosophy, but rather as an aid to analysing thought. Before looking for truth outside of yourself, they contend, you must first become aware of the modes by which you conceive of truth. This involves analysing those frameworks of understanding which are handed down to you in the language you learn to think with. This position is surprisingly close to the one espoused by Humboldt two hundred years ago. Indeed, to a great extent, Humboldt's manifold concept of *Sprache* ('language') resembles the cognitive unconscious as Lakoff and Johnson understand it. Humboldt's concept of *form*, far from retaining the merely formalistic, non-semantic elements invariably associated with our term 'form' in poetics or comparative linguistics, meant the frameworks of understanding, the links between words and the conceptual paths taken by individuals in their struggle towards meaningful expression. Like Lakoff and Johnson, Humboldt believed that creativity could be enhanced by taking stock of the patterns of thought of our language.

**Cold War clichés** Ideas generated by the two superpowers and which gained wide currency during the period 1945–89. These ideas enabled each of the superpowers to build a negative representation of the opposing power in order to induce the inhabitants of its own zone of influence to reject the lifestyles of the other and the ideals which belonged to it. Being binary, these ideas were often of an almost absurdly simplistic nature. Indeed, the propaganda used by each superpower was often found to be amusing and ridiculous to those of the other camp. Since the end of the Cold War, the peoples of Eastern Europe and the ex-Soviet Union have been forced to reappraise their own Cold War clichés. This reappraisal has led them into a 'binary world conception' which might be compared to crossing a river on stepping stones: those who live 'between worlds' can look back and forth to both banks. While both the world conceptions of capitalism and communism can be seen, the person does not live, think or 'feel' fully in either one. In the West, in contrast, politicians of both the Clinton and Bush administrations, and thinkers, such as Fukuyama, perceived the West as having 'won' the Cold War. Following the same reasoning, most Westerners have not been forced to question their own world conception. Their Cold War clichés remain, as a result, very much intact. We continue to affirm that the West means freedom, communism means slavery. Until the world economic crisis of 2008, we affirmed that our economy works, theirs did not. Western powers persist in representing themselves not as states seeking to impose their will and achieve objectives favourable to their countries' economies, but rather as powers in a harmonious political cosmos which are endowed with the vocation of serving the good of other states. Conceptual metaphors have been adopted and adapted to consolidate the views of Western states: man's taming of nature, conceived of in Christian imagery as 'stewardship', had been adopted by states since the Middle Ages to defend their diplomatic and colonial policies and strategies. But during the build-up to the second war in Iraq, we witnessed a forceful return to such rhetoric in propaganda used by the Bush and Blair administrations, when it came to 'looking after' the people of Iraq.

**Conceptual cluster**  A series or network of related concepts, the definitions of which are vague and ill-defined. The relationships between conceptual clusters are often ambiguous, fluctuating and instable. Conceptual clusters can form semantic systems used by political parties and political regimes which seek to manipulate the worldview we inhabit, but they do also often structure the organisation of the worldviews of subcultures. Individuals often betray an incapacity for clarity in conceptual thought when they express their ideas in confused conceptual clusters (as in the case of prejudice). A member of the British National Party, for example, may think and feel with a conceptual cluster which lumps together British-born blacks and Pakistanis, immigrants and foreign mafias of Chinese and Russian origin. In contradistinction to this complex and confused conceptual cluster, he may generate an 'ideal' form of culture which blends together whites, Christianity, the work

ethic, progress and civilisation. The complexity of semantic confusion often contrasts with the simplicity of reasoning and action.
Conceptual clusters often serve as simplifications to those of
limited awareness and understanding, allowing such people to set
up categories of good and evil. The logic of such reasoning invariably generates a We = Good *vs* Them = Evil paradigm. At a political level, conceptual clusters allow radical movements to mobilise
members around an attack–defence strategy.

**Conceptual frame** Relying on Fillmore 1982, Lakoff and
Johnson (1999: 116–17) defined conceptual frames as semantic
frames which 'provide an overall conceptual structure defining the
semantic relationships among whole "fields" of related concepts
and the words that express them' (116). At the heart of the matter
is the rejection of the conception of meaning as the addition of a
series of elements, words. Rather than ascribing meanings to words
themselves, the concepts of semantic frame and conceptual frame
remind us that it is the context of conventional social situations
that enables us to define and understand what meaning individual
acts, words and intentions are to be given within those situations.
For example, waiters, cheques and menus take on a certain signification within the restaurant frame which they do not have in
other situations in which they may arise. Conceptual frames are
obviously implicitly a part of our cognitive unconscious. They are
at work when we express ourselves and when we interpret what
others say. They constitute those elements which need not be
mentioned. Conceptual metaphors such as 'Love is a Journey' are
at work when a lover claims, 'You and me are going nowhere fast'.
In this example, it goes without saying that love should 'take you
somewhere'.

**Conceptual metaphor** (Originally referred to by Lakoff and
Johnson as 'protometaphor' (1980) and referred to before them by
other scholars as 'root metaphor'.) Term denoting an underlying
metaphorical equation. If a teacher tells a student who hesitates
about taking an exam to 'pick up the gauntlet', the teacher conceives
of the exam as a fight, a duel. If a Czechoslovak communist claims
certain members of society have 'lost their way' and no longer 'walk

with the people', he is positing the building of socialism as a path along which the 'enlightened people', the 'awakened masses', must walk together. Any refusal to conform to party doctrine, as defined by the 'people's nucleus', the State, will be considered as 'straying from the path'. The religious overtones are palpable. Defying the Party will be construed as a perverse refusal to realise one's nature by fusing with the 'will of the people'. The path constitutes the conceptual metaphor upon which extensions such as 'straying' and 'losing one's way' are superimposed. If we did not understand and accept the underlying conceptual metaphor, such extensions would be quite simply incomprehensible.

**Cultural mindset**  Term used in this work to designate that relatively rigid and fixed way of seeing the world which frames our perception and conception of politics, society, history, behaviour, the individual's place in the world and social relations as a whole. When groups and generations who speak the same language fail to understand each other, it is because their cultural mindsets have grown into very different expressions of the world. It is significant, however, that those differing expressions are derived from the same world-perceiving and world-conceiving which organises the language shared by all groups within a single linguistic community. In this sense, the worldview of the language may contain (or generate) multiple 'worldviews', if cultural mindsets are to be meant by that term as is commonly the case in the fields of sociology and philosophy.

**Cultural relativism**  The idea that all cultures (and consequently all world conceptions) are ultimately of the same value. It is worth remembering that, though relativists refuse hierarchies which posit superior and inferior cultures, they do not reject value judgements. They reserve the right to judge the value of a culture, but consider all cultures to be of equal value. The opposition between cultural relativists and defenders of cultural hierarchies can be partially explained by the fact that these two groups invariably hold a different definition of 'culture'. For cultural relativists, each one of us has his or her own culture. This view will allow us to speak of 'working-class culture', 'football culture', 'gay culture' or 'pop culture', terms which hold a special resonance for sociologists and academics working in the field of cultural studies. We are invited to respect each of these forms of cultures just as, in civil society, we are asked to respect the rights of all individuals. (Respect does not necessarily imply admiration here.) This idea of culture is descriptive not prescriptive. For the defenders of cultural hierarchies, on the other hand, culture is not simply a type of lifestyle or set of customs and beliefs, it is the means by which a man or woman fulfils his or her nature. This idea of culture is teleological. Just as the acorn should strive to fulfil itself by growing into the oak, so the individual should be nurtured by culture in order to develop in a way appropriate to his or her essential nature. Christians, Marxists, Platonists and Aristotelians are only a few of the groups which hold culture to be a necessary teleological project. When they perceive this project to be perturbed on a large scale, they will tend to speak of decadence. The concept of decadence has no meaning for the cultural relativist, on the other hand. Democracies seem to offer more fertile ground for cultural relativism; monarchies and oligarchies are probably more likely to engender cultural hierarchies with fixed ideals.

**Cultural superiority** The idea that one culture is more 'worthy' or has reached a higher level than other cultures. Academic disciplines such as ethnology, sociology and democratic culture as a whole have tended to make this is a rather unpopular idea in recent times. Claude Lévi-Strauss, for example, reminds us that only the culture concerned can, in any profound and immediate way, grasp the significance, meaning and 'value' of an element of culture for the community itself. Outsiders' judgements of the 'value' of cultural elements are inevitably naïve and opportunistic. We tend to value a culture in terms of what it can offer us, and we can never enter into a foreign culture sufficiently to enable ourselves to discard our own cultural modes of understanding which form the prism through which we view and 'understand' a foreign culture. Although the tide may be turning in favour of relativism in many academic fields, our language and culture are both full of traces of the hierarchical conception of culture. We speak of a 'rich culture' (which implies that other cultures are 'less rich' or

'poor'). We speak of a 'golden age' in a culture, meaning the best
moment of that culture's history (for example, the Elizabethan
age of theatre in England, seventeenth-century France, the
period of Corneille, Racine and Molière, the period of Herder,
Goethe, Schiller and the Grimm brothers in Germany at the end
of the eighteenth and the beginning of the nineteenth centuries).
Though many philologists have at times adopted fully or partially
relativistic positions, the history of philology has its roots in the
idea that some cultures are superior to others. For the Renaissance
scholar, the Greco-Latin culture was the superior model to which
our cultures should aspire. And when the nation states began
to abandon Latin in favour of their own languages, they relied
heavily upon borrowed words from Latin and Greek in order to
'ennoble' their own languages. Only when cultures had 'elevated'
themselves to the level of competitors with Latin, did scholars
start to claim that their languages and cultures were, if not superior to those of the Romans and the Greeks, at least their equals.
This process of 'elevation' took a considerable period of time. In
French, it might be considered to have begun around the time
of du Bellay, in the middle of the sixteenth century, and to have
been completed by the time of Malherbe, at the beginning of the
seventeenth century. Many writers and thinkers seem to feel that
German underwent a similar period of elevation at a somewhat
later period which began with Goethe in the 1770s. This period
was, however, somewhat shorter and can be considered to have
been largely completed within the lifetime of Goethe, who died in
1832. By that time, German music had offered the world Mozart.
German philosophy had provided Kant and Hegel. In literature,
the German Romantics had already provided a second generation
of writers and they themselves were shortly to be followed by Late
Romantics such as Heine. Despite the fact that cultural relativism
has become fashionable on the campus in recent generations, the
raison d'être of language departments (including English) and the
syllabuses that structure them rely heavily upon the belief in a
cultural wealth that must be preserved and disseminated. A failure
to recognise the importance of this task is invariably considered as
an ignorant and 'uncultured' reaction, and is accordingly frowned
upon or openly scorned.

**Dead metaphor**  A lexicalised metaphoric expression which goes unnoticed in everyday speech, for example, 'to fly into a rage' or 'the mouth of the tunnel'. We do not tend to notice dead metaphors such as these. They have undergone a process of 'literalisation': that is to say, they have been assimilated into what is currently considered to be 'literal speech'. If we say, for example, 'Her sweet voice was music to my ears', we respond to 'music' as a metaphor, while we treat 'sweet' as straightforward, though upon analysis it proves no less metaphoric than 'music'. This raises the question of convention, and implies that a model of metaphor which does not take into account chronology and the 'ageing' of metaphors cannot fully account for the way we respond to figurative language, analogies and metaphors.

**Defamiliarisation** (*ostranienie* in Russian, 'making strange', term coined by Shklovski) This term is often confused with the term coined by Mukarovský, 'foregrounding' (*aktualizace* in Czech). Such confusion is not surprising since both refer to literary effects in which attention is drawn to certain elements of the text. 'Foregrounding', however, refers to any means by which an element of discourse draws attention to itself. 'Defamiliarisation' designates that process in literary texts (often modern and contemporary) by which an object or person is presented from a strange new angle in order to allow us to perceive them as strange. Defamiliarisation strives to make us see the world as if we are seeing it for the first time. Shklovski suggests art aims to make a stone seem 'stony'. Art tries to show a man his wife as though he had never set eyes on her before. Defamiliarisation invites us back into that atemporal space, the state of wonder, which is both the stimulus and the raison d'être of much art.

**Disanalogy**  Term used to describe the trope or conceptual mode of understanding which enables us to distinguish, by opposition, two elements which are comparable on a different level. The Pacific and the Atlantic, for example, are both oceans. This fact allows us to contrast them. Though they may be set up as direct opposites in an example, they do, of course, bear more in common with one another than the Atlantic Ocean does to a brick, for example. The latter pair are not 'disanalogous', the former two are. Fauconnier and Turner rely heavily on the concept of 'disanalogy'. That it forms a fundamental mode of understanding seems undisputable. Fauconnier and Turner (2003: 255) offer the example 'If I were you, I would hire me', in which they argue: 'The "you"-to-"me" outer-space disanalogy connector is compressed in the blend into a unique person'. Though the reasoning is sound here, there is little new in this discussion of contrast and comparison. Grammarians, translators and linguists in general are, in fact, perfectly well aware of the processes which Fauconnier and Turner define as 'disanalogous' since they are widely used in conditional phrases and all forms of hypothesis and speculative thought.

**Discourse** Form or style of language which can be attributed to an individual, a group, an institution or a period of a culture's history. We might speak of the discourse of Marx and Engels, which in turn would be held to be distinct from the Marxist discourse adopted by those who claim alliance to the ideas of those thinkers. We might speak of the institutional 'bla bla bla' of European Union discourse. We might speak of a Christian discourse, though we might in turn make a distinction between ideas commonly expressed in protestant and catholic discourse.

**Discursive strategy** Term used by Eubanks to denote the arguments and positions we formulate by harnessing conceptual metaphors and directing them in ways which serve our purposes and consolidate our positions. Early formulations of the Lakoff–Johnson position stressed that conceptual metaphors would at times direct and determine the way we conceive situations, express ourselves and act within those situations. Love was experienced as a 'journey', for example. Metaphor theory was thus posited as a 'solution' to the naïve thinking of people who allowed themselves to be seduced by the metaphors of their language. Lakoff and Johnson were claiming such people 'lived by' metaphors, and the lucid critique they were providing of such metaphors was implicitly intended 'to liberate' those people from such conceptual and behavioural constraints. Eubanks's study of 'Trade as War', on the other hand, showed that speakers generally adapt metaphors in a conscious manner to reflect their views in a favourable light. Trade was often conceived of as war, but the analogy was used in such a way as to manoeuvre opponents into being those supporting such a position. In this way, Eubanks demonstrated that we are often aware of the constraints metaphors entail and we negotiate those constraints by using a great deal of subtlety and creativity.

**Ecolinguistics** A discipline practised by a group of linguists, including Hagège in France and Crystal in the English-speaking world. Ecolinguists have been militating since the 1980s to safeguard dying and endangered languages in order to preserve what these linguists claim to be the essential specificity of each language as an expression of the world.

**Essentialisation** Process, common to many European languages, in which the various members of a group are reduced to the category in which they are enclosed. The most fundamental example would be 'Man', whose use often bears little relation to many of the 'men' it is believed to refer to and to enfold. That the term also applies to women is obviously problematic. Different languages generate different strategies of essentialisation. 'Man', for example, is translated into German as *Mensch* ('the human', 'humankind', 'mankind'), while *Mann* is reserved exclusively for those of a masculine gender. Interestingly, however, neutral expressions such as 'One could say that' are translated into German using the masculine form (*Das kann Mann sagen*), rather than the neutral, impersonal form, *Mensch*. Essentialisation excludes and all but denies difference. It is fundamentally anti-empirical in that it starts out from the category and proceeds to take into account the specific examples existing in reality. It is perhaps the empirical bent of the Anglo-American mindset that has induced us to be wary of essentialisations. Though spoken and written English provide such examples as 'the customer', 'the client', 'the citizen' and 'the man in the street', far fewer examples can be found in English than in French, for example, which, of the four languages studied (English, French, German and Czech), showed the greatest propensity towards essentialisation. Translators regularly find themselves faced with the problem of essentialisation when translating from French into English, and will often opt for a plural in place of a transcendental, all-embracing singular. They will, for example, regularly translate *la femme française* as 'French women', *l'étudiant* as 'students' and *le contribuable* as 'tax payers'. These French examples of essentialisation are not necessarily manipulative or perverse. Essentialisation has, however, been criticised by both Klemperer and Meschonnic, who see it as a rhetorical strategy which can be used to enclose individuals within dehumanised categories and thereby enables them to be marginalised and stigmatised. Indeed, expressions such as 'the Jew' and 'the Black' or 'the Nigger' are obviously harnessed in racist discourse to deprive those enclosed in such a category of any real existence as individuals. Essentialisations of such a kind act upon the imagination of those who allow themselves to think and feel with the category, while closing up their emotions to any possible relation to those imprisoned within the category.

**Ethnolinguistics** In English-speaking linguistics, this term is often considered to be a synonym for *linguistic anthropology*. Though it has gained little or no recognition in English-speaking countries, and though few encyclopaedias or linguists list the term in their contents or indexes, the Lublin School of Poland has been developing a forceful analysis of language and culture in its brand of ethnolinguistics since the 1980s. (See Bartmiński in Polish, and, in English, Wierzbicka.) Bartmiński is involved in a vast synthesis of philological approaches ranging from the study of Polish folklore to the study of everyday language. This work bears some similarity to Humboldt's linguistic anthropology, especially regarding his concept of worldview, *Weltansicht*, a fact which can be seen in Bartmiński's attempt to reconstitute the worldview of a 'model' Pole with the archetypes (or 'stereotypes', as he calls them) which shape and condition the way individuals perceive their world. Wierzbicka, for her part, has attempted to bridge the gap between continental scholarship on worldview, philology and linguistic difference on the one hand, and the quest for universals on the other. She has stressed the limited extent to which we can legitimately establish, by informed research, the universals of language, though she does accept pronouns such as 'I' and 'you', quantifiers such as 'many' and 'all', intercausal linkers 'if' and 'because', and spatial terms such as 'far', 'near', 'here' and 'inside', among her list of universals. Her main challenge to 'Anglo' culture is to make an attempt to describe the linguistic contours of the English-speaker's worldview. This involves forcing English-speakers to see themselves as part of an *ethnie*, a linguistic community which has no direct link to reality and to the categories thereof, but which negotiates its relationship to the constructed reality which the English language opens up to them (that is to say, 'us'). For Wierzbicka, 'emotion', 'sense' and 'evidence' are cultural concepts, fundamental to our worldview: but these terms do not translate easily into other languages, nor do they have any more primary basis than the cultural concepts found in the worldviews of other languages. Unlike much scholarship in English-speaking countries, both Wierzbicka and Bartmiński have maintained a philological approach which preserves a concern for the interaction between literature and the language system. This makes their approach interesting for readers of the present book in that it contributes to Humboldt's project to uncover the character of languages as both collective and individual manifestations.

**Expression**   Term also referred to as 'idiom', denoting a colourful metaphoric phrase which constitutes one of the resources of a language for describing things, people and events, for example, 'like it or lump it' or 'easy come, easy go'. When expressions are felt to encapsulate a truth concerning human nature or the workings of the world, that is, when they are moralistic in nature, they are invariably referred to as 'proverbs'. Proverbs such as 'The early bird catches the worm' and 'A guilty conscience needs no accuser' can be regarded as belonging to a subcategory of the expression. Expressions were obviously originally coined by imaginative and original thinkers, and can often be traced back to written literature. But they also form part of our oral tradition and may well have been coined in conversation, jokes or oral literature. Expressions provide useful paths for expression and categorisation. Unlike 'clichés', they do not feign originality or pretend to be poetic.

**Family resemblance** Term designating the association of various related frames of meaning which contribute to forming the complex network of concepts we can evoke by using a single term. Wittgenstein's concept of definition relies upon the idea that one word may constitute a variety of concepts, 'a complicated network of similarities intersecting and overlapping one another – similarities large and small' (2001: §§66f.). Wittgenstein used the analogy of the various similarities we recognise in the members of a family to express the diverse and related meanings designated by a single term. Contrary to much lexical analysis and to traditional philosophical investigation, Wittgenstein argued that most concepts were nebulous:

> We are unable clearly to circumscribe the concepts we use; not because we don't know their real definition, but because there is no real 'definition' to them. To suppose that there *must* be would be like supposing that whenever children play with a ball they play a game according to strict rules. (1969: 25)

He rejected the quest for the essence of a concept. Thinking, for Wittgenstein, is creative, and the concepts we think with are approximate and often metaphorical. Wittgenstein himself relied heavily upon analogies (like these very references to 'family resemblances' and 'game-playing') in order to further his own philosophical investigations.

**Folk theory** A model or framework of understanding shared by a linguistic community. Folk theories are often unconscious or subconscious paradigms used to interpret and understand the world around us. The division of a person into body and soul, for example, is one of the fundamental givens of the Christian worldview: in this sense it may be described as a 'folk theory' by those who do not adhere to it as 'revealed Truth'. Most contemporary cognitive linguists (Lakoff, Johnson, Fauconnier and Turner, et al.) make use of the term 'folk theory'. Lakoff and Johnson, for example, describe the way we conceive of an object as being made up of 'elements' to be a folk theory derived from the Milesian nature philosophers (1999: 351–2). They also consider us to share a 'folk theory of meaning', which involves 'picking out things in the world and [. . .] assigning meaning to words [which they argue] makes all meaning mind-independent, objective and publicly accessible' (1999: 442). Since Lakoff and Johnson see all categorisation as mind-dependent, and since their work on conceptual metaphor aims to outline the frameworks of understanding, they conceive of their work as an aid to circumscribing the limits of this naïve view of meaning.

**Foregrounding** Term which refers to any means, be it formal, semantic or both, by which an element of discourse draws attention to itself. Metaphors, enigmas and repetition of all kinds are regularly used in literature to highlight the importance of certain aspects of a work. Alliteration, for example, is used in *Macbeth* to underline the intimate and inseparable relationship between Good and Evil when those two concepts are linked by the repetition of *f* in '*F*air is *f*oul and *F*oul is *f*air' (Shakespeare, *Macbeth*: I, ii, 776).

**Form** In Humboldt's thought, the patterns which, through the mind's struggle towards expression in language, come to *form* enduring and reusable channels and constellations of meaning.

**Grounding** The idea that certain expressions, idioms or metaphors are based on, or inextricably bound up in, other metaphoric language. To speak of one's wife as one's 'partner' is 'grounded' in the conceptual metaphor according to which a relationship is a contract binding two equal parties who agree as individuals as to what they 'put in' and what they should 'get out' of their 'shared venture'. The conceptual frame of 'Marriage as Partnership' is, of course, transposed from the world of work, into which many women have launched themselves in recent decades, and it constitutes a critique of the conceptual metaphor, 'Marriage as Possession of One's Spouse', which allows individuals to believe their spouses 'belong' to them.

**Ideology** This controversial term is attributed various meanings. Firstly, it can be applied in the widest sense to any 'system of ideas'. In fact, before Marx, it referred to a supposed 'science of ideas' in the work of the French philosopher and political reformer, Destutt de Tracy (1754–1836). Napoleon was highly critical of the Ideologists for overestimating the reasonableness and malleability of human nature, and the way in which they discounted religion. This derogatory connotation has tended to stick to the term. During the Cold War, Marxists were often taxed for their ideology, but Marx himself also used the term in a negative sense, maintaining that an ideology was a 'world picture', or body of ideas held by a certain group, as opposed to the real world, which the ideology of that group (mis)represented. The historical materialism which Marx advocated was intended to demystify the ideological misconceptions of morality, religion and metaphysics. One of Humboldt's French translators, Thouard, proposes to translate Humboldt's term *Weltanschauung* as *idéologie* ('ideology'), but given the lingering negative connotations of the term, it may be wiser to translate it into English as 'system of ideas' or, as I have done, as 'cultural mindset'.

**Idiom (idiomatic expression)** Synonym for expression. Examples include, 'He's got a finger in every pie', 'He's streets ahead of the others', 'It's better than a poke in the eye with a pointy stick' or 'You couldn't damage his face with a pick axe'. Idioms seem 'poetical' and original to non-native students when they first learn them. And translators often enrich the target language when they translate expressions directly from the source language. This transforms a commonplace expression in one language into a novelty in the foreign language. English-speakers will no doubt find intriguing expressions which go almost unnoticed in the languages from which they sprout. Take, for example, 'Dogs don't have kittens' (from French, *Les chiens ne font pas les chats*) or 'Don't hurry. The lake's not on fire' (equally from French, *Il y a pas le feu au lac*). Or consider 'Lies have short legs, they don't get you very far' (found in both German, *Die Lügen haben kurze Beine*, and in Czech, *Lží májí krátký nohy*).

**Irreconcilable world-conceptions** Conceptions of the world which are contradictory and mutually exclusive, for example, scientific conceptions of mankind and reproduction which are incompatible with religious views on the family, the destiny of individuals or their obligations to God, the Church and to one another. The confrontation of irreconcilable world-conceptions can (and invariably does) exist within cultures. One group perceives the aims of society and the roles of individuals in a way that does not coincide with, opposes or excludes the way another group perceives them. This may be because the two groups speak different languages or because they use the same language in different ways. Some immigrants may not adapt to the conception of the world held by the dominant population. It is important here to stress, though, that the dominant population is often far from homogeneous in the way it perceives the world. Conservatives and radicals can be said to inhabit different 'worlds' to some extent, and this is reflected in the language they use and the concepts they think with. Irreconcilable world-conceptions can also exist within one person, either because he or she is bilingual or because he or she has had to become accustomed to existing in very different social spheres. To some extent, acculturation to a different class will often force someone to adopt a different conception of fundamental concepts such as responsibility, ambition and pleasure. In this sense, the great wave in upward mobility in the 1950s and 1960s in Britain produced a middle-class population which still clung to (or claimed to cling to) 'working-class values'. From office to pub, from dinner parties with colleagues to Sunday lunch with parents, moving between different social situations requires a change in the way we act and express ourselves. To some extent, this can give rise to a duality in perspective which is rarely fully reconciled within the individual's consciousness, in his or her deeper feelings, or in the way they perceive the world in which they must live and act.

**Juxtaposed world-conceptions** This term is closely linked to 'irreconcilable world-conceptions', but 'juxtaposed world-conceptions' does not imply that the different worldviews involved necessarily exclude each other or create a tension in society. The Canadian 'mosaic cultural model' is a product of the belief that a nation's collective culture will be 'enriched' by the free 'cross-fertilisation' of different cultures. The fact that different world conceptions exist side by side is not considered to be a problem in the Canadian view, and, indeed, multilingual, multicultural, multi-ethnic and multireligious societies seem to have been the rule rather than the exception throughout history. Only with the rise of the nation state in Western cultures did the concept of a monoculture come to be seen as the 'natural' state of things.

**Language** Term so pervasive that to abandon it would be absurd. However, speaking of 'language' in this work will lead to confusion, if it is not borne in mind that several concepts inhabit this single word. Language can mean 'speech', as in the faculty of speech, but it can also mean the act of 'speaking'. It can refer to the 'discourse' of an individual at a given time or to that individual's 'habitual speech patterns'. Similarly, it can be applied to the 'discourse' of a group, an institution, a world-conception or even a period in a people's history. We might speak of the 'language of Elizabethan English', for example. Finally, language, when used with an article (a language), refers to the linguistic system of a given community, such as English, Polish or Urdu. Similarly, some distinctions should be made when considering 'speech'. The linguistic models which were developed in Western countries in the twentieth century were heavily influenced by the 'exchange principle' fundamental to the capitalist conception of social organisation. In such a conception, social relations are invariably reduced to the exchange of goods between two individuals. Individuals 'put something in' and expect 'to get something out' of a relationship. Even in the most intimate of relationships, they make an 'emotional investment'. In terms of linguistics, this reductive-exchange model tends to obscure many forms of social and linguistic interaction which will, to such a conception, inevitably appear to be 'non-profitable' or pointless. In such a conception, it is difficult, for example, to account for the sharing involved in 'phatic communication', the recognition of a person's presence and the ongoing social games involved in maintaining contact, without seeking an exchange of information. In general, linguistic schools in the West have tended to impose a model of 'dialogue' at the expense of other forms of communication, such as conversation, teaching, public speaking, TV and radio broadcasting, literature, and so on, which necessarily require a more complex model and which do not necessarily entail the equal participation of all parties involved.

**Linguistic anthropology** Term used in English-speaking countries to designate the study of language as one essential aspect of anthropology as a whole. Modern linguistics has often chosen to privilege the study of language structure and formal detail, a fact which prevented many linguists from concentrating on social interaction and the expression of meaning. In reaction to this trend, linguistic anthropology developed as an attempt to study the use of speech and the relationship between language and culture. Traditionally speaking, for the anthropologist, Man is a social animal. Consequently, it is the study of individuals as socially interacting, meaning-making members of a social group that is the focus of linguistic anthropology. There exists, however, a tension in this discipline between the desire to analyse speaking in social contexts and the desire to draw conclusions regarding the long-term evolution of a language as the tool of and the expression of a cultural group. Because linguistic anthropology as it is practised in the USA derived from anthropology, it is important to stress that it does not coincide with what has come to be called in France, in recent decades, *anthropologie linguistique. Anthropologie linguistique* has its roots in philology, not anthropology, and has grown up around a renewed interest in the linguistic philosophy of Wilhelm von Humboldt. For two of the main exponents of linguistic anthropology, the French thinker, Henri Meschonnic, and the German philologist, Jürgen Trabant, what I have been forced to translate into English as 'linguistic anthropology' should be reserved for the investigation of individuals as expressive subjects. This approach overlaps the US form of linguistic anthropology in that Meschonnic and Trabant are concerned with the way people define themselves as a linguistic subject in relation to others in the act of speaking. But the concern for the colouring of individual discourse, accentuation, expressive links between patterns of sound and repeated phrases, which is characteristic of Meschonnic's approach to discourse, finds little echo in English-speaking linguistics, which tends to relegate such questions to literary criticism or stylistics. In contrast, for Humboldt and Meschonnic, such 'formal' patterns are fundamental to the work of the mind. Only Sapir, with his study of personality in language, preserved this aspect of linguistic study in American linguistics. Boas used language principally as an entrance into social anthropology, and Whorf was concerned more with the language system and less with the discourse of individuals and specific forms of expression. Linguistic anthropology might be considered as a synonym for 'ethnolinguistics' in the English-speaking world. The linguistic anthropology of Meschonnic would be better understood as the crossroads at which stylistics meets critical discourse analysis, philology and translation studies.

**Linguistic relativity hypothesis** Term widely used in linguistics, sociology and cultural studies and usually associated with what has come to be known as the 'Sapir–Whorf hypothesis'. Since this term is essentially reductive in that it marginalises differences between the linguistics practised by both Whorf and Sapir, and since those who use the term often have no direct knowledge of the work, concepts and preoccupations of either of the linguists, some redefinition is required here. In Whorf's opinion, all languages are 'thought worlds' impenetrable to the speakers of another language. Whorf seems to have believed that the thought world involved a series of constraints which limit the individual's thought, but Whorf envisaged an interaction and mediation between language and culture. In his model, the thought world embraced both language and culture. The interaction between language and culture also took place within the thought world. Whorf did not exclude the idea of creativity and freedom in linguistic expression, but this was not a main focus of his concern with language. Because Whorf conceived of languages as being instruments which channelled thought and fundamentally limited our conception of the world, he was attracted to 'exotic' languages, whose study, he believed, would enable him to reach beyond English and allow him to transcend the limits of its thought world. From this perspective, the more exotic the language, the greater the adventure into freedom would be. And in a very real sense, all language-learners find themselves struggling to assimilate the foreign language's patterns and conceptual categories into their own consciousness. Sapir, on the other hand, concentrated much more fully on the freedom a language opens up for the mind, and, unlike Whorf, his approach took on board literary expression. This preserved Sapir from falling into the implicit pessimism which underlies Whorf's negative definition of language as a series of constraints. When Sapir elaborated his ideas on linguistic patterning, he spoke of 'grooves' rather than 'constraints'; and these grooves themselves were made by speaking individuals for speaking individuals. They could, therefore, be modified at any time. In this sense, his model of language was much closer to that of Humboldt, for whom 'linguistic form' is simply the apparatus for thought which has been evolved and maintained in speech by people for people. Sapir's concept of linguistic relativity does, however, coincide to some extent with that of his student, Whorf, in that he believed that different languages were different systems of thought, infinitely complex and intricate configurations of patterning, which were formed by living speech as expression in speech crystallises over time. For Sapir, these systems were 'incommensurable'. Like Whorf, Sapir believed that thought is language-bound and language-dependent. Consequently, he believed that the fundamental differences between languages would induce the speakers to both conceive of the world and express their experience of it in a distinctly specific mode. Sapir's model embraced creativity and freedom of expression, however. Individuals are not the 'slaves' of language, but neither is language a 'tool' wielded by the conscious individual who can reach outside of language, unfettered by its patterning. For Sapir, the creative individual was capable of self-liberating expression, but the expression of his or her creativity in language, Sapir believed, took place within language and took conventional speech patterning as its starting point. Sapir defined linguistic relativity as:

> a kind of relativity that is generally hidden from us by our naïve acceptance of fixed habits of speech as guides to an objective understanding of the nature of experience. This is the relativity of concepts or, as it might be called, the relativity of the form of thought. (Sapir, qtd in Lucy 1996: 20–1)

The innovative speaker takes stock of those 'fixed habits of speech' and reflects upon them critically and creatively, and this is what allows him or her to formulate new configurations of thought. It is important to remember, nonetheless, that it is our native language system which, as a mode of expression, opens up to us the possibility of creative expression.

**Literalisation** Process by which an original metaphor becomes established as a common expression until finally, with use, it becomes assimilated into the lexical structure of the language. An 'English rose' might be considered an expression in that it still draws attention to itself as a comparison. 'Blossoming youth' and 'budding genius' would, on the other hand, probably be taken as non-metaphorical expressions by most people. That is to say, speakers do not realise they are making a comparison when they use such a phrase. Of course, poets invest a great deal of energy in digging up dead metaphors, that is to say, 'reliteralising' them. This creative enterprise aims not only at achieving a novelty effect; by 'reliteralisation', literary texts demonstrate the limits of the language we use. 'Reliteralising' expressions proves that language is no prison house that confines us, but rather a creative space in which we construct and reconstruct our concepts, thereby pushing back the limits of language and ideas, thought and feeling.

**Literarity** Term derived from the Russian formalists (*literaturnost*), and disseminated largely thanks to Roman Jakobson and other members of the Prague Linguistic Circle such as Jan Mukařovský: that quality which allows us to distinguish between non-literary and literary texts. For Russian formalists and Prague linguists, 'literarity' implied a distinction between literary and non-literary (ordinary) language. Analyses tended to stress the importance of form for generating meaning in the literary text which, to put it in Mukařovský's terms, draws attention to a text's mode of expression. Such a term cannot be defined in formal terms alone, however, by referring, for example, to the use of rhetorical language, such as alliteration, metaphor, and so on, since many non-literary forms of language use such elements. A literary text usually strives to be innovative and fresh. Advertisers, on the other hand, have no such pretensions, and playfully accept the idea that they distort reality in order to embellish their product and seduce the audience, that is, pervert the consumer's impression of a product.

**Metaphor** A non-explicit comparison between things, people, activities or qualities. As Brooke-Rose's study of metaphor revealed, contrary to the most widespread definition, most metaphors are not nominal, that is, they do not consist in the transformation of one object into another (for example, Macbeth and Banquo into 'hawks' and their foes into 'doves'). Verbal metaphors such as 'the boat slices through the water' and metaphors using adjectives ('rosy' cheeks) or present participles ('overflowing' love) turn out to be far more common and they tend to be more fully integrated into the lexicon. See 'Conceptual metaphor'.

**Metaphoric amalgam** Pejorative term designating the blurring of concepts resulting in an absurd or illogical structure. The metaphoric amalgam constitutes a form of blend commonly found in discourse which is hostile to logic and lucid reasoning. Racism and bad faith offer plentiful examples of metaphoric amalgams. In the language of the Third Reich, for example, Jews were declared to be the enemies of the 'Germans'. This entailed the denaturalisation of Jewish Germans. But as World War II generated new enemies for the Germans, these enemies were subsumed in the logic of the Jews-versus-Germans, and considered to be 'Jews' also. Communists had long been considered 'Jews'. The Marx-inspired communist Russians were, by the same logic, represented as waging a 'Jewish war' upon the German people, and upon civilisation itself, whose defenders the Nazis held themselves to be.

**Metaphoric confusion** Neutral term for a certain degree of confusion at the level of implicit comparisons made in metaphoric thinking. Conceptual frames are often at odds with each other. Love, for example, can be represented in English as being something we can hold within ourselves as containers: a man or woman can be 'full' of love or 'loveless'. Love can also be seen as a treasure we seek to uncover or possess, but it can also be seen as a force that penetrates us and transforms us, a force which plays with us. Shakespeare amuses us by juxtaposing such incompatible metaphoric representations in the famous rhetorical joust between Romeo and Mercutio in which Romeo complains that love is not the tender thing it is said to be:

> ROMEO: Is love a tender thing? It is too rough,
> Too rude, too boisterous; and it pricks like thorn.
> MERCUTIO: If love be rough with you, be rough with love;
> Prick love for pricking, and you beat love down.
> (Shakespeare, *Romeo and Juliet*: I, iv, 705)

Love is in turn represented as a tender lover, a bully, a thorn and finally as an opponent who can be subdued.

**Metaphoric contradiction** A metaphor which arises though the combination of mutually exclusive terms. The language of the Third Reich offered a grotesque example of metaphoric contradiction when it was declared that Jews were 'intellectual beasts'. In this absurd construct, two incompatible hierarchies are superimposed. In the first hierarchy, we oppose Man and Beast, an opposition in which the former is, of course, held to be superior. In the Nazi version of this opposition, the 'German', the Teutonic warrior, is placed at the peak of the hierarchy while the Jew is held to represent the lowest form of human life, a degenerate form of humanity. In the second hierarchy, the resentment felt by pragmatists, active men, and soldiers for intellectuals, whose ideas they fail to understand, generates a hierarchy which extols feeling and action while disparaging intellectualism. The Nazis obviously felt that in classing Jews as 'intellectual beasts' they were doubly disparaging them. However, since the Man–Beast hierarchy is meaningful only in that it stresses the intellectual superiority of man over beast, and since it celebrates the faculty for analysis and reason which sets mankind apart from the animals, the metaphoric contradiction of the 'intellectual beast' breaks down.

**Metaphoric importing/exporting** Languages import conceptual metaphors and metaphoric frames from other languages just as they export them to other languages. This does not necessarily imply exchange, however. Importing and exporting are usually one-way processes and depend upon the status of the languages and cultures involved. Just as eighteenth-century French exported ideals of liberty and the Rights of Man, so the Bush administration at the beginning of the twenty-first century exported conceptual metaphors such as the 'War on Terror', and concepts such as 'rogue states' and 'politician-gangsters', to French, Spanish, German, Czech and Russian. Given the advances in IT communication, the World Wide Web and the fact that news agencies often base their articles on US sources, and demand almost hour-by-hour translations, the exportation of US conceptual metaphors is at present an unstoppable force, one which is likely to continue to grow in future decades. The economic and cultural status of a country is, however, only one of the factors which determines the exportation of metaphors. In wartime, a conquered culture will often adopt the worldview of the conquerors and the conceptual metaphors which serve to frame that worldview. Collaborators and institutions usually play a crucial role in the 'colonisation' of a country by a new worldview. On the other hand, often the invaders find themselves transformed by the worldviews of the cultures they conquer. Alexander the Great alienated himself from his Macedonian officers when he adopted the customs of the Persians he had conquered. The Romans conquered the Greeks militarily, only to find they themselves were conquered by Greek culture which Roman writers assimilated, extolled and imitated. This involved the integration of Greek ideals, concepts, words and conceptual metaphors. When the Romans were in turn 'conquered' by Jewish mysticism in the form of Christianity, it was the neo-platonic philosophy inherited from the Greeks which enabled them to assimilate concepts of the soul and its raison d'être. It is, therefore, by virtue of a complex process of importing and exporting that many of Plato's metaphors survived in Christian cultures. Metaphoric importing and exporting can also result from alliances between states, friendship between statesmen, and from commerce.

**Metaphoric resuscitation** The act of bringing back to life, or 'reawakening', dead or 'dormant' metaphors, literal metaphors, expressions, idioms or clichés.

**Metonymy** Term, like metaphor, denoting a change in meaning. Unlike metaphor, however, which depends upon incongruity, opposition and surprise, in metonymy there exists some form of logical link between the two elements in the transposition. This link may be material, causal or conceptual. Cognitive scholars, who seemed to feel they had exhausted the subject of metaphor by the end of the 1990s, began a vast project of research into metonymy. Lists of the different forms of metonymy had, however, already been drawn up by classical scholars such as Quintilian, and the rhetorical traditions of European languages have regularly redefined that list. Dupriez (1984) lists nine forms: the French examples he uses have been adapted to make the definitions more accessible to the English reader:

1. The cause for the effect: Shakespeare for his works.
2. The instrument for the person who plays or uses it: the first violin.
3. The effect for the cause: Socrates drank death (that is, took the poison, hemlock).
4. The container for the contents: to drink a glass.
5. The place of origin for the object: Washington seems dubious about London's proposal.
6. Synecdoche, a sign or part for the whole: the Crown for the King or Queen.
7. The physical element for the moral quality: a lily-livered man, or a great-hearted man.
8. The master for the object: Saint Mary's for the church, or Notre Dame for the cathedral.
9. The object for the person: two uniforms just walked in.

**Mixed metaphor** An unintended clash of metaphorical frameworks. Mixed metaphors are rightly condemned since they are the product of an unreflecting mind which puts pieces of different puzzles together. Someone who claims that an opportunity is 'virgin field pregnant with possibilities' clearly does not realise that the two hackneyed expressions are mutually exclusive (outside of the logic of the *New Testament*). See 'Metaphorical amalgam', 'Metaphorical confusion' and 'Metaphorical contradiction'.

**Negated metaphor** Term designating the process of debunking a metaphor. Negated metaphors are parasitic because they depend upon existing metaphors. Common targets for negation are romantic ideas about life and love, expectations of work and relationships and traditional representations of women. Women's magazines provide a vast number of negative forms of representation. Some women declare that men cannot be the 'centre' of their lives. Others claim to be in search of sexual experiences which do not entail commitment, that is, 'no-strings sex'. Negated metaphors critique and reject traditional metaphors, but they have no independent basis. In other words, they become meaningful only in relation to what they debunk.

**Noumenon** In Kant's 'phenomenon-noumenon distinction', the latter refers to the 'object of intellectual intuition'. Derived from Greek, the 'noumenon' (that which is perceived) is used to refer to the construction of 'objects' by the mind when it draws them into itself and conceptualises them. It refers to the idea we have of a ball, an apple or a book, for example. Noumenon is therefore used to highlight the activity of the mind in intuiting and understanding reality. While phenomena exist in and of themselves outside of our perception of sensible reality, we cannot perceive them. Because the categories we use to conceive of reality (existence, negation, substance causality, and so on) serve to order and organise our understanding of our perceptions, they are of no use in ordering our intellectual intuitions of the noumena. Humboldt was to adapt this distinction. For Aristotle, the categories were found in nature and formed part of it. For Kant, the categories were found in the mind. For Humboldt, the categories were found in language, that is to say, in languages. For Humboldt, concepts only enter into man's consciousness by a mental activity which defines objects and distinguishes between them. This becomes all the more clear in the construction of abstract concepts (such as love, wisdom or goodness) which refer to no immediately tangible reality but which nonetheless have a very real meaning for us and an impact upon our lives. The concept of the noumenon and Kant's theory of understanding was to have a great influence on Humboldt's linguistic philosophy. Far from refusing meaning (as our contemporaries often do), Humboldt shared Kant's belief that the mind would always (and should always) strive towards an understanding of things in themselves. In this sense, he considered each language as a means of formulating abstraction and objectivity by moving beyond the sphere of subjective perception. Where he differed from Kant was in his belief that all objectivity originated in subjectivity. For Humboldt, objectivity is 'supra-subjective' and interactive. This is logical (or rather 'dialogical'), since for Humboldt we become 'subjects' as we assume the 'I' in addressing the 'you' of our interlocutor. While Kant focused on the processing of perceptions by and in the mind, Humboldt envisaged the greater part of the work of the spirit to be a shared interactive process, though the internalisation of language in the individuality of each man and woman also played a role in fashioning language for Humboldt.

**Obfuscation** The wilful blurring of concepts in discourse. Obfuscation serves to manipulate the thought of others. It often harnesses metaphors in order to exploit their emotive potential while obscuring the concept described. Considering Jews as 'vermin' in the National Socialist worldview allowed the Party to obscure and veil the real nature of existing individuals, who became hidden behind a grotesque figurative conceptualisation. The 'Final Solution', the eradication of the Jewish people, shows the horrific extent to which blurred and confused analogical concepts can intervene and displace actual experience: living people become replaced by the caricatures of stigmatised groups. The 'logical' consequences entailed by obfuscation would be literally 'unthinkable' without the conceptual blurring of confused metaphorical reasoning.

**Objectification** The reduction of a person or an animal to an object (the converse of 'personification' or 'animation'). Certain metaphors will impose upon us conceptual frameworks which encourage us to perceive people as things. The Bolshevik project for the rapid industrialisation of Russia made mechanical metaphors not only widespread (as they were in the West) but also very fashionable in Russia. Stalin liked to call himself the 'Engineer of human souls'. The contrast between mechanical and spiritual language must have pleased those who saw Russian Socialism as a form of idealism which would help modernise society and educate mankind by leading it out of the dark ages of religion, much in the same way as we represent the conquest of the Church by Science and the Enlightenment. The unfortunate logical consequence of the metaphor representing the leader of the state as the Engineer of human souls is that the 'souls' are considered as little more than the nuts and bolts of the system; and the system is sacrosanct, of course, while the nuts and bolts are dispensable. Working with – or rather living out – such a metaphor, the 'Engineer' could hardly be expected to feel any regret at 'changing the parts' of the 'machine' or 'throwing them out', as Stalin might be said to have done when he decimated the generals of the Red Army in his purges during the 1930s. Neither would such a metaphor leave much space for self-recrimination when Russian infantrymen were sent to fight Panzer tanks with Molotov cocktails instead of guns and bazookas. Objectification does not exclude sympathy, but in treating people as things, it does tend to make sacrificing people and causing them suffering to seem logical, justified and above all necessary. This example should not, however, imply that objectification is more present in communist societies than in capitalist societies. In the West, we speak of staff in terms of 'human resources' that can be used, disposed of or 'rationalised'. Objectification is frequently encountered in the representation of sexual desire in which the person desired is reduced to the status of an object which is coveted or consumed. Contrary to feminist critiques of sexism, which tend to attribute objectification exclusively to men, contemporary studies of women's discourse and historical studies of slang show that women have always had recourse to forms of representation which reduce men to sexual objects. Men have, with varying degrees of frequency, been considered as 'hunks', 'beefcakes' and 'bolt-on boyfriends'. And men are increasingly represented in the media as consumer items which can be 'tried out' by women.

**People** A group of people belonging to a culture or a nation. This term is relatively simple to handle when used with an indefinite article (a people) or with a defining adjective: to speak of the

'Scottish people' or the 'Dutch people' is to refer to a fairly clearly defined and straight-forward concept. On the other hand, when the term takes a definite article, as in 'the People', it is invariably found to be functioning as part of a rhetorical strategy used by one group or class to motivate or mobilise another group or class. Those who use the term 'the people' in public often refer to this same group as 'the masses' when speaking among members of their own group which is implicitly held apart from, and usually felt to be superior to, 'the masses'. The term, 'the People' has been harnessed by political regimes of all creeds and colours. Capitalist systems tend to extol the individual and disparage 'the masses', but are not above making calls to 'the People' to endorse Liberal and Right-wing parties at election time, or in order to incite people to buy homemade products and thereby defend against foreign imports. 'The people' is, of course, one of the founding pillars of socialist thought, though the implicitly global aspirations of *The International* and world revolution make the concept somewhat difficult to define. At times, communists have used 'the people' in a restrictive meaning to denote the citizens of the land who are asked to retaliate against foreign 'imperialist' forces. At other times, a universal meaning is attached to the term: 'the People' become the workers of the world who should unite and rise up to fight against all forms of imperialism, irrespective of national borders. In the socialist and communist systems of thought, the Party is held to be the nucleus of 'the People'. The role of the Party is to awaken the 'sleeping masses' and guide them by teaching them to rise up in order to fulfil their historical role in founding the social-ist state. According to this ideology, only in the socialist state can 'the People' freely found a harmonious society in which they are neither 'exploited' nor subjected to the tensions of class conflict. The obvious shortcoming of this concept of 'the People' is that it is exclusive: those who do not agree with the Party (which forms the State) are held to go against 'the People', and in so doing they are believed to be going against both society and history. Not only are they held to be enemies of the Party, they are also seen to be either the agents of foreign revisionist states, or dangerously unbalanced psychotics. The latter interpretation was used to justify the treat-ment of dissidents by psychiatrists. In the Nazi system of ideas 'the People' (*das Volk*) was also used in a restrictive sense. *Volk* referred to a group related by blood, the 'noble' Germans, the Teutonic warriors, the Aryans. The 'idealistic' concept of an essential German soul and an ideal German people was used to classify Germans in terms of race and to deprive many individuals of their rights as citizens. The Jews are the most obvious example, but they were in fact only one of the groups to be excluded: others included blacks, Slavs and communists.

**Personal world** Term used in this work to designate the mode of perception and conception of the world which is specific to each individual. This 'personal world' constitutes the individual's own version of the 'cultural mindset' he or she adheres to both consciously and unconsciously. This world constitutes a stance, and as such it may change over time. Nevertheless, the personal world remains coherent and, to a large extent, a permanent aspect of the life and personality of the individual to whom it attributes a certain coherence. Though malleable, the personal world cannot be abandoned or supplanted. In contrast to this, an individual's 'perspective' changes with circumstances and as the individual interacts with others.

**Personification** The representation of an object or an idea in terms of a person, for example, 'Time and tide wait for no man' or 'Your country is calling to you'. Certain concepts, such as ideals, seem to attract personification more than others. Truth, for example, is frequently personified in many languages: in English we 'unveil' truth, in Czech we speak of 'naked' truth, while in French truth has been compared to a queen. In a corpus derived from women's magazines in English, French and Czech (Underhill 2007), personification was as common as reification, if not more so. In an English example, DNA was said to 'take over' and direct the course of behaviour in sexual relations.

**Perspective** Term used in this work to designate the changing nature of the way individuals perceive and conceive of the world. A person's 'perspective' changes as he or she moves through the world, interacting with others and discovering new and different experiences. In this, 'perspective' contrasts to the individual's 'personal world' (see above), which can be said to be a more or less stable form of consciousness which frames the individual's experience, worldview and identity. Perspective is active, or rather interactive, and for that reason it is constantly changing. Just as the changing nature of the world to some extent fashions the perspective we have of it, so we ourselves change, as we adopt new ideas and expressions with age and experience.

**Polysemy** The state of having multiple meanings. A tripartite distinction should be made between 'dictionary polysemy' and two forms of 'conceptual polysemy'. Dictionary polysemy involves the fact that one word can be used to serve multiple meanings in different contexts, for example, I can sit on a 'chair' or 'chair' a meeting. Contextual polysemy is divided into two categories. Firstly, we have simple ambiguity: if we say an Alpinist has 'his head in the clouds', it will be uncertain whether a literal or figurative meaning should be attributed to the phrase. Secondly, polysemy can involve a play on words: this form of polysemy is frequently found in both advertising and literature, in which the meaning of a word in a given context can be enriched by the juxtaposing of different meanings. In one recent French advert for the Renault car whose name, *l'Espace*, means 'space', spectators are asked 'What if true happiness was space?' (*Et si le vrai bonheur était l'Espace?*). This phrase also means, of course, 'What if this car was true happiness?'

**Protometaphor** Synonym for 'conceptual metaphor', used by Lakoff and Johnson (1980). Since the 1990s, this term has fallen into disuse.

**Proverb** Expression often of a colourful and metaphoric form which usually offers a moralistic maxim or truth concerning mankind, its nature and its fate, for example, 'You can take a horse to water, but you can't make it drink'.

**Reciprocal metaphor** Term used to translate Morier's term (*métaphore réciproque*) (Morier 1989: 744). In the 'reciprocal metaphor', the term compared and the means of comparison are interchangeable: that is to say, A is described in terms of a metaphoric term, B, while B, in turn, is described in terms of A. In French, for example, the tube of the syringe is known as the 'cannon' while, in the language of artillery, the cannon is known as the 'syringe'. While the compass, in French is said to have two 'legs' (*jambes*) the walker, in lengthening his stride, widens his 'compass' (744).

**Regrounded metaphor** Metaphor which reactivates or resuscitates a dead metaphor which has become so commonplace in the spoken language that it no longer functions as a colourful or literary expression. The metaphors used to express love and desire in a trilingual corpus (Underhill 2007) frequently made explicit the implicit reference to the symbolic frameworks of the concepts we think and feel with. The sensual nature of 'ego-stroking" was exposed when juxtaposed with stroking the clitoris in the English corpus. Another English article (*Glamour*, 06/07) played with the sexual implications which English prepositions allow, using puns such as the 'ins and outs ... of our latest encounters' (Underhill 2007).

**Rhetorical strategy** Term used by Eubanks to describe the way in which speakers harness words, concepts and metaphors and tailor them to their needs in order to promote and defend their own positions in relationships and negotiations. One rhetorical strategy he recognised was the tendency to adopt the terms of a conceptual metaphor while attributing it to an opponent in a confrontation. Those advocating an 'aggressive' commercial practice often justified their position in claiming that their counterpart had started a 'trade war'.

**Reification** Synonym of 'objectification', process by which people or animals are considered in terms of objects.

**Second degree metaphor** Term used to designate a metaphoric innovation which takes for its vehicle or source a term which is already in itself a metaphorical construct. The expression 'the Cold War' is obviously based upon a heat metaphor. But with use, the metaphor became assimilated into the concepts of our language. If, for example, we say that a couple has been living through a year of 'cold war', then we enter into a second layer of figurative language. The metaphoric frame 'Love is War' is transposed onto the frame 'Coldness is Contempt' which was commonly used to characterise the hostile diplomacy that existed between the superpowers in the post-war era.

**Sense of language**  Term used to translate a central concept in Humboldt's theory of language, *Sprachsinn*. Humboldt used the term to define the activity of the mind which struggles towards expression by giving a linguistic form to its perceptions and conceptions. Since for Humboldt, the broadening of the mind was inconceivable without a simultaneous and inextricable broadening of the patterns of language, he believed that a culture's mode of expression, its worldview and its identity could only be furthered or maintained by a lucid reactivation and critique of the formal structures of thought-patterning in word construction, collocations and metaphors. Humboldt believed that grammarians, philosophers and poets were all involved in the process of refining the language as a mode of expression. Such people were animated by the 'sense of language' (*Sprachsinn*). In contrast to these, people who simply accept terms and concepts as tools, and who unthinkingly use metaphors without recognising the patterns and frameworks they open up for the mind, show a dull capacity for creative expression. Naïve and unreflecting speech cannot, consequently, revitalise language. While ethnolinguists, 'ecolinguists' and defenders of the French language, for example, demand the preservation of languages, what Humboldt and advocates of linguistic anthropology such as Meschonnic claim must be preserved is our awareness of the essentially creative potential of our language. From their perspective, only a language's speakers can 'save' it.

**Simile**  Term derived from the Latin word for 'like' (in the neuter form of *similis*), used to designate an explicit comparison. While metaphors take it for granted that we will make the connection between two conceptual domains, similes use the word 'like' or 'as' to signal that we are required to make the effort of trying to understand something in terms of something else. For this reason, similes are often used for more original comparisons than metaphors. Michael Dorris, for example, opted for the simile form in his novel, *Cloud Chamber* (qtd in Hodgson 2006: 143), when he invited readers to imagine two fairly demanding comparisons: '[He looked] like a suit of clothes on a padded hanger or a three-storey house with a fat central chimney'. Conventional similes do exist, however: take, for example, 'good as gold' or 'to get on like a house on fire'.

**Specificity** Literary term used to translate Meschonnic's term *spécificité* from French. 'Specificity' is used to refer to the essentially individual and original quality of a literary writer's work. While 'literarity' is used to distinguish between literary and non-literary texts, 'specificity' distinguishes between the work of one writer and that of another. A text can be 'literary' and a poem can be 'poetic' without showing any 'specificity'. Ironically, the attempt to sound 'poetical' is often the hallmark of bad poems which abound in clichéd, florid metaphors and rehashed 'poetical' phrases. 'Specificity' is a concept which is closely bound up in Meschonnic's reinterpretation of Humboldt's concept of *Sprachsinn*, the 'sense of language' (see above). For Meschonnic and Humboldt, what matters in literature and in creative speech is the degree to which a person strikes his or her roots into the language, transforms it, and thereby reawakens its vital elan as a mode of expression. While both the unthinking use of concepts and collocations, and literature which conforms to the norms of established literary usage, tend to blunt the instrument of language, specificity in literature refreshes language and forces readers to focus on the mode of expression and on the limits and possibilities of linguistically patterned thought.

**Subject** Term used to translate the French term *sujet* used by Meschonnic. While sociologists are content to use the term 'individual' for the person who thinks and acts within society and in his relationships, linguists posit that the 'subject' does not exist outside of language. We can, of course, separate a man from his society and his language: like Robinson Crusoe, we could leave him alone, washed up upon a shore. Nevertheless, people construct their identity interactively with others using language. Our ideas of history and society themselves are transmitted to us through communication. The concepts we think with are carved into our consciousness by the speech into which we spiral, as we create our ideas of the world and of our own selves, when, time and time again, we strive to define and express our ideas. We cannot cut ourselves off from this linguistic consciousness. Even Crusoe writes a diary, proving thereby that language remains essential for him, even though communication with other human beings is impossible. To this extent, the physical individual and the linguistic subject do not coincide. For Meschonnic, the 'I' we encounter in a literary text is a subject who creates himself or herself by means of the text. The subject of literature is, therefore, very different from the 'real' individual (the individual of which biographies are written). The linguistic subject fashions his or her identity within language by positing an 'I-you' relationship: an 'I' reaches out to a 'you' in a communicative act. The writer may find no readers, just as Robinson Crusoe might send messages in bottles out to sea in vain, but inasmuch as the 'I' of the text reaches out, striving towards expression in language, he creates himself. Meschonnic refers to this act of creation as the 'invention' and the 'adventure' of the subject.

**Synecdoche** Specific form of metonymy, the substitution of a thing by one of its parts, as for example when we want someone to help us, we ask them to 'give us a hand'. Similarly, we say, 'It's nice to see a friendly face around the place'. Different languages use different synecdoches. In French, for example, someone whose parents are of North African origin might complain that a person is racist because the latter makes it plain that all he notices when they meet is his *tête d'arabe* ('Arab head').

**System of ideas** Term largely synonymous with 'ideology' though it does not have the negative connotations sometimes associated with the latter term. Ideology is often used to denote a system which 'deludes' a group of people and 'perverts' their way of perceiving the world. Those who use the term in this fashion clearly assume that they themselves hold a privileged insight into the real 'nature of things'. 'System of ideas' is a neutral term. It implies that we are always subject to the influence of frameworks of thought which we inherit through language from society and from history.

**Thought** Since all literary and cognitive approaches to metaphor participate in the debate on the relationship between language and thought, it is important to define what we mean by the seemingly simple term 'thought'. This term refers to various modes of apprehension and reflection which can be organised into two broad categories, conscious and unconscious thought. Under unconscious thought, we can list perception, feeling, contemplation, dreaming and daydreaming. Under conscious thought, we can list reflection, logical reasoning, analytical thought, reading and conscious learning, criticism and evaluation, inspiration, speculation, and creative forms of thought such as allegorical thinking. While few people would contest that language is important in such forms of thought as analysis and logical reasoning, much doubt has been expressed concerning the significance of language for creative thought and perception. Language, however, seems to be fundamental to both forms of thought. We frame new inspired conceptions in terms of existing language-bound frames of conception. Fresh metaphors spring from the roots of existing conceptual metaphors. Dreams would seem to be heavily reliant on the associations which structure the linguistic frameworks and contours of our cognitive unconscious. Even perception is, to some extent, language-bound: we tend to notice what we recognise. Children, for example, notice a church or a hospital once they learn the meaning and the role of such institutions in their own lives. Categories, such as the names of birds or insects, direct the gaze of our analytical eye to help it perceive differences, just as academic disciplines with their own terminology allow us to formulate ideas and arguments which would be 'unthinkable' without that terminology.

**Thought world** Term used by Whorf to designate the complex frameworks of meaning and understanding by which a culture understands the universe. Though 'thought world' is at times expressed as *Weltanschauung* in Whorf's thought, it seems clear that what he has in mind when he uses both terms is closer to Humboldt's concept of *Weltansicht*, which I have carved into the distinction world-perceiving and world-conceiving.

*Weltanschauung* Term widely used in German, and often attributed to Humboldt, though he rarely used the term. In contemporary German, French and English, this term designates a world-conception, a system of ideas or ideology, for example, the dogma of the Catholic Church, the principles of the US Democratic party, or the Nazi Party's doctrines. A *Weltanschauung* involves not only the aims and sympathies of those who adhere to it but their acceptance of a series of related frameworks of conceptual metaphors which serves to give form and coherence to the system of belief in question. The *Weltanschauung* structures not only the discourse of those who adhere to it, but also partakes in the development of their ideas, beliefs and desires. Ultimately, the sentiments of those that adhere it are shaped by the world-conception 'within' which they live and from the perspective of which they perceive the world. An essential distinction that should be made in linguistic philosophy was made by Jürgen Trabant, who contrasted the meanings of *Weltanschauung* and *Weltansicht* as the latter term was used in Humboldt's conception of language. According to Trabant (1999), a world-conception (*Weltanschauung*) is elaborated and maintained through dialogue with others; such dialogue can involve a self-critical and analytic discussion of the principles on which the world-conception is founded. Priests can discuss the immaculate conception and the vocation of the human soul. Marxists can debate and reappraise Marxist-Leninism. In contrast to this, the organ of world-perceiving and world-conceiving, the *Weltansicht*, precedes all analytical or dialectical discussion. The organ of world-perceiving and world-conceiving enables us to formulate concepts as we draw the world into our consciousness. Without the *Weltansicht* – which comes to us through our assimilation of words, concepts, frameworks for understanding and conceptual metaphors – no discussion of the world is possible.

*Weltansicht* In Trabant's *Weltansicht–Weltanschauung* distinction inspired by Humboldt, the capacity which language bestows upon us, allowing us to form the concepts with which we think and which we need in order to communicate. While the *Weltansicht* of a language is implicit to it and inseparable from it, *Weltanschauungen* are not dependent upon the language system in which they are found. Several contradictory *Weltanschauungen* can exist within the same language, and they can migrate between radically different language systems. Religious and political worldviews which spread throughout the world, taking root in different cultures, testify amply to the truth of the fact that *Weltanschauungen* are not language-bound. In contrast to *Weltanschauung*, the *Weltansicht* constitutes the organ of understanding which develops the mind and allows it to first gather and draw its perceptions into itself in order to elaborate a complex organised understanding of the world and the way it works. Contrasting two conceptions of one question should clarify this fundamental distinction. We might discuss the role of the individual in society and in history in different systems of ideas. Though perhaps no agreement on such a question may finally be reached, the very discussion of such concepts (and the oppositions that may arise during the discussion of the question) depend upon the apparatus for understanding concepts such as the 'individual', 'society' and 'history'. It is language which provides us with these concepts. If we content ourselves with discussing the role of the individual, we remain at the level of ideology. If we begin to question the very concept of the 'individual', by, for example, comparing it with the concepts evolved in different languages and at different periods in time ('person' or 'soul' in English, *Mensch* in German, or *osoba* or *člověk* in Czech, for example), then we begin to reflect on our mode of expression and the very nature of our consciousness itself. At this level, we find ourselves questioning the *Weltansicht*, the worldview that language opens up for us.

**Work of the mind** The mental activity of negotiating with, and in, language in order to express ideas. While the mind can accept the form of language as adequate to its needs for expression, it can also innovate while using given concepts, channels and constellations of meaning. A third alternative remains open to the mind, however: it can refuse both existing patterns of thought and the temptation to adapt them, by striking out in an entirely new direction.

**World-conceiving** Term used in this work to designate one aspect of Humboldt's concept of *Weltansicht*, namely the changing and developing manner in which we draw that world into the realm of thought to form concepts and frameworks of ideas to represent things and our experience of the world.

**World-perceiving** Term used in this work to denote one aspect of Humboldt's concept of *Weltansicht*, namely the changing and developing perception we have of the world.

**Worldview** Term redefined in an earlier work, *Humboldt, Worldview and Language* (Underhill 2009b), the aim of which was to investigate the relationship between 'language' and 'worldview', in particular with regard to Humboldt's conception of language. Since that work questioned the usefulness of maintaining 'worldview', a catch-all term, it may seem somewhat perverse to attempt to preserve it here. Indeed, 'worldview' encapsulates often incompatible meanings. However, since the term has gained wide currency in the disciplines of philosophy, sociology and cultural studies as well as in linguistics, and since it is not likely to be discarded, some attempt should be made to define it. Though any attempt at definition will be inadequate, it seems, nevertheless, reasonable to affirm that this term is used to denote five different concepts, which I have attempted to disentangle using the terms 'world-perceiving', 'world-conceiving', 'cultural mindset', 'personal world' and 'perspective', as defined in Underhill 2009b, definitions which are reproduced in the relevant entries found above.

# Bibliography

Abdulmoneim, Mohamed Shokr, 'The metaphoric concept "life is a journey" in the Qur'an: a cognitive-semantic analysis', *metaphorik.de*, October: 94–132, 2006, online: http://www.metaphorik.de/10/shokr.pdf.

Adorno, Theodor W., *Minima Moralia*, trans. E. F. N. Jephcott, London: Verso, [1951] 1991a.

—, *Notes to Literature*, ed. Rolf Tiedemann, trans. Shierry Weber Nicholsen, New York: Columbia University Press, [1958] 1991b.

—, *Théorie esthétique*, French trans. Marc Jimenez and Eliane Kaufholz, Paris: Klincksieck, [1970] 1989.

Aristotle, *The Rhetoric and the Poetics*, trans. Ingram Bywater, New York: Random House, 1954.

—, 'Metaphysics', in Albert Hofstadter and Richard Kuhns (eds), *Philosophies of Art and Beauty: Selected Readings in Aesthetics from Plato to Heidegger*, Chicago: University of Chicago Press, 1964.

—, *The Politics*, trans. William Ellis, New York: Prometheus Books, 1986.

—, *Poetics*, trans. Hippocrates G. Apostle, Elizabeth A. Dobbs and Morris A. Parslow, Grinnell, IA: Peripatetic Press, 1990.

Armstrong, Karen, *A History of God*, London: Mandarin, 1993.

Auroux, Sylvain, *La philosophie du langage*, Paris: Presses Universitaires de France, 1996.

Bartmiński, Jerzy, *Aspects of Cognitive Ethnolinguistics*, London: Equinox, 2009.

Baudelaire, Charles, *Œuvres Complètes I*, Pléiade edition, Ligugé: Gallimard, [1975] 1997.

Benrabah, Mohamed, *Langue et pouvoir en Algérie: histoire d'un traumatisme linguistique* (*Language and Power in Algeria: the History of a Linguistic Trauma*), Paris: Séguier, 1999.

—, 'Ecole et plurilinguisme en Algérie : un exemple de politique linguistique éducative "négative"' ('The Multilingual School in Algeria: an example of a "negative" educational policy'), *Éducation et sociétés plurilingues*, 13: 73–80, 2002.

Benveniste, Émile, *Problèmes de linguistique générale I*, Paris: Gallimard, 1966.

—, *Problèmes de linguistique générale II*, Paris: Gallimard, 1974.

Berlin, Isaiah, *Three Critics of the Enlightenment: Vico, Hamann, Herder*, Princeton: Princeton University Press, 2000.

*The Holy Bible: Containing the Old and New Testaments, King James, Authorised Version*, London: Eyre and Spottiswoode.

*La Bible: L'ancien Testament I*, trans. Édouard Dhorme, Paris: Gallimard, 1956.

*La Bible: L'ancien Testament II*, trans. Édouard Dhorme, Paris: Gallimard, 1959.

*La Bible de Jérusalem*, reference edition with notes, Rome: Fleurus/ Cerf, 2001.

*Die Bibel nach der übersetzung Martin Luthers*, Stuttgart: Deutsche Bibelgesellschaft, 1999.

Boas, Franz, *Introduction to Handbook of American Indian Languages*, Lincoln, NE: Nebraska University Press, [1911] 1973.

Boers, Frank, '"No Pain, No Gain" in a free market rhetoric: a test for cognitive semantics?', *Metaphor and Symbol*, 12(4): 231–41, 1997.

Brooke-Rose, Christine, *A Grammar of Metaphor*, London: D. R. Hilman and Sons, [1958] 1965.

Buber, Martin, *Ich und Du*, Stuttgart: Reclam, [1923] 1983.

—, *I and Thou*, trans. Ronald Gregor Smith, Edinburgh: T. & T. Clark, [1937] 1958.

—, *Je et Tu*, trans. G. Bianquis, Paris: Aubier, 1969.

Cassirer, Ernst, *The Philosophy of Symbolic Forms, Volume one:*

*Language*, trans. Ralph Manheim, New Haven, CT and London: Yale University Press, [1925] 1968.

—, *Language and Myth*, trans. Susanne K. Langer, New York: Dover, [1946] 1953.

Chabrolle-Cerretini, Anne-Marie, *La vision du monde de Wilhelm von Humboldt: Histoire d'un concept linguistique*, Lyon: ENS Éditions, 2007.

Charbonel, Nanine, *Les Aventures de la métaphore*, Strasbourg: Presses Universitaires de Strasbourg, 1991.

Chomsky, Noam, *Language and the Mind*, 2nd edn, New York: Harcourt Brace, [1968] 1972.

Clément, Michèle, 'Chvéïk héros cynique?', in *De Hašek à Brecht: Fortune de la figure de Chvéïk en Europe*, *Les Cahiers de l'ILCEA*, No. 8, Grenoble: ILCEA, Presses Universitaires de Grenoble, 2006.

Čmejrková, Světla, *Reklama v Čestině* (*Publicity in Czech*), Prague: Leda, 2000.

Colin, Jean-Paul, *Dictionnaire de l'argot français et de ses origines*, Paris: Larousse, 1990.

Collombat, Isabelle, 'Le Discours imagé en vulgarisation scientifique: étude comparée du français et de l'anglais', *metaphorik. de*, May: 36–61, 2003, online: http://www.metaphorik.de/05/collombat.pdf.

Copleston, Frederick S. J., *A History of Western Philosophy*, 9 vols, New York: Image Books, 1962.

Crystal, David, *The Cambridge Encyclopaedia of Language*, 2nd edn, Cambridge: Cambridge University Press, 1997.

—, *Language Death*, Cambridge: Cambridge University Press, 2000.

—, *English as a Global Language*, 2nd edn, Cambridge: Cambridge University Press, [1997] 2003.

Cuddon, J. A., *Dictionary of Literary Terms and Literary Theory*, 3rd edn, London: Penguin, [1976] 1991.

Dalby, Andrew, *Language in Danger*, London: Penguin, 2003.

Dalrymple, Theodore, *Life at the Bottom: The Worldview that Makes the Underclass*, Chicago: Ivan R. Dee, 2001.

Dalzell, Tom and Terry Victor, *Sex Slang*, New York: Routledge, 2008.

de Beauvoir, Simone, *The Second Sex*, trans. H. M. Parshley, London: Picador, [1949] 1988.

de Certeau, Michel, Dominique Julia and Jacques Revel, *Une politique de la langue: La révolution française et les patois – l'enquête de Grégoire*, Paris: Gallimard, 1975.

de Gobineau, Arthur, *Oeuvres*, Pléiade edition, Dijon: Gallimard, 1983.

de Man, Paul, *Allegories of Reading: Figural Language in Rousseau, Nietzsche, Rilke, and Proust*, New Haven, CT: Yale University Press, [1979] 1982.

Derrida, Jacques, 'La mythologie blanche', in *Marges de la philosophie*, Paris: Editions de Minuit, [1971] 1972.

de Swaan, Abram, 'Le sentimentalisme des langues', in Michael Werner (ed.), *Politiques & Usages de la Langue en Europe*, Condé-sur-Noireau: Collection du Ciera, Dialogiques, Éditions de la Maison des sciences de l'homme, 2007, pp. 81–98.

Dirven, René, 'Metaphor as a basic means of extending the lexicon', in Wolf Paprotté and René Dirven (eds), *The Ubiquity of Metaphor: Amsterdam Studies in the Theory and History of Linguistic Science*, Amsterdam and Philadelphia, PA: John Benjamins, 1985, pp. 84–119.

Dubois, Jean, Mathée Giacomo, Louis Guespin, Christiane Marcellesi, Jean-Baptiste Marcellesi and Jean Pierre Mével, *Dictionnaire de linguistique et des sciences du langage*, Paris: Larrousse, 1994.

Ducrot, Oswald and Jean-Marie Schaeffer, *Nouveau dictionnaire encyclopédique des sciences du langage*, Paris: Seuil, 1995.

Dupriez, Bernard, *Gradus, Les Procédés Littéraires (Dictionnaire)*, Paris: Union générale d'Editions, 1984.

Eckermann, Johann Peter, *Gespräche mit Goethe in den letzen Jahren seines Lebens*, Berlin and Weimar: Aufbau-Verlag, 1982.

—, *Conversations with Goethe*, trans. John Oxenford, ed. J. K. Moorhead, New York: Da Capo Press, 1998.

Emanatian, Michele, 'Metaphor and the expression of emotion: the value of cross-cultural perspectives', *Metaphor and Symbolic Activity*, 10(3): 163–82, 1995.

—, 'Congruence by degree: on the relation between metaphor and cultural models', in Raymond W. Gibbs, Jr. and Gerard J. Steen (eds), *Metaphor in Cognitive Linguistics*, New York: Cambridge University Press, 1999.

Encrevé, Pierre, 'Conditions d'exercice d'une politique linguistique en démocratie aujourd'hui', in Michael Werner (ed.), *Politiques & Usages de la Langue en Europe*, Condé-sur-Noireau: Collection du Ciera, Dialogiques, Éditions de la Maison des sciences de l'homme, 2007, pp. 121–36.

Eubanks, Philip, *A War of Words in the Discourse of Trade: The Rhetorical Constitution of Metaphor*, Carbondale and Edwardsville, IL: Southern Illinois University Press, 2000.

Fauconnier, G., *Mental Spaces: Aspects of Meaning Construction in Natural Language*, Cambridge, MA: MIT Press, 1985.

Fauconnier, Gilles and Mark Turner, *The Way We Think: Conceptual Blending and the Mind's Hidden Complexities*, New York: Basic Books, [2002] 2003.

Fergusson, Rosalind, *The Penguin Dictionary of Proverbs*, London: Penguin Books, 1983.

Fidelius, Petr, *L'esprit post-totalitaire*, Paris: Bernard Grasset, 1986.

—, *Řeč komunistické*, Prague: Triada, 1998.

*Filozofický slovník (O–Z) (A Philosophical Dictionary)*, Prague: Svoboda, 1985.

Fingl, J., M. Klivar, J. Klofáč, V. Krechler, L. Myška, J. Poláček, J. Potoček and E. Zahrádka, *Stručný politický slovník (Concise Dictionary of Political Terms)*, Prague: Nakladatelsví Politické Literatury, 1962.

Fontaine, Jacqueline, *Le cercle linguistique de Prague*, Tours: Mame, 1974.

Fontanier, Pierre, *Les figures du discours*, Paris: Flammarion, [1830] 1977.

Foucault, Michel, *Philosophie, Anthologie*, Paris: Gallimard, 2004.

Garton Ash, Timothy, 'Orwell for our time', *The Guardian*, 5 May 2001, online: http://www.guardian.co.uk/books/2001/may/05/artsandhumanities.highereducation.

Goatly, Andrew, *Washing the Brain: Metaphor and Hidden Ideology*, Amsterdam and Philadelphia, PA: John Benjamins, 2007.

Goebbels, Joseph, *Kampf um Berlin, Der Anfang*, Munich: Zentralverlag der NSDAP, 1937.

—, *Die Tagenbücher: Sämtliche Fragmente, Teil I, 1924–1941, Band I, 27.6.1924–31.12.1930,* ed. Elke Frülich, Munich: K. G. Saur Verlag, 1987.

Goschler, Juliana, 'Embodiment and body metaphors', *metaphorik. de,* September: 33–52, 2005, online: http://www.metaphorik. de/09/goschler.pdf.

Grady, J., *Foundations of Meaning: Primary Metaphors and Primary Scenes* (PhD Thesis), Berkeley, CA: University of California, 1997.

Grijelmo, Álex, *Defensa apasionada del idioma español* (*A Passionate Defence of the Spanish Language*), Madrid: Punto de Lectura, [1998] 2006.

Guillemin-Flescher, Jacqueline, *Syntaxe comparée du français et de l'anglais: problèmes de traduction,* Paris: Ophrys, 1981.

Hagège, Claude, *L'homme de paroles: Contribution linguistique aux sciences humaines,* Paris: Fayard, 1985.

—, *Le français: histoire d'un combat,* Paris: Editions Michel Hagège, 1996.

—, *Le souffle de la langue,* Paris: Odile Jacob, 1992.

—, *Halte à la mort des langues,* Paris: Odile Jacob, 2000.

—, *Combat pour le français: Au nom de la diversité des langues et des cultures,* Paris: Odile Jacob, 2006.

Hansen-Løve, Ole, *La révolution copernicienne du langage dans l'oeuvre de Wilhelm von Humboldt,* Paris: Vrin, 1972.

Hersant, Yves, *La métaphore baroque: D'Aristote à Tesauro, extraits du Cannocchiale aristotelico,* Paris: Seuil, 2001.

Hobbes, Thomas, *Leviathan,* London: Penguin, [1651] 1985.

Hodgson, Terrence, *Eyes Like Butterflies: A Treasury of Similes and Metaphors,* Edinburgh: Chambers, 2006.

Holub, Josef, and Stanislav Lyer, *Stručný Etymologický Slovník Jazyka Českého* (*A Short Dictionary of Etymology for the Czech Language*), Prague: Statní Pedagogické Nakladatelsví, 1978.

Howe, Irving (ed.), *1984 Revisited: Totalitarianism in Our Century,* New York: Harper Row, 1983.

Humboldt, Wilhelm von, *Linguistic Variability and Intellectual Development,* trans. George C. Buck and Frithjof A. Raven, Philadelphia, PA: Pennsylvania University Press, [1836] 1971.

—, *On language: On the Diversity of Human Language Construction and its Influence on the Mental Development of the Human Species*, trans. Peter Health, ed. Michael Losonsky, Cambridge: Cambridge University Press, [1836] 1999.

—, *Schriften zur Sprache*, Stuttgart: Reklam, Universal-Bibliothek, 1995.

—, *Sur le caractère national des langues et autres écrits sur le langage*, trans. Denis Thouard, Paris: Seuil, 2000.

—, *Über die Verschiedenheit des menschlichen Sprachbaues / Über die Sprache*, Berlin: Fourier Verlag, 2003.

Ibn 'Arabï, *Traité de l'amour*, trans. Maurice Gloton, Paris: Albin Michel, 1986.

Jaspers, Karl, *Plato and Augustine*, trans. Ralph Manheim, ed. Hannah Arendt, New York: Harcourt Brace Jovanovich, 1962.

Johnson, M., *The Body in the Mind: The Bodily Basis of Meaning, Imagination and Reason*, Chicago: University of Chicago Press, 1987.

Joseph, John E., *Language and Identity: National, Ethnic, Religious*, New York: Palgrave Macmillan, 2004.

—, *Language and Politics*, Edinburgh: Edinburgh University Press, 2006.

Kant, Immanuel, *Critique of Pure Reason*, a revised and expanded translation based on Meiklejohn, ed. Vasilis Politis, London: Everyman, 1993.

Klemperer, Victor, *LTI: Notizbuch eines Philogen*, Leipzig: Reklam Verlag, 1975.

—, *LTI: la langue du IIIe Reich*, trans. Élisabeth Guillot, Paris: Albin Michel, 1996.

—, *Tagebücher 1933–1934*, Berlin: Aufbau-Verlag, [1998] 1999.

—, *The Language of the Third Reich: LTI Lingua Tertii Imperii*, trans. Martin Brady, London and NewYork, NY: Continuum [2000] 2006.

—, *I Will Bear Witness, 1942–1945, A Diary of the Nazi Years*, trans. Martin Chalmers, New York: The Modern Library, 2001.

Kliment, Jan, 'Umění pokroku lidskosti, života' ('The art of progress of humanity and of life'), *Rudé Právo*, 4 August 1979.

Kövecses, Zoltán, *Metaphors of Anger, Pride, and Love: A Lexical Approach to the Structure of Concepts*, Amsterdam and Philadelphia, PA: John Benjamins, 1986.

Kristeva, Julia, 'É comme écrire en français', in Bernard Cerquiglini, Jean-Claude Corbeil, Jean-Marie Klinkenberg and Benoît Peeters (eds), *Le Français dans Tous ses États*, Paris: Flammarion, 2000.

Kundera, Milan, *Směšné Lásky*, Brno: Atlantis, [1968] 2000a.

—, *The Unbearable Lightness of Being*, London: Faber, 2000b.

Lakoff, George, *Women, Fire and Dangerous Things: What Categories Reveal about the Mind*, Chicago: University of Chicago Press, 1987.

—, *Moral Politics*, Chicago: University of Chicago Press, 1996.

—, 'Metaphor and war: the metaphor system used to justify war in the Gulf', Parts 1 and 2, *Viet Nam Generation Journal & Newsletter*, V3, N3, November 1991, online: http://www2.iath. virginia.edu/sixties/HTML_docs/Texts/Scholarly/Lakoff_ Gulf_Metaphor_1.html.

Lakoff, George and Mark Johnson, *Metaphors We Live By*, Chicago: University of Chicago Press, 1980.

—, *Philosophy in the Flesh*, Chicago: University of Chicago Press, 1999.

Lakoff, George and Mark Turner, *More Than Cool Reason: A Field Guide to Poetic Metaphor*, Chicago: University of Chicago Press, 1989.

Langham Brown, Roger, *Wilhelm von Humboldt's Conception of Linguistic Relativity*, The Hague and Paris: Mouton, 1967.

Lee, Penny, *The Whorf Theory Complex: A Critical Reconstruction*, Amsterdam and New York: John Benjamins, 1996.

Leech, Geoffrey, *Semantics: The Study of Meaning*, 2nd edn, London: Penguin, [1974] 1990.

*Le Figaro*, 11 January 2005, online, www.lefigaro.fr.

*Le Monde de l'Éducation. Quelles langues pour demain*, 367: 28, 2008.

Levinson, Stephen C., *Space in Language and Cognition: Explorations in Cognitive Diversity*, Cambridge: Cambridge University Press, 2003.

Lévi-Strauss, Claude, *Race et Histoire*, Paris: Gonthier, 1961.

Littré, Emile, *Dictionnaire de la langue française*, France: Gallimard/ Hachette, 1962.

Locke, John, *An Essay Concerning Human Understanding*, Glasgow: Fontana/Collins, [1689] 1964.

Lucy, John A., *Language Diversity and Thought: A Reformulation of the Linguistic Relativity Hypothesis*, Cambridge: Cambridge University Press, [1992] 1996.

McArthur, Tom, *The English Languages*, Cambridge: Cambridge University Press, 1998.

*Malá Československá Encyklopeie (I–L)* (*The Shorter Czechoslovak Dictionary*), vol. III, ed. Miroslav Štěpánek, Prague: Akademia, 1986.

Malmkjaer, Kirsten, *The Linguistics Encyclopedia*, London: Routledge, 1991.

Malotki, Ekkehart, *Hopi Time: A Linguistic Analysis of the Temporal Concepts in the Hopi Language*, Berlin: Mouton, 1983.

Manchester, Martin L., *The Philosophical Foundations of Humboldt's Linguistic Doctrines*, Amsterdam and Philadelphia, PA: John Benjamins, 1985.

Matoré, Georges, *L'espace Humain*, Paris: La Colombe, 1962.

Meschonnic, Henri, *Critique du rythme: anthropologie historique du langage*, Paris: Verdier, 1982.

—, *Les états de la poétique*, Paris: Presses Universitaires de France, 1985.

—, *Politique du rythme: politique du sujet*, Paris: Verdier, 1995.

—, *De la langue française: Essai sur une clarté obscure*, Paris: Hachette, 1997.

—, *L'utopie du juif*, Paris: Desclée de Brouwer, 2001.

—, *Heidegger ou le national-essentialisme*, Paris: Laurence Teper, 2007.

— (ed.), *La Pensée dans la langue, Humboldt et après*, Paris: Presses Universitaires de Vincennes, 1995.

Messling, Markus, 'L'homme? Destruktion des Menschen in der Humboldt-Rezption bei Gobineau', in Jürgen Trabant and Ute Tintemann (eds), *Wilhelm von Humboldt: Universalität und Individualität*, Munich: Fink, 2010.

Michelet, Jules, *Le Peuple*, Paris: Marcel Didier, [1846] 1946.

Mikołajczuk, Agnieszka, 'The metonymic and metaphorical conceptualisation of *anger* in Polish', in Angeliki Athanasiadou and Elżbieta Tabakowska (eds), *Speaking of Emotions: Conceptualisation and Expression*, Berlin and New York: Mouton de Gruyter, 1998, pp. 153–90.

—, 'ANGER in Polish and English: A semantic comparison with some historical context', in Christian J. Kay and Jeremy J. Smith (eds), *Categorization in the History of English*, Amsterdam and Philadelphia: John Benjamins, 2004, pp. 159–78.

Mleziva, Emil, 'Vliv společenských změn na vznik nových významů a výrazů v českém jazyce' ('The influence of social developments on the creation of new meanings and new expressions in the Czech language'), *Slovo a slovesnost*, 57: 283–96, 1996.

Morier, Henri, *Dictionnaire de poétique et de rhétorique*, 4th edn, Paris: Presses Universitaires de France, [1961] 1989.

Mukařovský, Jan, *Kapitoly české poetiky*, vols I and II, Prague: Statní Pedagogické Nakladatelsví, 1948.

—, 'Standard language and poetic language', in Joseph Vachek (ed.), *A Prague School Reader in Linguistics*, Bloomington, IN: University of Indiana Press, 1964.

Müller, Ralph, 'Creative metaphors in political discourse: theoretical considerations on the basis of Swiss speeches', *metaphorik. de*, September: 53–73, 2005, online: http://www.metaphorik. de/09/mueller.pdf.

Naugle, David K., *Worldview: The History of a Concept*, Grand Rapids, MI and Cambridge: W. B. Eerdmans, 2002.

Nerlich, Brigitte, Craig A. Hamilton and Victoria Rowe, 'Conceptualising foot and mouth disease: the socio-cultural role of metaphors, frames and narratives', *metaphorik.de*, February: 90–108, 2002.

Nettle, Daniel and Suzanne Romaine, *Vanishing Voices: The Extinction of the World's Languages*, Oxford: Oxford University Press, 2000.

Nieztsche, Freidrich, *On the Genealogy of Morals and Ecce Homo*, trans. Walter Kaufmann and R. J. Hollingdale, ed. Walter Kaufmann, New York: Vintage, 1989.

Noguez, Dominique, 'C comme une crise du français?', in Bernard Cerquiglini, Jean-Claude Corbeil, Jean-Marie Klinkenberg and Benoît Peeters (eds), *Le Français dans Tous ses États*, Paris: Flammarion, 2000.

Orwell, George, *The Collected Essays, Journalism and Letters of*

*George Orwell. As I Please, 1943–1945*, vol. III, ed. Sonia Brownell Orwell and Ian Angus, London: Camelot, 1968.

Oster, Pierre, *Dictionnaire de citations françaises I, de Villon à Beaumarchais*, Paris: Robert, 1990.

—, *Dictionnaire de citations françaises II, de Chateaubriand à J. M. G. Le Cézio*, Paris: Robert, 1993.

Paprotté, Wolf and René Dirven (eds), *The Ubiquity of Metaphor*: *Amsterdam Studies in the Theory and History of Linguistic Science*, Amsterdam and Philadelphia, PA: John Benjamins, 1985.

Picoche, Jacqueline, *Le Robert dictionnaire étymologique du français*, Paris: Robert, 1994.

Plato, *The Collected Dialogues*, ed. Edith Hamilton and Huntington Cairns, Princeton: Princeton University Press, 1961.

—, *The Republic*, trans. Allan Bloom, New York: Basic Books, 1968.

Plotinus, 'Ennead', *Philosophies of Art and Beauty: Selected Readings in Aesthetics from Plato to Heidegger*, ed. Albert Hofstadter and Richard Kuhns, Chicago: University of Chicago Press, 1964.

Poldauf, Ivan, *Česko-anglický slovník*, 2nd edn, Prague: Státní Pedagogické Nakladatelství, 1986.

Preminger, Alex and T. V. F. Brogan, *The Princeton Encyclopedia of Poetry and Poetics*, Princeton: Princeton University Press, 1993.

Rey, Alain, *Dictionnaire historique de la langue française*, Robert: Paris, [1992] 1998.

Rey-Debove, Josette, *Le Robert Brio, Analyse des mots et régularités du lexique*, Paris: Robert, 2004.

Rey-Debove, Josette and Gilberte Gagnon, *Dictionnaire des anglicismes: les mots anglais et américains en français*, Paris: Robert, 1980.

Rey-Debove, Josette and Allain Rey, *Le Nouveau Petit Robert*, Paris: Robert, 1993.

Ricœur, Paul, *La métaphore vive*, Paris: Seuil, 1975.

Riley, Philip, *Language, Culture and Identity*, London: Continuum, 2008.

Ripert, Pierre, *Dictionnaire des citations de la langue française*, Paris: Booking Internationale, 1993.

Russell, Bertrand, *History of Western Philosophy*, London: Unwin Paperbacks, [1946] 1979.

Saint Augustin, 'De Musica', in Albert Hofstadter and Richard Kuhns (eds), *Philosophies of Art and Beauty: Selected Readings in Aesthetics from Plato to Heidegger*, Chicago: University of Chicago Press, 1964.

—, 'De Ordine', in Albert Hofstadter and Richard Kuhns (eds), *Philosophies of Art and Beauty: Selected Readings in Aesthetics from Plato to Heidegger*, Chicago: University of Chicago Press, 1964.

—, *Les Confessions*, Paris: Garnier Frères Flammarion, 1964.

Salzmann, Zdenek, *Langage, Culture, and Society, An Introduction to Linguistic Anthropology*, 2nd edn, Boulder, CO: Westview Press, 1999.

Sapir, Edward, *Language: An Introduction to the Study of Speech*, New York: Harcourt, Brace & World, [1921] 1949.

—, *Selected Writings in Language, Culture, and Personality*, ed. David G. Mandelbaum, Berkeley, CA: University of California Press, [1949] 1985.

Scholze-Stubenrecht, W. and J. B. Sykes, *The Oxford-Duden German Dictionary*, Oxford: Clarendon Press, 1999.

Schulte, Joachim, *Wittgenstein: An Introduction*, trans. William H. Brenner and John F. Holley, Albany, NY: State University of New York Press, 1992.

Scruton, Roger, *Kant*, Oxford: Oxford University Press, [1982] 1996.

Šefčík, Vladimir, 'Ekonomická válka – Staronový fenomén mezinárodní bezpečností' ('Economic war – ancient-new phenomenon of international security), 2002, online: http://www.army.cz/avis/vojenske_rozhledy/2002_3/89.htm.

Shakespeare, William, *The Illustrated Stratford Shakespeare*, London: Chancellor Press, 1992.

*The Shakespeare Collection: All 37 Productions from the BBC Television Shakespeare Series*, DVD, directed by Alvin Rakoff. London: BBC Worldwide, 2005.

Sire, James W., *Naming the Elephant: Worldview as a Concept*, Downers Grove, IL: InterVaristy Press, 2004.

Steiner, George, *After Babel, Aspects of Language and Translation*, 2nd edn, Oxford: Oxford University Press, [1975] 1992.

Sweetser, Eve, *From Etymology to Pragmatics: Metaphorical and Cultural Aspects of Semantic Structure*, Cambridge: Cambridge University Press, 1990.

—, 'Negative spaces: levels of negation and kinds of spaces', in Stéphanie Bonnefille and Sébastien Salbayre (eds), *La négation: formes, figures, conceptualisation*, Tours: Presses Universitaires François Rabelais, 2006.

Sweetser, Eve and Gilles Fauconnier, *Spaces, Words, and Grammar*, Chicago: University of Chicago Press, 1996.

Taylor, John R., *Linguistic Categorization*, 3rd edn, Oxford: Oxford University Press, [1989] 2003.

—, *Cognitive Grammar*, Oxford: Oxford University Press, 2002.

*The Aristocats*, film, directed by Wolfgang Reitherman. USA: Walt Disney Productions, 1970.

*The Unbearable Lightness of Being*, film, directed by Philip Kaufman. USA: The Saul Zaentz Company, 1988.

Thomas, Linda, Shân Wareing, Ishthla Singh, Jean Stilwell Peccei, Joanna Thornborrow and Jason Jones, *Language, Society and Power: An Introduction*, 2nd edn, London: Routledge, [1999] 2004.

Trabant, Jürgen, *Traditions de Humboldt*, French edn, Paris: Maison des sciences de l'homme, [German edn 1990] 1999.

—, *Humboldt ou le sens du langage*, Liège: Madarga, 1992.

—, *Mithridates im Paradies: Kleine Geschichte des Sprachdenkens*, Munich: Beck, 2003.

—, 'L'antinomie linguistique: quelques enjeux politiques', in Michael Werner (ed.), *Politiques & Usages de la Langue en Europe*, Condé-sur-Noireau: Collection du Ciera, Dialogiques, Éditions de la Maison des sciences de l'homme, 2007, pp. 67–79.

—, *Was ist Sprache?*, Munich: Beck, 2008.

Turner, Mark, *Death is the Mother of Beauty: Mind, Metaphor, Criticism*, Chicago: University of Chicago Press, 1987.

—, *The Literary Mind: The Origins of Thought and Language*, Oxford: Oxford University Press, 1996.

Underhill, James W., 'Meaning, language and mind: an interview with Mark Turner', *Style: Resources in Stylistics and Literary Analysis*, North Illinois University, 36(4): 700–17, Winter 2002.

—, 'The switch: metaphorical representation of the war in Iraq from September 2002–May 2003', *metaphorik.de*, December: 135–65, 2003, online: http://www.metaphorik.de/05/underhill.pdf.

—, 'Métaphores dans le marché, ou le marché en métaphores', in *Traduction/adaptation des littératures et textes spécialisés, Les Cahiers de l'ILCEA*, No. 6, Grenoble: ILCEA, Presses Universitaires de Grenoble, 2004.

—, ' "Having" sex and "making" love. Metaphoric patterning in representations of the sexual act in Czech, French and English', *Slovo a smysl: Word and Sense*, 8: 84–112, 2007, online: http://hum.uit.no/lajanda/mypubs/slovo%20a%20smysl%20cultural%20ling.pdf.

—, 'War and peace: a story of international trade: a critical appraisal of Philip Eubanks' *A War of Words*', in Sina Vatanpour (ed.), *L'argent*, Lille: Presses universitaires de Lille, 2008.

—, 'Dérive et déformation de la pensée: Vision du monde et métaphore', in Denis Jamet (ed.), *Dérives de la métaphore*, Paris: Harmattan, 2009a.

—, *Humboldt, Worldview and Language*, Edinburgh: Edinburgh University Press, 2009b.

—, *Ethnolinguistics and Cultural Concepts: Truth, Love, Hate and War*, Cambridge: Cambridge University Press, in press.

Vaňková, Irena, *Nádoba plná řeči* (*Dishes Full of Speech*), Prague: Karolinum, 2007.

— (ed.), *Obraz světa v jazyce* (*The Picture of the World in Language*), Prague: Desktop Publishing – FF UK, 2001.

Vaňková, Irena, Iva Nebeská, Lucie Saicová Římalová and Jasňa Šlédrová, *Co na srdci, to na jazyku* (*What's on your Heart is on the Tip of your Tongue*), Prague: Karolinum, 2005.

Vlasák, Vaclav and Stanislav Lyer, *Česko-Francouský Slovník*, Prague: Státní Pedagogické Nakladatelství, 1987.

*West Side Story*, film, directed by Robert Wise and Jerome Robbins. USA: Mirisch Pictures, 1961.

Whorf, Benjamin Lee, *Language, Thought and Reality: Selected Writings*, ed. John B. Caroll, Cambridge, MA: MIT Press, [1956] 1984.

Wierzbicka, Anna, *Semantics, Culture and Cognition: Universal*

*Human Concepts in Culture-Specific Configurations*, New York: Oxford University Press, 1992.

—, *Understanding Cultures through their Key Words*, Oxford: Oxford University Press, 1997.

—, *Emotions across Languages and Cultures*, Cambridge: Cambridge University Press, 1999.

—, *Semantics: Primes and Universals*, Oxford: Oxford University Press, [1996] 2004.

—, *Experience, Evidence & Sense: The Hidden Cultural Legacy of English*, Oxford: Oxford University Press, 2010.

Williams, Raymond, *Keywords: A Vocabulary of Culture and Society*, rev'd edn, Oxford: Oxford University Press, [1976] 1983.

Wittgenstein, Ludwig, *Tractatus logico-philosophicus*, French trans. Gilles-Gaston Granger, Paris: Gallimard, [1922] 1993.

—, *The Philosophical Investigations, The German Text with a Revised English Translation*, 3rd edn, trans. G. E. M. Anscombe, Oxford: Blackwell, [1953] 2001.

—, *The Blue and Brown Books*, 2nd edn, New York: Harper and Row, 1969.

—, *Remarques mêlées*, trans. Gérard Granel, Paris: Flammarion, 2002.

# Index